SOCIAL STUDIES FOR ELEMENTARY TEACHERS

David Warren Saxe
The Pennsylvania State University

Allyn and Bacon
Boston • London • Toronto • Sydney • Tokyo • Singapore

Series Editor: Virginia Lanigan
Editorial Assistant: Nicole DePalma
Cover Administrator: Suzanne Harbison
Composition Buyer: Linda Cox
Manufacturing Buyer: Megan Cochran
Editorial-Production Service: Progressive Typographers
Photo Researcher: Susan Duane
Production Administrator: Ann Greenberger

Copyright © 1994 by Allyn and Bacon
A Division of Simon & Schuster, Inc.
160 Gould Street
Needham Heights, Massachusetts 02194

Library of Congress Cataloging-in-Publication Data

Saxe, David Warren, 1953–
    Social studies for elementary teachers / David Warren
Saxe.
        p.   cm.
    Includes index.
    ISBN 0-205-15224-4 : $22.50
    1. Social sciences—Study and teaching (Elementary)—United
States.   I. Title.
LB1584.S35 1993
372.83'0973—dc20   93-1561
                                               CIP

Printed in the United States of America

10 9 8 7 6 5 4 3 2 1   98 97 96 95 94 93

*To Danny, Andy, Debbie, and Kathryn;
remembering those who came before and considering
those who will follow . . .*

CONTENTS

PREFACE

This book began with a simple idea: to bring social studies experiences to children. The success of this idea rests with you. The production of this book, however, rests with the many students, teachers, and researchers who worked with what we came to call the "synoptic method" over the six years this project was in development. While I assume responsibility for the project and the contents of this textbook, I wish to thank the many who helped make this textbook a reality.

The project began on a lunch break with graduate assistants. There, literally on the back of a napkin, I discussed with students how ideas from our rich educational past might be applied to present conditions in elementary schools. For their courage to try something new and patience during revisions, I thank instructors Brad Smith, Margaret Pursell, and Julie Weber of The Pennsylvania State University and instructors Zonnel Crandall and Bob Wyatt of the University of Oklahoma. Over the past six years some 1500 teachers in training from The Pennsylvania State University, the University of Oklahoma, and the University of Illinois worked to give form to the synoptic method. Through weekly journals, these students sharpened the clarity of the text's many ideas and added a number of helpful comments; all of which worked to shape the project-in-process.

I owe a special debt to Professors C. Benjamin Cox of the University of Illinois and Gail Tompkins of California State University, Fresno who each provided opportunities and encouragement to try new ideas within "established" programs. In addition, I want to acknowledge the help of the six anonymous reviewers as well as to extend a special thanks to Cindy Cason and Professor Douglas Anderson of Penn State, who read and commented on earlier drafts.

My many thanks to the production crew at Allyn & Bacon, who patiently answered questions and worked tirelessly to shepherd the project through the narrows of the commercial publishing world. I wish to express my appreciation to former editor Sean Wakely who was willing to take on an idea that worked against the grain. I am also in debt to Virginia Lanigan and her staff who tenderly picked up the project and moved it forward. I also wish to single out the efforts of Ann Greenberger and Suzanne Mescan for their expert attention to detail.

Finally, I wish to recognize the immeasurable debt I owe to my wife Laura, daughters Debbie and Kathryn and sons Danny and Andy; each gave openly and lovingly toward the success of the project.

A BRIEF WORD BEFORE WE START

"A journey of a thousand miles begins with the first step."
A Confucian saying, circa 500 B.C.

The distance between your student days at college and teaching in an elementary school may appear far apart at this point of your professional preparation. Indeed, the vision of a classroom full of youngsters eager to join you in learning about the world may be so removed from your present experience that this happy image appears more dream-like than real. However, the journey from college student to professional teacher is one that virtually every elementary teacher has made, and, you, too, shall soon join their select company.

As for any trip, we need to make preparations for our arrival. Together with other courses in your teacher education program, one important component of your professional preparation is to learn something about the teaching of social studies. As used here, social studies[1] is activated through experiences that highlight the world and its people, our nation, different states, regions, and local communities. Social studies also provides opportunities to explore political, economic, and social systems and includes experiences about our rich past and our hopeful future. Most importantly, however, social studies serves to facilitate the shift from children acting as individuals to children acting as informed and engaged citizens.

On our journey to the elementary classroom, as employed here, education is not conceived as a vehicle to train children to function as workers or technicians for some predetermined industrial or business destination. Rather, education, through social studies, is viewed as a means to help teachers activate the development of liberal democratic citizenship. In this view, social studies is a means toward raising the quality of the individual's life as well as that of the

---

[1]Although social studies appears in plural form, as used in this textbook, view its meaning as grammatically singular.

community. In short, social studies is not something teachers try to make children learn for their own good.

The search for a stable foundation upon which to build lesson experiences has been the "Holy Grail" of education throughout the past one hundred years. Indeed, the search for a powerful, comprehensive, consistent, and fully functional base for elementary curricula has persistently eluded educators. This textbook represents a bold attempt to claim a portion of that elusive prize. It will be argued here that the exploration for a sound curricular base not only begins with children, but can be found within children, or more directly, within any child.

In the context of our attempt to introduce children to their world, the term *synoptic method* is used to describe how social studies is activated with children. Like social studies (and education in general) the synoptic method is not conceived as a noun, but as a verb, a deliberate action. In this sense, synoptic method involves:

1. bringing together ideas, materials, children, adults, values, beliefs, behaviors, teaching and learning strategies and more
2. selecting, planning, organizing, and presenting specific learning experiences from a pool of possibilities
3. assessing the degree of success of these experiences

When a teacher uses the synoptic method for social studies, he or she is demonstrating the notion of consciously choosing a particular learning experience(s) as the best selection among a number of different possibilities for one particular group of children. This empowered teacher is not simply taking a prepared textbook of one-size-fits-all curricula and presenting it to children. The teacher as the intellectual leader of the class begins his or her educational efforts by first taking into account a whole range of ideas and then identifying what appears to be the best fit for children given prevailing conditions and/or context of the learning experience.

When used in social studies, the synoptic method draws upon four central strands of theory and practice in education: holistic education, cognitive science, social reconstruction, and child-centered approaches.

1. Holistic Education: To take into consideration individual children, communities, and contexts of learning experiences; cognizant of different capacities, abilities, skills, and dispositions of individuals—to be aware of implications, resources and challenges of holistic approaches to education
2. Cognitive Science: To foster and provide practice for a child's growing ability to direct and focus his or her own individual learning (metacognition)—to create an environment in which children can explore ways to become more efficient learners with careful and loving guidance

3. Social Reconstruction: To develop a sense of the empowerment of individuals as integral participating members of a liberal democratic community—to seek out ways to help children identify and explore models of equity and justice and to look for opportunities to improve the social and cultural life of the child's community

4. Child-centered Education: To place emphasis on meeting/satisfying needs of children—to appreciate interests of children and the powerful role they play in the young lives of children, to make use of a child's native skills and dispositions, and to provide direct supervision of a child's activities

Although the synoptic method applies to selected elements of these important educational initiatives and research areas, it would be incorrect to assume that the synoptic method follows any single one of these in terms of theory and practice. The synoptic method has at its roots a synergistic quality, in that the construction of learning experiences from parts of these various positions creates a curricular idea that is decidedly different (and expanded) from the application of any single one tradition.

Specifically for social studies, like the vision of a rainbow of many colors, the synoptic method is activated by applying different ideas that retain individual characteristics, but when viewed as a whole create a new pattern of ideas. Thus, as we shall discover, the synoptic method brings together a number of distinct ideas such as: the four universal needs of children, engaging children with acceptance and thought and action dispositions and skills, and by introducing children to the social studies formula. At the core of the synoptic method is the notion of providing meaningful experiences that allow for the direct enlargement of the child's experiences.

Given these elements, within schools synoptic teachers are responsible for and empowered to generate, foster, and/or facilitate experiences in which not only individual needs can be met, but also experiences in which learning can occur. Synoptic experiences, however, are not centered on specific skills, a "great books" curriculum, or five thousand cultural literacy terms. The synoptic method focuses upon what teachers can do to make learning experiences meaningful to every child. As we shall see later, given this view, the synoptic method represents a theory of instruction more than a theory of learning.

Because instruction will be keyed to meeting the four universal needs of children, no special claim is required to explain how children learn. Synoptic teachers do, however, make a prediction that if experiences are well designed, executed, monitored, and assessed, in addition to meeting four real needs of children, learning will take place at some perceptible or measurable level and perhaps even at significant levels of understanding and application.

Each of these exciting proposals for teaching (some that are perhaps new to you and some that are familiar) will be presented in the following chapters. In the exploration of this new approach toward teaching children through social studies, I invite and challenge you to experiment with these ideas as you probe and extend the frontiers of your own experience. I hope as you become a teacher of children you will in turn guide and support young minds and bodies as they encounter the perplexities and wonders of living in our world—that your efforts will help children build rainbows to the world.

1

BUILDING A TEACHING KIT

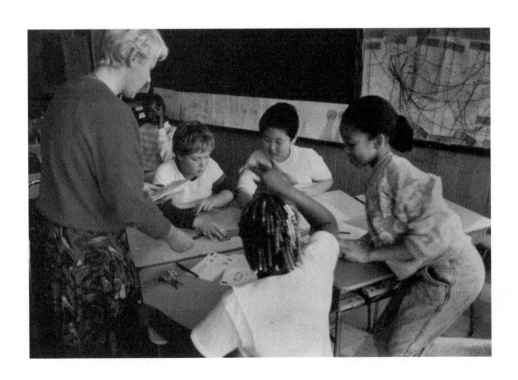

In this chapter you will

- Learn how to put together a teaching kit.
- Identify an exciting social studies topic.
- Begin to explore new sources and materials.
- Practice research skills.

Welcome! You are about to begin an edventure in social studies. Edventure is short for educational adventure. Many elementary education experiences begin this journey with a description of social studies and its teaching methods. Our social studies program is divided into three basic components that engage teachers in curricular development at the outset, rather than at some later point.

Instead of just reading about social studies, we will learn about social studies as we practice social studies. Thus, the start of your expedition into teaching elementary social studies does not begin in a chair reading a book or listening to a lecture, but on the move—thinking about exciting lesson ideas and gathering up materials and supplies for teaching social studies.

First, you will need to identify and cultivate a broad social studies topic. Next you will explore and/or generate whatever materials and supplies you may think useful to create experiences for children to be introduced to or exposed to your topic. This accumulation of materials, tools, books, objects, and more—all related to one particular topic—is called a teaching kit. Depending upon the circumstances, time, and resources of your teacher education program or school, much of the teaching kit will only exist as a list of materials. Whether or not you will be able to actually find and literally use the materials and supplies found in your kit is not the point of our program. The point is for you to have a strong grasp of developing potential teaching ideas and materials as well as for you to gain experience discovering and applying what is available and what you might want to use for your lesson experiences.

The second part of the course will be devoted to practice in designing lesson experiences for a particular group of children. Drawing upon the teaching kit as a base, you will organize a collection of lessons into potential learning experiences for children. Typically this unit or module of experiences will cover portions of ten to fifteen teaching days (or less) depending upon the demands of your teacher education program or existing school program.

The third component of the program is designed to help you present sample lessons to peers. Perhaps you would provide a particular example from your topic or even explain your approach to the learning experience for your peers. The lesson presentations furnish not only the opportunity for you to practice your teaching skills in front of a group, but, more importantly, the presentations provide the chance to learn valuable lesson ideas from others.

Because this might be your first teaching experience, the teaching kit model offers an opportunity to explore the variety of materials and supplies necessary for effective and successful teaching. This sharing of ideas also provides an opportunity for you to test your creative powers. In addition, the kit model offers the opportunity to practice four basic experiences: planning lesson experiences, organizing actual lesson experiences, presenting lesson experiences, and assessing each of these three steps.

This book emphasizes holistic teaching. Holistic teaching implies a strong sense of teacher empowerment in the planning, organization/preparation, presentation, and assessment of learning experiences. Teachers who apply holistic models view the child as a whole entity, considering the contextual environment of each child and not separating the child from this experience. Holistically minded teachers attempt to avoid viewing the child as a receptacle with parts clearly marked, "place social studies there, mathematics here, language arts there, reading here, and science there, and everything else over there."

The common division of curricula into distinctive parts is called analytical sense; this happens when you explore, teach about, and keep separate, certain elements of the whole curriculum. The maintenance, integration, or construction of distinct parts into meaningful wholes is called holistic sense; this happens when elements of the whole curriculum are not separated or investigated independently. The approach of this course acknowledges the discrete, yet interconnected, nature of the various disciplines of study. However, the application of analytical sense (the division of social studies subject matter into areas such as history, geography, political science, economics, anthropology, sociology, and psychology) is not encouraged or endorsed for elementary-age children (see explanation in chapter 5). By permitting the intermingling of various subjects with the experiences of the child, the holistic approach facilitates metacognition (literally helping children to learn how to learn).

Holistic sense extends beyond social studies to other school subjects such as language arts, science, reading, and mathematics. While our first focus will be on using holistic sense within social studies patterns, you will also need to look for intersections and possibilities that unify and build bridges of experiences across all curricular areas. In many school districts, seeking bridges to other subject areas of elementary curricula is becoming accepted as a critical part of education.

Three Components of Course-Textbook

- Teaching kit
- Planning and preparation of lesson experiences/unit
- Presentation of lesson experiences

A Rationale for Teaching Kits

As a basic rule, the assembly of a large number of resources permits the builder to fashion his or her work into any variety of forms depending upon circumstances and needs. For example, given a wide assortment of building blocks or Legos, a child can put together any number of structures or things. Although the child is limited to the building medium (Legos), since the task of construction possibilities is large, the outcome will not be limited either. Combined with their own imaginations and your helpful suggestions and given a supportive environment for learning, children can produce amazing results.

No one would think of limiting a songwriter to one or two notes in the composition of a melody, yet some teachers would not think twice about teaching a lesson about Scotland (or any other topic) with only one resource. Many teachers rely wholly upon a single textbook and its worksheets when teaching social studies to children and give little consideration to the use of other materials.

Consequently, rather than beginning specific lessons with a few resources in hand, you will first develop a grasp of the topic and its teaching possibilities. The purpose of the teaching kit is to assemble as much background information, supplies, and materials about a social studies topic as possible. Although you may not be able to actually have on hand all the materials and supplies listed in your kit, you will know where you might obtain these items when needed.

With the kit materials collected, we will begin to assemble lesson ideas into a unit. Defined here, a unit is a set of teaching experiences that may be organized as individual lessons that can stand alone or perhaps as a group of lessons that are designed to highlight a specific theme that will be repeated in other units during the school year. Throughout the process of lesson experience planning you will want to add to your teaching kit as needed. Thus, the teaching kit is a literal expansion of interests and needs, rather than a set or fixed body of materials. As your experience grows, you will add to the volume of ideas and materials in your teaching kits, carefully modifying the kits according to you and your children's needs and interests.

Generating a Topic

The first question for many new teachers (and veterans also) is the challenge: What should I do first, where do I begin? Prepare lessons? Gather materials? Both? When given the curriculum in the form of a basal or other curricular guide, accepted practice is to follow the book. However, what happens when

1. The book does not suit your or your children's needs?
2. The reader is poorly written or designed?
3. The fixed curriculum does not account for circumstances and situations, creating unforeseen concerns and challenges?
4. As a professional educator you are not empowered to create and experiment with curricular ideas?

Although following the curricular patterns of the district or school is important, every professional teacher needs to be ready to make curricular as well as other important decisions daily—decisions that may include supplementing standard curricula or creating new curricula. Your first task is to decide upon a topic or theme for your teaching kit, such as "Pioneer Days," "People of the Congo River," or "Foods of America." This topic-theme will be used later in the development of your unit. You may wish to assemble your kit around an idea that will be expressly used for just this unit. That is, the kit will represent teaching materials to be used for a single, stand-alone unit. In contrast, you may want to think of the kit as a springboard/resource guide to a number of units that will be taught over the course of the school year. This use of the kit captures the sense of using a thematic approach to planning.

Your teaching kit will be used throughout the course, so you will need to think carefully when selecting a topic-theme. You may want to consider starting with a broad topic such as "Living in Far-off Places" or "Endangered Animals" or "Knights and Castles." Then, later, when you have brought together a number of materials you could decide to narrow your topic-theme to determine a few exciting lesson experiences you will want to try during the course or when you begin to work with children in the field.

The general-to-specific format is helpful because it affords you the opportunity to comprehend and appreciate the range and depth of the topic-theme. The more materials you can find, the greater the teaching possibilities, which also increases the learning possibilities for children as well. Having more ideas and materials to choose from that add range and depth should prove beneficial when you plan your lessons.

Sources of Topics-Themes

In social studies the number of topics-themes to choose from is enormous. You may want to look over a list of topics-themes from your instructor to get ideas or you may have some ideas in mind. We should all try to avoid limiting the possibilities. If we draw limits upon our own work, even when unintended, we are also drawing limits upon our children. Although it may take time and practice to get it right, let imagination, common sense, and your own creative talents and potentials guide your selections.

Although some may say "You can't do that!" or "The kids will never understand this" or "I've tried that idea before and it doesn't work," your teaching ideas have not been tested. And your children have not had you as a teacher before. You might be the one who makes a difference, who opens new worlds of ideas and possibilities to a child, who dares to dream new dreams, who lights new fires of learning. If you believe opportunities for learning are endless, your teaching and the experiences you offer children must reflect this belief.

Topics or themes do not define social studies, people do. In deciding upon your social studies topic or theme two general rules apply: first, the topic or theme must be directly related to human life and our use of our planet/ universe, and second, the topic or theme must possess the potential for exploring the past, present, and future in a number of dimensions. This may appear to imply the sky is the limit, and in one sense it is; however, every teacher must work within some boundaries—boundaries that are often defined by circumstance, conditions, abilities, energy, and other characteristics. Although holistic teaching highlights teacher empowerment, you will also need to know local and/or state curricular requirements.

Review of Your First Tasks

- Generate a topic or theme
- Explore and identify potential materials based on topic-theme
- Keep a complete running record of your activities and ideas

Commercial Sources for Teaching Kits

Typically when new teachers begin to prepare units for their children they turn toward commercially available textbooks, basals, trade books, journals, and other printed materials. These are excellent places to begin your work because they offer a variety of ideas as well as concrete examples. You can find many of these materials in your college library and the children's section of your local library or media center. You may even know an elementary teacher who might be wiling to share sources with you. If you would like to purchase your own materials you might want to investigate ordering catalogs or materials from your local bookstore (which may already have a good selection of books on hand to examine) or ordering from a commercial publisher or supplier (addresses listed in the appendix).

As good as commercial materials may be, alone they are insufficient for holistic teaching. Holistic teaching requires learning about the child and his or her world by looking into the context of the child's experience—to examine social, cultural, and other important elements of the child's life. Holistic teaching involves introducing the child to the world of possibility, rather than fitting the child into a predetermined life. In this spirit, using holistic sense means treating the child as part of the teaching experiences, not as an entity outside of the experiences. With these ideas as guideposts, other sources must be explored, examined, and secured.

Creative Sources

One rule when building a teaching kit is to study children in various contexts— to go where children play, shop, live, worship, and do whatever it is they do today. Explore any place where children are the focus of activity. Sources for kit materials can be found at the mall, church, mosque, synagogue, restaurants, playground, parks, street corners, and more. Even watching children's television programming on Saturday mornings and other times during the week can be a helpful source of information.

You need to explore what toys children play with, what clothes they wear, what music they listen to, what fads they copy, and what foods they eat. Popular magazines, television commercials, Christmas catalogues, and department and specialty stores offer a wealth of information about children. Even a visit to the local pediatrician's office may reveal valuable information about how children deal or cope with stress and illness. Schools, too, are an excellent place to observe and identify children's needs and interests.

What do observations of children (between the ages of five and twelve) in these many settings have to do with building a teaching kit? The observations reveal a wealth of information about children: what they like, what they dislike, what activities they enjoy, how they behave in a variety of situations, and more. Knowing that children like dinosaurs, horses, or baseball cards, for instance, may have a direct bearing upon the selection of materials for your kit if your topic is "Prehistoric Life," "Native Americans from the Great Plains," or "Popular Culture." Knowing that children like rap music, particular foods, certain stories, or movies may also directly influence your kit if your topic is "The History of Musical Instruments," "Foods from Europe," or "Children Around the World." The point of these observations is to gain an appreciation of the life of the child by utilizing the child's own experience in your teaching.

For example, if your topic is "Colonial American Life", you might include selected groups of Americans living in North America during the mid-1750s. In your explorations you may find dolls or other toys, such as puzzles, boats, and toy soldiers. You may also find information about Native American handcrafts, recipes, or clothing. Or you might use information about ship building and architecture from European-Americans. Films, songs, stories of children, stamps, biographies, and a host of materials not found in textbooks might help you plan experiences for children to learn about the lives of African-Americans.

This expansion of multiple historical perspectives and materials (of depth and breath) increases the potential (what could be) and possible (what can be) learning experiences. Variety and choice add excitement, fun, and enjoyment to learning that otherwise might have been reduced to mere workbooks and worksheets.

Suggestions: Things to Look for

After you have located books from children's literature, trade publications, textbooks, and other printed materials, you may also want to examine books that include general and specific information about your topic. Also be on the lookout for leads to other sources. Encyclopedias, atlases, dictionaries, and almanacs have both general and specific information about social studies topics or themes. Some encyclopedias, such as *The World Book,* publish materials and guides especially for children.

> **Consider This:** *Public libraries often have excellent selections of children's books and materials.*

Audio-visual materials such as commercial films, documentaries, and film shorts—available on video tape—should also be examined. In addition, filmstrips, vinyl records, cassette tapes, videodiscs, transparencies, still pictures, posters, and slides should be located and noted. Check the running time, suggested audience (K–3, elementary, etc.), supplier, costs, and summary of contents. Make note of any special equipment or other materials needed to use the audiovisual materials (video tape machine and television monitor, projectors, etc.). As you examine these materials, it may be helpful (as an aid to remembering or grading materials for later use) to construct an annotated bibliography to add to your kit.

Computers, printers, and necessary software are rapidly becoming standard equipment in many elementary schools for all traditional curricular areas, including social studies. At present, due to costs, space, staff confidence and competence with computers, and time factors, the challenges of using this equipment can prove formidable. While some schools may have a computer for each child and others none at all, many schools have only a classroom set of computers that must service the computer needs of every child and staff member in the whole school. Thus, waiting for computer time may limit some of your efforts. Nonetheless, most schools rely on Apple and IBM (and their clones) to provide most of the operational hardware. Typically, Apple products and compatible software are more popular, but this may not be reflective of the actual number of Apple products in schools. Despite the challenges of using computer technology, the payoffs are many. When used as tools to enhance learning experiences, computers can clearly increase the activity, enthusiasm, and creativity of children.

> **Follow-up Question:** *What makes computer knowledge and skills important for our children's future?*

Visual exhibits and presentations such as bulletin boards, wall posters, freestanding displays, and dioramas (life-like representation using figures and models) add much to not only the learning possibilities, but also to the classroom environment. Your kit should include enough materials to design, build, and present these visual projects—construction paper, tacks, stencils, staples, scissors, and glue. You may, however, want to add magazines, catalogues, and other printed materials for cutting out pictures and letters. If you have your children build a diorama or other display, you will have to include the necessary materials.

> **Follow-up Question:** *How might visual aids stimulate and motivate children?*

Children enjoy making things. For example, it can be fun and personally satisfying to plan and construct your own projects, such as building a Sioux

Indian or Viking village or perhaps a Roman town or a model of their own neighborhood. Your children could build a spaceship, country store, castle, apartment building, race car, or farm. Large cardboard boxes from your local appliance dealer can become any sort of object with a little imagination. If you have the space, you might want to consider building a house right in your classroom. For flexibility, the house should be put together with portable walls and roof that can be reworked, repainted, removed, and easily reassembled. Depending on the unit, topic, or season, your flexible house can be transformed into an igloo, log cabin, Indian log house, country store, grass hut, Viking long house, or anything else desired.

Follow-up Question: Why do children like building things?

Another interesting and inexpensive idea that you might want to explore with your children is use of an old carpet as a building surface. This can be accomplished by turning the carpet over on the back side; you can paint on it, staple or nail on it, build up areas with plaster, cut it and more. What is good about old carpets is that they can become a country or lunar landscape or a city or world map, all this fun can be had for next to nothing, and then the carpet can be thrown out when the project is finished. (Do not be surprised if some children want to take the project home.) Moreover, when old carpets are used properly, custodians also like them because they leave classroom floors clean. Other construction projects will require building blocks, sand and stone, popsicle sticks, plaster of Paris, and lots of water and flour (for making papier mâché). You will also need hammers, saws, drills, levels, pliers, screw drivers, wrenches, and a good supply of nails, screws, bolts, staples, and other fasteners.

Literally any material, used for construction that can be made safe for the classroom should be added to the list. As you, your principal, your children, and your children's parents and guardians will expect, safety must be a major consideration with any construction project. You must be sure to include instruction and demonstration of the proper care and use of every tool and procedure and make children aware of general safety rules as well as specific safety requirements for all equipment for each project. While fun and enjoyable experiences are our goals, safety must be a prime consideration.

Consider This: Always provide important dos and don'ts for every activity; having a fun time is great, but safety has to come first.

Since social studies draws upon the world and its people, we will want to include sources of information about what is happening in other parts of the world as well as in our own nation, state, region, or neighborhood. Newspapers, periodicals, other print media, telecasts, and radio can bring the world into your classroom. With a satellite link you can bring television broadcasts from around the world and nation to your children. With a more modest budget, shortwave radio can bring radio broadcasts from Rome to Rio de Janeiro to London to Beijing to Cairo to Mexico City and points all over the globe, or perhaps, you could explore a telecommunications link by computer and modem.

> *Follow-up Question: How might children benefit from exposure to different and varied cultures?*

Newspapers are also an excellent source of social studies materials. There are local newspapers, regional papers, and even nationwide papers *(USA Today)*. You may want to explore the possibility of getting a classroom set of newspapers, or perhaps a class subscription to a weekly news magazine such as *Time* or *Newsweek* or a quality monthly such as *National Geographic* or *National Geographic's World*. In addition, a number of national organizations produce magazines for children that you might want to include in your kit. The National Geographic Society, the National Council for Social Studies, and the Organization of American Historians all publish journals, magazines, and materials with exciting ideas for elementary teachers and children. Newspapers and periodicals with illustrations can be used not only for class projects, but they also can be useful for the construction of collages or bulletin boards, or for other experiences.

We all love to eat interesting and new foods. Although serving a full, several-course Cantonese (Chinese) dinner may seem out of place at school, you could make preparing and eating such a meal part of a cultural experience unit. Cooking is fun for boys and girls. You may consider getting a hot plate, authentic recipes, cooking utensils, paper plates, forks, knives, spoons, and whatever else you need to make a perfect traditional Japanese, French, Russian, Bantu, Brazilian, or Hebrew dinner. Be sure to have a good supply of clean-up materials—cooking and eating can be messy.

As miscellaneous materials, your kit should include enough pens, pencils, crayons, paints (water and acrylic clean up the best), and markers for written work and illustrations. You will also need cutting and pasting materials and tools for art work and sewing and weaving materials and tools for making costumes and other handicrafts. Play money, pocketbooks, wallets, and store items can be very useful. You could have your children open a school store where toys, foods, clothes, and whatever you have handy could be sold. Children might collect old boxes and containers to sell, collect and deposit their money in the bank, pay for supplies, hire employees, and make profits.

Creating a Positive Environment for Learning

The teaching kit represents a host of materials from which you will develop lesson experiences. You may also want to include a number of other objects to create an inviting and stimulating learning environment. Children love to travel, to dream of far-off exotic places. Since traveling to Kenya or Australia is not usually practical, you may be able to bring a bit of Africa or the "Land Down Under" to your classroom. Obtaining and displaying artifacts, souvenirs, clothing, and other objects from around the world can create some exciting lessons. You may want to use a camera and copy stand to prepare your own slide presentations of your favorite projects.

There may be a number of people in your community who would be happy to share their traveling experiences with your children. You (and others in class) may have been to Europe or Asia or even Central America. Just being able to touch something from a far-off land can create a sort of magic for children. Clothing, shoes, hats, toys, art-crafts, and more can become fashioned into lesson experiences. This variety of objects enriches and expands the classroom in ways that books or films cannot.

Historical objects and clothes are both interesting and educational. Your children might want to dress up in old-fashioned shoes and hats or pants and shirts. Dress-up and pretend games/roles create a number of teaching possibilities. You may want to find a trunk or big box to store shoes, belts, topcoats, nightshirts, and whatever else you can find. Some commercial manufacturers sell period costumes that you may want to model for your children. Instead of the typical Halloween costume, you may want to stage a historical fashion show. Old clothes can be found at garage sales or second-hand clothing stores or from volunteer organizations.

> **Consider This:** *Look for dress-up clothes at second-hand stores; garage sales are also great (and cheap) sources of fun clothes and shoes.*

Geography is a central part of social studies. You should include a number of wall or pull-down maps, charts, and globes in your class that help children put people and places together. Location is an important dimension of social studies and every event or group of people can be represented on a map. The National Geographic Alliance and National Geographic Society have a number of excellent materials available for children (the use of geography will be discussed in chapter 5).

Finally, no elementary classroom would be complete without music—song and dance. Music set to rhymes and rhythms (that your children can make up) can truly add fun and help create a happy atmosphere for your classroom. You may either find old musical instruments or have children improvise and explore music by making their own sets of drums, chimes, bells, and various other things that make sounds. A good rule is to keep the music simple (simple patterns, simple verse, simple dance); it is easier for children to enjoy and follow. Standard favorites should be mixed with contemporary sounds as well as sounds from other cultures and lands. Mixed with history, geography, and other social studies, music adds a wonderful and magical dimension to learning.

Summary of Some Suggested Teaching Kit Materials

- Books
- Reference materials

- Audiovisual materials
- Computers and software
- Visual displays
- Construction materials
- Newspapers, print, and other media
- Foods
- World cultural objects, clothing
- Musical instruments and sheet music
- Historical objects, clothing
- Geographic materials

Depending upon your individual circumstances, your kit should stimulate a wide variety of teaching ideas. It is probably best to have more materials to choose from than less; however, you and your instructor should agree what is enough to complete the next assignment (designing lesson experiences).

A Look Ahead

For the next several weeks you will be busy finding and cataloguing materials for your teaching kits. After you have assembled these materials in some form, you will be ready to progress to developing these materials into teaching lessons for elementary-age children.

As you are working on your kits, we will begin to examine and to explore a viable context for teaching in a liberal democracy. The next five chapters present a number of ideas for you to think about as you develop and expand your personal philosophy of teaching. After you have had time to consider these ideas and perhaps opportunities to generate discussions with you peers, you will then begin to organize your lesson experiences into units. Toward the end of your class experience, if time and circumstances permit, you might even have the chance to present your unit to your peers.

Beginning Tips to Think about and Explore

- Try out a few broad topics; remember that look is one of the most inviting words in the English language. As you explore your library card catalog, shelves, and other places, check out just how much information you can find about your topic. Be persistent, keep on the trail of your idea . . . and keep looking. If you find that the trail of materials and ideas is getting cold, consider switching to another topic that seems more promising. Be flexible. If you experience difficulty getting materials from your library or other sources, you may want to set your idea aside for now and pick it up at another time. Also, ask yourself, does the idea excite you? If you think the topic is fun and interesting, use your enthusiasm to build your kit.

Remember children can recognize whether or not you are really excited; use this to your advantage.

- If you wish, find a book with lots of color illustrations and/or suggestions. Look through the pages, list some ideas, and check up on the resources in appendices. As you begin your kit, there are a number of excellent places to look for ideas. Some of my favorites are *The World Book Encyclopedia,* current and back issues of *National Geographic Magazine,* catalogs from commercial publishers of children's materials, *Reader's Digest's* special books series, and the exquisitely illustrated and detailed Usborne family of publications (particularly the *Usborne Children's Encyclopedia*).

- Another excellent source for teaching materials/ideas is the Broderbund Company's family of *Carmen Sandiego* computer games (currently four titles are available).

- For a hands-on approach to child's play (and learning), the Playmobil Company's toys are difficult to beat for imagination and action. Of special note: none of the toys require batteries. Because the toys are specifically designed as a system (that is, all the toys and their component parts are interrelated and interchangeable), children can easily move from a western town to a medieval castle to a modern train station in one day and each toy in the series is compatible with every other!

- Although some might believe that most elementary-age children have outgrown *Mister Rogers' Neighborhood,* I think the accompanying *Mister Rogers' Plan and Play Book* is a first-rate source for a host of fun-tested, marvelous ideas for children.

- While the *Children's Books in Print* continues to be the authoritative index to children's books, your library may also have the now available *Children's Reference Plus* computer program on CD-ROM. This up-to-date, easy-to-use reference contains fully annotated publishing information such as current prices of items, suggested grade levels, and an overview of contents all indexed by author, subject, and title. In addition, you might want to browse through *Best Books for Children* by John T. Gillespie and Corinne J. Naden as well as *Our Family, Our Friends, Our World* by Lyn Miller-Lachman; both references are published by R. R. Bowker. *Best Books* gives you the information found in its title and *Our Friends* provides a wealth of information about currently available multicultural titles. If your library does not own these, ask to have them ordered. (Tell the librarian they will be put to good use.)

- Finally, no kit search would be complete without consulting the single most comprehensive guide for films and video, *The Educational Film and Video Locator.* Packaged in two full volumes of more than 4,000 pages, the *Locator* not only gives you an annotated guide to available films and video materials, but describes each item and gives the source.

This beginner's list is not exhaustive; these suggestions are given merely to get you up and running . . . so, keep looking.

Guide to Possible First Sources

The World Book Encyclopedia sets the standard for a comprehensive, user-friendly encyclopedia. Its excellent, well-written articles with fine illustrations and graphics make it a must for every classroom. Although *World Book* is most helpful for upper grades, the fifteen volume *Childcraft—The How and Why Library* is expressly designed for elementary-age children. Full of first-rate stories, activities, ideas, and illustrations, *Childcraft* combines truly exciting and fun educational ideas with learning.

Send for catalog of current titles and services to:

World Book Educational Products
101 Northwest Point Blvd.
Elkgrove Village, Illinois 60007
(800) 621-8202

Cost of full set exceeds several hundred dollars.

National Geographic Magazine is the best general source for social studies teaching. Superior writers, stunning photographs, and excellent maps make this magazine the single best educational value available in any medium. General articles are good for all ages. For some articles special attention by teachers may be needed to help children understand controversial issues or material. The *National Geographic World Magazine* is also great for children. The society's *Picture Atlas of the World,* suitable for all elementary grades, offers not only the superb *Geographic* pictures and easy-to-read information on the various nations and regions of the world, but does so with a keen sense of humor.

Send for current catalog of titles. Subscription available:

National Geographic Society
P.O. Box 2895
Washington, DC 20077-9960

Cost: $21.00 (US)

Social Studies School Service Catalogs, available from the *Social Studies School Service* company offer a wide variety of social studies texts, trade books, computer software, games, and many other special items. Just about anything currently available for the general social studies market from the elementary grades (K–6) and up to high school can typically be found. Although the variety of materials available is better than any store could provide, prices generally run at full retail (no discounts, except if you buy in bulk quantities).

All the catalogs are free, the 800 number is handy, and the customer service is excellent. Be sure to order at least the general catalog (K–12 materials) and the special social studies catalogs for grades K–6 and 4–8.

Order catalogs from:

Social Studies School Service
10200 Jefferson Boulevard
P.O. Box 802
Culver City, California 90232-9983
(800) 421-4246 toll-free customer service

The *Usborne Children's Encyclopedia* is the most visually engaging set of children's materials on the market. *Usborne* presents history, geography, and a host of other topics in ways that children of any age can readily grasp and enjoy. If you have not seen the Usborne catalog, order one. The quality and quantity of titles available at reasonable prices is impressive.

Available from most book stores and department outlets. Send for catalog of titles:

EDC Publishing
10302 East 55th Place
Tulsa, Oklahoma 74146

Titles range in cost from $5.95 to $19.95

Where in the World Is Carmen Sandiego? is part of the *Carmen* series from Broderbund, which markets a number of computer games for social studies. Available in Apple and IBM forms, the games are wonderful assets for teaching about time (history) and space (geography). Be sure to look carefully at these products. Younger children and less patient others will need careful guidance and attention. Available at most computer and department stores. Request catalog from:

Broderbund Company
P.O. Box 6125
Novato, California 94948-6125

Cost for games is about $35.00

If your budget permits, an investment in *Playmobil* toys can lead to a wealth of quality imagination experiences as well as valuable learning experiences about history, geography, and economics. Because imagination and building exercises are integral to the action, *Playmobil* toys can be enjoyed by all elementary-age children. Of special importance are the medieval castles, trains, and authentic farming village. Although cost is always a factor, not only are these toys the most interesting and creative, but they are also (perhaps more importantly) the best made, most durable products of this kind on the market. Visit your local retailer to view these products and to observe children carefully eying these wonderful toys.

Send for full color catalog to:

Playmobil USA, Inc.   Playmobil Canada, Inc.
11-E Nicholas Court   7303 Danbro Crescent
Dayton, New Jersey 08810 or Mississauga, Ontario
                             L5N 6P8

Reader's Digest's Special Books include a wide variety of quality hard-bound books for social studies, especially history and geography subjects. Most combine excellent pictures and story lines that really help children grasp ideas, content, and perspectives. They are best for older children, but are excellent sources for teachers exploring lesson ideas.

Send for current catalog of titles to:

Reader's Digest Association, Inc.
Pleasantville, New York 10570

Titles cost about $25.00 and up

Mister Rogers' Plan and Play Book, like *Mister Rogers' Neighborhood* consistently for some thirty years the single best all-around children's program on television, emphasizes the emotional well-being of children. The *Plan and Play Book* offers brief, doable hands-on activities that will delight, puzzle, and intrigue children. Many of the ideas can easily be combined with or converted to social studies lessons, especially for lower elementary grades. Check through the program sketches, select those ideas that seem interesting, and try them.

Available from:

Family Communications, Inc.
4802 Fifth Avenue
Pittsburgh, Pennsylvania 15213
(412) 687-2990

Cost: $12.95

For thematic ideas, *Kids Discover* is the single best magazine available. Each of the ten yearly issues highlights a single theme such as Volcanoes, the Roman Empire, the Mayas, Trains, Space, and more! Full of careful charts, beautiful illustrations and pictures, explanations, puzzles, teaching ideas, and more a copy should be available to every elementary class for study, projects, or just plain fun.

Available from:

Kios Discover
170 Fifth Avenue
New York, New York 10010
(212) 242-5133

Cost: $14.95 ($3.00 for back issues)

Marking Your Progress

1. Topic/Theme Selections _____

    _____

    _____

2. Important Sources Found _____

    _____

    _____

3. Potential Teaching Ideas _____

    _____

    _____

4. Materials Needed _____

    _____

    _____

2

THE CHILD AND YOUTH CULTURE

In this chapter you will

- Be asked to find out more about children.
- Consider differences and similarities between children and adults.
- Generalize about children's views of the world.
- Discuss using imagination, interests, and needs to motivate children.

What are kids really like? Although we were all kids at one time, children of today seem different from our memories of our own youth. When we look at a group of boys with thunderbolt designs cut neatly into the hair by their temples, we wonder "What are today's kids coming to?"

> *Follow-up Question: In the 1990s Teenage Mutant Ninja Turtles, Nintendo, Jurassic Park, Where's Waldo, Ren and Stimpy, and Troll dolls have found a happy audience among many children. What other interests do children have?*

In our observations of children some of us may even think we have literally lost touch with the youth culture of today and become anxious at the prospect of facing thirty little strangers on our first day of teaching. At the beginning of your classroom career you may be struck by the differences between your perceptions of what you think children will be like and what they really are like. Because our knowledge of children varies widely, we are going to take some time to look at children, not just at what makes them appear different from the memories of our youth, but also what makes them the same.

> *Follow-up Question: What was your life like during childhood? Your interests? Fun things to do with friends? Your imagination games?*

Children are not merely the topic of this chapter, they are the focus of this textbook and its methodology. Children are the reason we are teachers. You have chosen a very important career—to become an elementary teacher. Knowing more about children is simply a necessary part of your professional development. Possessing textbook knowledge of subject matter is important too, and learning to teach about content is also significant. The foundation of our work, however, is learning to deal with content, methodology, and children in the context of our world.

As we think about the "same but different" description of children, we find it awkward and contradictory. How can children be the same and different? Perhaps you are a typical precertification teacher, born in the late 1960s through the early 1970s. Think back upon the experiences you shared with others of your age as you grew up. Maybe you and millions of others tuned television sets to episodes of *The Brady Bunch, Wonder Woman,* or even reruns of *Gilligan's Island* or the more serious saga, *Roots.*

Possible you wore your designer jeans while listening to your favorite "Jackson Five" records or played with your Barbie dolls; you may have even taken care of your older sister's Pet Rock. Perhaps you spent your summers with GI Joe and Matchbox cars in the backyard or playground. After Dorothy Hamill skated her way to an Olympic gold medal at the 1976 Innsbruck Games maybe you were one of millions of girls who rushed to get the latest "Hamill hairstyle." Pet rocks, Wonder Woman, Hamill hair styles, Barbie and GI Joe dolls, heart-throbs Andy Gibb and Shawn Cassidy, J.J. from the hit show *Good Times,* Vinnie from *Welcome Back Kotter,* "the Fonz" from *Happy Days*—all were part of the youth culture of the 1970s.

Although much of your shared youth culture was found on television, you also saw images of the nation's 200th birthday on July 4th, 1976. Perhaps you wondered about the fuss over President Jimmy Carter's brother Billy or the death of Elvis Presley? You may have stood in a long line at the movie house to wait your turn to be thrilled by the films *Star Wars* and *Superman,* or maybe you were frightened when adults talked about the nuclear accident at Three Mile Island in Pennsylvania.

You may remember some special experiences that you shared with a few of your friends from school or with your family. A special trip, or perhaps a tragedy, such as the death of a grandparent, may have drawn you and your friends together in ways that others did not share. Although millions of children your age laughed at the antics of *Laverne and Shirley,* some of your early joys and sorrows are known only to your family and a few of your old childhood friends. And some of your experiences are known only to you.

> **Consider This:** *Investigate life for children in large cities, towns, farming, and other rural areas.*

In theory, this phenomenon of sharing some experiences, but not others, captures the "same but different" description used for comparing youth cultures. In application, this description, although seemingly contradictory, does provide an apt characterization of youth culture. American youth culture of today is simultaneously similar to and decidedly different from our own earlier experiences. Moreover, the differences as well as similarities among various contemporary youth groups in a particular time frame are the same and different, too. For example, although city, suburban, and rural children share many experiences, there are many experiences that are not shared. You may share many experiences with children, yet because of personal situation and/or circumstance you do not share other experiences. To capture the idea in another way, if you have attended your five or ten year high school reunion you might have experienced the same but different phenomenon. You are the same person, but you are different. Your old friends are the same, but they, too, are different. In another sense, imagine how much technology has changed our lives in the past decade. Think of all the new inventions that we did not have in our youth but today are now central to our modern lives—VCRs, CDs, video stores, personal computers, portable phones, microwave ovens, fax machines and more. Imagine the changes that inventions of the next ten years will hold for our lives.

Understanding the paradoxical nature of youth culture (the same but different phenomenon) helps us to make sense of our feelings toward children. Through our teaching this understanding facilitates building networks of sympathy, tolerance, sensitivity, and empathy toward children. Understanding children assists teachers in becoming not merely better teachers, but better human beings. We must recognize, however, that the concept of understanding children must be embraced and lived. That is, teachers need to continuously work toward understanding children and make applications of their understandings.

Behaviors, Beliefs and Values

To assist our understanding of children, teachers must come to recognize the role that behaviors, beliefs, and values play in the lives of children. Taken as a living interaction, these three elements constitute a child's personality: behaviors are defined as a summary or characterization of a child's observable actions; beliefs are defined as that which a child holds as truth, the child's perception of reality; and values are defined as those things that are treasured by the child as well as those feelings that may govern or direct a child's thoughts and actions.

Follow-up Question: How important is it for teachers to recognize differences among children?

For example, after closely observing Bobby at school for a week, Mrs. Rama decided Bobby really likes school, as in "Bobby has a good attitude about school" (his behavior shows through his observed attitude). To confirm her statement, Mrs. Rama asked Bobby why he liked school so much he replied, "because going to school is the best way to get a good job." "Do you really mean that Bobby?" asked Mrs. Rama. "Oh yes," claimed Bobby, "that's how my father got his job."

Although he has not verified it, through these comments Bobby communicates his belief that going to school produces certain acceptable results. In the third sense, we move another step closer to assessing Bobby's personality when he reveals his values to us. Because Bobby said he loves history and wants to be a history teacher when he grows up, we assume that he is identifying a value. Thus, although she may be mistaken, Mrs. Rama believes that Bobby cherishes history, that is, he values history.

Notwithstanding these definitions and examples of behaviors, beliefs, and values, there are several complexities to attend to. For instance, using the latter example of Bobby's love for history, Mrs. Rama may say Bobby has a good outlook about history (behavior), that Bobby believes history will provide him with a good living (belief), and, of course, that Bobby cares deeply about history (value).

Essentially one action (loving history) can reveal all three personality qualities; however, Mrs. Rama could be incorrect in her assessment of Bobby's behavior, belief, and value toward history—Bobby might not be telling the truth. It is possible that Bobby is merely acting as if he cares about history to impress Mrs. Rama, when in reality, although his outward personality supports Mrs. Rama's assertions, Bobby inwardly could care less about history.

Despite this problem, identifying the current behaviors, beliefs, and values of a child is an important task for teachers because knowing about these elements of personality provides an essential understanding of the child. Identifying their behaviors, beliefs, and values can be challenging. As the child's interests and view of the world are in a state of constant flux, so, too, are his attitudes, beliefs, and values still forming.

Those who celebrate religious or social events such as Christmas may recall feelings as this special time or season nears. For instance, one critical element of the approaching excitement was a belief in Santa Claus, that is, that Santa Claus was real and that he would bring toys if you were a good boy or girl. The Santa Claus phenomenon is common in the United States as can be seen through the tens of thousands of children who write Santa Claus at his home address at the North Pole every year. To these children Santa is real, he exists, and, his existence is confirmed by parents, grandparents, other adults, television programs, print media, stories, and songs.

Given the context of Sara's world and her emotional state (she wants to believe in Santa Claus), she is supplied with enough reasons to verify Santa Claus. Ultimately, with maturity and adult-like reasoning, Sara begins to uncover the inconsistencies of her own observations; she begins to doubt. This rising doubt highlights a shift in her beliefs. Eventually, she begins to view Santa Claus and Christmas in a new way; her beliefs have changed. This change of belief signals growth. It is measurable phenomena that mark the changes from one attitude, belief, or value to another. As teachers (on behalf of children), we often call such changes learning or education.

For the child, this changing process is constant. In handling behaviors, beliefs, and values, adults must first become sensitive to this process by accepting, uncritically, the child's behaviors, beliefs, and values as they appear to us and understanding that these behaviors, beliefs, and values are subject to alteration, conversion, correction, exchange, and outright replacement. Adults know that a child's behaviors, beliefs, and values will probably undergo radical changes; however, children are not as aware of the phenomenon of change. Even though some may have recognized a change in their own behaviors, beliefs, and values, they often rely heavily upon their present behaviors, beliefs, and values as being real and fixed.

In this process of change, when the child reveals these elements of personality she is also disclosing the behaviors, beliefs, and values of parents, peer group, and significant others. Television may also have an influence. Thus, by accepting and recognizing the child's particular character dispositions, you are also recognizing the source of these elements, which often means accepting the behaviors, beliefs, and values of parents.

Some behaviors, beliefs, and values are in an early formative stage, such as placing a value on responsibility or the respect for the property of others. Other dispositions are nearly gone, such as a belief in the "tooth fairy" or that anybody can become an astronaut. Teachers and other adults need to recognize what a child's behaviors, beliefs, and values consist of as well as to identify the developmental stages of these three elements. In recognizing and identifying the development of any shift in behaviors, beliefs, and values, teachers come to understand the importance of encouraging and fostering the growth of positive personality elements and reject or let pass negative personality elements.

For example, when Danny grows in maturity and mixes with other children in school, his behaviors, beliefs, and values will be in constant close contact with the behaviors, beliefs, and values of teachers, peers, and a host of other influences, good and bad. To Danny, many of these behaviors, beliefs, and values are in conflict with his own. This conflict can be troubling for Danny for just when the world appears in focus, someone challenges one of his beliefs. "Presidents always do the right thing!" exclaims Danny, "but how come people say President Smith should go to jail? Jail is the place people go when they are really bad. Because President Smith is going to jail, President Smith must be bad; but how is that possible?"

Danny is puzzled by this inconsistency and may need your assistance to sort it all out. At other times, it may be prudent to let Danny work out this conflict of experience on his own. Children often identify national leaders, sports figures, and entertainment personalities as heroes and heroines and the pedestal they are placed on is often too high for mere mortals. When some conflict, contradiction, or inconsistency repeatedly challenges a child's behaviors, beliefs, and values regarding such heroes and heroines or some other issue, it is important to the child that some exploration and resolution of the issue be provided. Without our attention or at least understanding, the issue will probably persist.

Even when adults do not challenge children's dispositions or acknowledge a child's present and forming beliefs, inevitably, many questions are asked:

- Whose values do you encourage? Discourage?
- Why are some beliefs reinforced, while others are discarded?
- Are children ready to have their values challenged?
- Is school the appropriate place for behaviors, beliefs, and values to be explored and tested?
- Are teachers prepared, competent, and willing to teach about behaviors, beliefs, and values?

Do we want to change the child's behaviors, beliefs, and values or do we merely want children to be able to recognize their own behaviors, beliefs, and values? Do we want children to learn how to cope with challenges to their behaviors, beliefs, and values? How can we answer these questions? Do answers exist?

The Child's View of the World

Our varying perspectives of children are developed and dependent upon our own remembrance of childhood as well as experiences with children since our youth. Most adults have developed a view of the world that is beyond the ability and comprehension of the child. One critical difference between the child and adult is that the child views his world as a whole—a complete entity. The child has made sense of this world (on his own terms) long before attending school. Although much is still puzzling and misunderstood, by the time a child enters school he or she has developed a rather embryonic understanding of life.

> *Consider This: What are the differences between what a child perceives and what adults perceive?*

The adult, however, knows from experience, that the child's view of the world is woefully incomplete and will change and become enlarged with new experiences. The adult, then, divides the curricular whole into parts, such as mathematics, science, literature, social studies, and more. Ostensibly, to the adult, it is thought to be easier for the child if the whole of a child's learning is dissected and explained as separate parts. Although children may tacitly accept these divisions, they do not see these adult divisions as natural, nor do they understand them.

Whether in school or out, the child sees information as complete. Moreover, without information or experience to the contrary, children also view their world in a literal sense. For example, one child may actually think that when the sun disappears in the early evening, it goes to sleep for the night. Another child may think that the reason a baby grows in mother's stomach is because her mother ate a special baby egg. And still another child may believe that putting Tylenol on your head will stop a headache. The seemingly illogical perceptions of children often astound adults who have long organized their world and have forgotten how children view or organize their world. Still, some adults continue to feed incorrect perceptions in order to mask or gently coerce a child to do something, such as "You will see better if you eat your carrots!"

> *Find It Out: Ask children their perceptions of things such as where lumber comes from, what the President does, or what happens to the sun at night. Cross-check responses across grade levels/ages/genders.*

Over time, with the enlargement of experience, most childhood misconceptions will be clarified. Even though experience changes perspective, the child retains the notion that the world is a whole. This observation is significant and has a direct bearing upon how much, if any, long-term learning will take place. Perhaps, what the child may learn throughout childhood, in a collateral manner, is not to invest much time in learning specific details because they will change at the next level of experience.

Often unknowingly teachers heap information and new data upon children that makes the world more complicated, intricate, and complex. One result of the information-loading process, to the child, is known as a "rude awakening," or in another adult term "welcome to the real world, kid, learn to live with it." The opposite effect, that teachers certainly do not desire, is for the child to reject altogether the new and the different. Another facet of the holistic to analytic development (the separation of wholes into parts) is that adults expect children to reconstruct the dismembered parts of the whole.

For instance, with history and geography as typical subject matters, adults often teach about historical events independently of geography as well as teach geography without any historical contexts. Thus, children may know that the Constitution was written in Philadelphia, but have no idea of Philadelphia's location. Likewise, teachers often present geography lessons without references to human connections. Thus, children may come to know Philadelphia's location but have no idea that the Declaration of Independence, Constitution, and the Bill of Rights were first heard there. Other parts of school curricula are also segmented—teachers may not prepare experiences for children to read and write clearly while doing current events, or science lessons are presented without any relationship to arithmetic.

When analytic sense is applied, teachers (adults) are assuming that the children will be able to construct the appropriate associations independently. Consequently, not only is the world made more complicated by adults when they split intact perceptions of a child's world into seemingly incomprehensible divisions, but adults expect children to accept adult abstractions as well as to reassemble these and other divisions into meaningful understandings.

The frustration level and patience of adults are often tested to their limits in vain attempts to convince children to follow their lead. Because adults have a firmer grasp of cause and effect (primarily due to their greater experience), they understand the consequences of certain actions and nonactions. For instance, most adults perceive the value and importance of brushing teeth. In contrast, children typically fail to agree that teeth brushing has any importance whatsoever. The long-term effects (or future) of brushing or not brushing is lost upon children. "Why do I have to brush my teeth?" questions Tommy. "Because I do not want you to get any cavities," declares his mother. Tommy replies in strong defiance, "I don't care if I get cavities! What's the big deal about cavities?"

The child's ability to forecast future outcomes is severely limited by his meager experiences. In brief, the future is one place that children have a difficult time putting themselves into. Tommy simply does not see the relationship between brushing teeth now and not getting cavities later. Tommy would rather not brush his teeth tonight and take his chances with the future.

This failure to project themselves into the future is directly related to the complexities of reassembling adult abstractions and divisions. Adults inevitably give children the feeble explanation that their abstractions and divisions of the world will be necessary later in life. To children, who lack a perception of the future, this talk of linking adult abstractions and divisions of the world to the child's future makes little sense. This problem is not without a solution, however.

The most powerful and effective method of synthesizing the complexities of life is within the grasp of every child and every adult. By the time formal school begins every child is supplied with the basic equipment needed to bridge the gap between the world inside a child's head and the wider world outside. The primary tool of this exchange is not didactic instruction with abstractions and divisions of the world known to adults, but with the power of imagination within every child. As John Dewey wrote many years ago, "Imagination is the only gateway through which meanings derived from prior experiences find their way into the present and make present experiences more conscious."[1] But imagination is more than understanding the present, it is also an excellent tool to help children understand their future as well.

Role of Imagination

Imagination plays an important part in the way children view the world. Because children lack experience and maturity, much of their understanding of the world appears to adults as fuzzy at best. To the child, however, even if aware of her "fuzzy thinking," she does not let this condition impede her thought process. Simply put, children use their own imagination to bridge gaps between the adult world and the child world by filling in all the necessary or missing connections. Moreover, the child's imagination can supply all the essential background information that enables the child to cope with new situations, information, and questions.

Imagination play, typically called pretending or make-believe, is an important part of coping with childhood. In fact, child psychologists have consistently argued that play is the work of the child. Play allows children to be part of the adult world, but not at the cost of becoming adult-like. For example, children often play house where they can imitate adult behaviors and values without having the adult responsibilities that comprise running a real household. When children decide to quit, they can walk away without penalty, perhaps to begin the activity anew some other day. Adults, however, cannot walk away as easily. Although the pretend play is not real to adults, role playing can be very serious to children. In fact, some children often create imaginary friends to play with that (although it may be distressing to adults) become a very real part of a child's life.

Imagination is a leap from the known to the unknown. It is a prediction of reality, an interpretation. For example, Andy (a child in your kindergarten class) loves milk. Milk is found in the refrigerator at his home, at stores, and even at McDonald's. Where does the milk come from? How is milk made (if it is made at all?) Who puts milk in the store? Even though he has been told

---

[1]John Dewey, *Art as experience* (New York: Minton, Balch, 1934), p. 272.

milk comes from cows, this idea does not make much sense to Andy. In fact, because Andy has not given these questions much thought, they have little meaning to Andy.

It is not even a case of "who cares about these questions"—Andy simply has never had to think about the source of milk, until, of course, on the day his milk cup is empty. Then Andy may ask the question, "Where is my milk?" Andy's parents may explain that the people who carry the milk to the store (truckers) are on strike and are refusing to make their deliveries. Andy's parents continue, "When the union negotiations with management are over, the milk will return to the store." To Andy, however, this explanation merely puzzles him.

All this talk about truckers, strikes, and union negotiations have no meaning to Andy; all Andy truly understands is that his milk is not available. Although initial adult explanations may not help Andy understand what happened, Andy is capable of making sense of the situation with his imagination. Using a parental-like tone (much like deciding the battle of Waterloo took place in water), Andy may suddenly declare that the truck drivers had better return the milk to the store because they had no right or reason to take it in the first place. Andy's explanation, however, misses the point.

The idea that the drivers do not own the milk, but merely carry it to stores may totally escape Andy. Andy's parents or another adult may try to explain the process of shipping goods to market, where the store sells the products. This explanation and more may be correct and perfectly logical to adults; however, abstract explanations may prove unintelligible to Andy. Between whatever adult abstract explanations are offered and more potent concrete observations (watching milk being drawn from cows, stored in tanks, and then loaded into trucks), Andy can use his imagination to fill in the gaps, that is, to provide whatever information is necessary to cope with the situation.

In this example, imagination offers children a means to test new experiences against known experience. In this manner imagination becomes an important part of the developing individual because it enables children to organize and conceptualize their world. After Andy makes up an explanation, he can test this explanation with adults. Although Andy may realize his own errors (self-discovery is important), adults have a responsibility to assist Andy by confirming/denying Andy's version of reality when it appears that he is unable to make his own confirmations of truth. Children progress developmentally using this technique of trial and error and it is critical that adults listen to children and respond to a child's imaginative stories in appropriate ways. A number of strategies are often applied by adults, such as identifying the truth for the child, assisting the child with finding the truth, admitting you do not know and working with the child to discover the truth, and allowing the child to continue seeking the truth without interfering.

Challenges to Imagination

In another context of school and life, the child must cope with a dilemma that he or she is incapable of recognizing: namely, that the world is in constant flux and he/she is blithely unaware of it. The move toward adulthood can generally be marked when the child realizes that few things remain the same for long. In the constant bombardment of information and experience, the child must eventually filter, order, and discard or incorporate most of the new and different. Imagination, however, may not always serve to organize the child's thoughts. Often organization and conceptualization become pragmatic matters; there simply is not enough time to grasp the meaning or significance of every new piece of information or experience.

When not able to cope, explain, or imagine away information overload, often the child simply ignores or blots out information and experience. This is precisely what the human body does with severe injuries in the short term. For example, you may cut your hand to the bone on a sharp piece of glass and literally not "feel" the real pain until your body has had time to process the sensory messages to the brain. Although pain may be manifested quickly, initially, when overloaded, the body shuts down the pain response. Similarly, for the child, overload of experience can produce a comparable response. The unique difference between cognitive overload and pain-sensory overload is that the cut in your hand remains a wound for a long time. By contrast, as soon as you physically or mentally escape the cognitive overload, the overload can be completely, conveniently, and painlessly wiped out.

In a different sense, nature has not afforded the child time to think things through due to profound physical, mental, and social changes that are part of the experience of growing up. Stress and disequilibrium can be handled through ongoing reflection, regrouping, and reorganizing new and old situations and information. Because time and experience have provided more practice and perfection of change and conflict situations, adults have a greater advantage in filtering life's realities, that is, to accept, reject, ignore, and/or incorporate change within their lives. Children, however, do not deal with stress and disequilibrium like adults. Because their understandings and experiences are not as well formed, children must often wait for time, maturity, situation, and increased experiences to mitigate experiences that create, prolong, and/or exacerbate stress and disequilibrium.

The adult division of things complicates life for the child. To the adult, dividing things is a necessary part of the developmental process toward adulthood. The adult makes these divisions so that the child can come to view the world through its parts. The problem, for the child, is that these parts are not viewed in relation to other parts. To begin with, the artificial division is an abstraction—an adult abstraction. If the child is unable to appreciate and understand the relationship of the abstraction according to his/her sense of reality, the lesson and learning are soon lost.

Without an eye toward connecting experiences to the child's world, the experience or learning may become plainly absurd to the child's sensibilities. To become effective facilitators of learning, teachers need to avoid presenting experiences without developing meaningful relationships between the experience and the child. Outside of accidental or collateral learning, the child may be able to assimilate his or her experience (simply by placing it within his/her own context of experience without any understanding). The distinction made here is that experience assimilated in this fashion rarely is transformed into learning.

For example, what information do you remember from elementary school? We need only survey our own experiences to realize the futility of rote efforts. For instance, you may remember that you studied history in grade school, but have completely forgotten what that history may have been. How sad to think that you spent all those years engaged in learning activities and cannot remember what was once learned! Rote learning may indeed be effective in the short term; however, the type of learning theory expresses in this textbook is a long-term approach toward the relationship between classroom experience and learning. A first step in this effort is to discuss the interests and needs of children.

Follow-Up Question: What do you remember from your grade school experiences?

Interests

Initially one of the easiest ways to understand children is to come to know their interests. In fact, while interest-centered teaching ideas are not infallible, the use of interest can be very effective. For example, the enormous popularity of the 1988 film *Teenage Mutant Ninja Turtles* that caught the fancy of children exemplifies the potency of their interests. Who could have predicted that four cartoon turtles—teenagers no less—with bandannas and Ninja weapons would have the power to influence the playing (and buying) habits of an entire generation of children?

Manufacturers and merchants have been quick to respond to the seemingly overwhelming demand of children to wear, sound, talk, think, eat, play, and pretend to be "Teenage Mutant Ninja Turtles" by providing an endless parade of T-shirts, dolls, food items, toys, magazines, live concert tours, and more Turtle merchandise than the earlier Batman or Dick Tracy crazes (the caped crusader and the 1930s detective may have suffered because they were not teenagers).

Adults can adjust and seek to promote what children like; however, they do not always know. For manufacturers and merchants, the Christmas toy season begins soon after the preceding Christmas. However, for parents and children, the Christmas toy season begins sometime in late September and early October. In either case, evaluating new toy products is a likely barometer of what adults want children to like and desire. Essentially, toy makers, through the child-oriented products they manufacture, make predictions based upon what adults perceive children to be. An accurate prediction can translate into millions of dollars in sales; an inaccurate prediction can spell financial disaster.

Find It Out: Describe popular toys over the past fifty years.

Unhappily, for manufacturers and merchants and often for parents as well, these predictions sometimes fall far short when toys and other items make it to store shelves and remain there well past the Christmas rush. Recently, retailers could not keep up with the demand for Teddy Ruxpin dolls; yet, unbelievably, Teddy's makers went bankrupt. In catching up with demand, among other problems, Teddy dolls suffered a drop in sales as competitors flooded the market with "talking-story dolls." In another boom-bust tale, the once coveted Cabbage Patch dolls also lost popularity and required sales, driving its maker (Coleco) into heavy debt and bankruptcy.

Paradoxically, both Teddy Ruxpin and Cabbage Patch dolls were smashing successes and utter failures. To the millions of children who held these toys and carried them throughout their world of bed, home, school, stores, playgrounds, and more, these toys represented an integral part of their young lives. Children loved them deeply. They cared for and thought about these dolls in ways that few adults could understand or remember (many adults also maintain a similar human attachment to things). Although these dolls were not flesh and blood, but merely objects of plastic, cloth, and metal, they represented more than just a plaything to children. Nonetheless, something strange happens with most children and their precious things—someday something else comes along and replaces Teddy Ruxpin, Barbie, or Troll dolls. The child psychologist can explain why and how this happens; however, it is sufficient for us to know that a child's interests change.

What was puzzling to the toymakers was that the next generation of children shifted their interests from Teddy Ruxpins and Cabbage Patch dolls to something else. To these adults, the dolls were a financial failure. But to one generation of children, at least, they were everything that was good, happy, and secure in the world.

The problem of adult perceptions of children stems from the misplaced theory of using the child's interest to guide adult relations with children. Adults often confuse a child's curiosity for a child's genuine interest. Recognizing and acknowledging curiosity is important for adults. Curiosity is the initial spark of interest that puts attention upon an object, activity, idea, and more (remember the power of the word *look*). Curiosity does not imply a child's commitment, it is simply an arousal of first interest that may lead to meaningful engagement with an interest. Interests often require a period of exposure before the child will seek to repeat involvement with the interest. The notion of repetition is the key to interests, forming an important part of what makes an interest an interest. That is, adults can usually suspect that the child has an interest in something if he seeks to repeat it. Interests also have a magical, sensual property that urges a child to touch, smell, and taste the object at hand—to play with, finger, and repeat the action.

In another sense, adults sometimes ignore a child's native interest and attempt to project adult interests upon the child. The imposition of adult interests conjure up the image of something like a "stage door" parent, who wants desperately for the child to become a star. The child becomes caught up in the excitement of show business, trying to please adult sponsors, and in the process is used as a pawn of what the adult wants. As a result, the child loses the opportunities of growing up and exploring her own native interests.

Another important aspect of interest is its source. Children are not born with an interest in specific things such as baseball cards or coin collections. Such interests are acquired by the child after exposure to and/or experience with something. What makes a child interested in baseball cards rather than another interest cannot be assessed with complete assurance; it is difficult to gauge or predict the interests of children. The true source of any child's interest may remain a mystery, not revealed or understood by you or even the child. The point is that children's interests vary in duration and intensity. As teachers, we need to be mindful of interests our children possess and work to understand the nature of these interests.

All children have interests—things they like to do, watch, handle, read, think about, and more. Many children adore animals of all types, others love to play games, and still many others would be happy just to watch their favorite television programs all day. A list of children's interests is limited only by an individual's experience, imagination, access, and opportunity. This is not to say that all interests should be accepted as equal by teachers; some children may enjoy pulling wings off of insects or chewing pencil erasers. For many the interests that are cultivated during childhood carry over into adulthood. You, too, may still have an interest in reading exciting stories or in collecting dolls, or even, baseball cards.

Despite generalizations of youth interests, there does not appear to be any uniformity or patterns of interests across class, gender, race or other characteristics. For example, however much adults may wish to promote gender-neutral toys, some girls (when free to choose) select dolls, and some boys (when free to choose) pick up trucks and cars to play. Regardless of the appearance of gender-determined toys, adults should not assume that interests are gender or even race-specific. Myths, such as all African-American children play basketball and listen to rap music or Asian-American children like computers and math, or Irish-American children like leprechaun stories, are more than inaccurate and misleading, they are patently wrong. While there are certainly children of these cultural groups who have these interests, there are many others of different cultural groups who also possess corresponding interests. The singling out of one group (defined by physical or other characteristics) and associating that group, and that group only, with a particular interest does not have a place in education. Let the child explore an interest in something, but never assume that another child should display a similar interest according to gender, race, age, or any other characteristic.

The notion of stereotyping interests according to standards such as gender or ethnicity is inappropriate and harmful for two reasons. First, stereotyping is unfair to the individual child, and second, stereotyping may restrict or eliminate many learning experiences for children. Although overviews of interests and needs are reproduced here, adults must keep in mind that this list of interests is not applicable to all youngsters. The interest list is reproduced merely as a guide and should not be taken as fact or as an unalterable conclusion.

Individual Development

(Generalizations)

Interests:	changeable, fickle, transitory, repetitive—tend to be focused within age group
Ages 5–8 Grades K–3	Make believe, play groups, singing songs, television, video games, video tapes, patterns and rhythms, drawing and painting, different animals, books with adventure as theme, collecting things, toy models, action toys, "repulsive things," games with rules, free play, stories with strong characters (right/wrong, good/evil), dolls, boy-boy and girl-girl groups, group activities, far-a-way places and people, imitation, ride bikes, puzzles, action toys, poems, posters
Ages 9–10 Grades 4–6	Team games, games that promote winning, foods, taking trips, reading, writing notes, rough play, "blood and guts," being in fashion, professional sports, collecting things
Ages 11–13	Hobbies, keeping pets, teen-age movies, hanging out with friends, using the telephone, "in music," being in fashion, opposite sex, dancing, active sports, professional sports, cars, famous personalities, having spending money (job), shopping
Needs:	Constant—tend to persist throughout age groups
Ages 5–8 Grades K–3	Outlet for physical activities, honesty, sensory experiences that highlight touch, sights and smell, support and encouragement, deserved praise, to feel part of a group, reassurance by adults, routines, adults who treat children with a smile, pleasant voice and accepting body language, adults who demonstrate patience (little people, not little adults), adults who make time for and give attention to the child, imitation, role models, outlet for imagination (make believe), to feel special
Ages 9–10 Grades 4–6	Continue with above, plus children begin to realize the need to be liked, also try to please adults
Ages 11–13	Continue with above, self-worth, a developed sense of identity (male/female/individual), to be accepted by peers (powerful need), a feeling of security with independence, a feeling of independence with security

Nonetheless, interests are powerful motivators. Teachers often rely upon knowing their children's interests in advance of designing activities and experiences. For instance, in a writing assignment for a third grade class, Mrs. Tompkins may ask Tommy to write a story about cars (his favorite interest). Julie may like collecting stickers and Mrs. Tompkins may ask her to write a story about her fine collection. It makes little difference if the children write about cars or stickers or anything else, so long as the children write. The idea behind exploiting the interests of children is that it helps the teacher meet her goals. Mrs. Tompkins wants her children to practice writing skills through stories. Rather than having all the children write about whales, which they may or may not like, she found the exercise goes smoother and produces better results when children can direct the activity through their own interests.

Using an interest approach to curricular planning is common and, at times, prudent. However, tying activities and experiences to interests as a motivator can lose its effectiveness. The reason is basic to a young person's human nature: children's interests tend to be transitory. In other words, a child's interests can and do frequently change. These changes may be due to physical growth, mental maturity, shifts in peer groups, and a host of other factors including the very powerful effect of television advertising.

Children are prone to change their minds and attitudes and do so very quickly. One day Tommy may love cars, the next day he wants to be a "Teenage Mutant Ninja Turtle." Julie may covet her stickers today, and be swooning over the "New Kids On The Block" tomorrow. Given the ephemeral quality of interests, planning lessons based upon children's interests can be much like building a house on sand. It may stand today, but tomorrow? Therefore, teachers must exercise caution with or build in flexibility to interest-oriented activities when designing projects and activities as well as other classroom or grade-level experiences.

Many of the interest examples presented here will certainly be out of date after the publication of this textbook. Because textbooks cannot be produced spontaneously, the interest examples presented will always be somewhat out of fashion and in need of updating: the Turtles, Trolls, and Mermaids of today will soon pass. Thus, ironically, just as we discuss this issue, our textbook provides a clear illustration of the fatal flaw of relying solely on interests for curricular guidance—interests simply change too quickly.

Another element to consider with interests is that you must act carefully to avoid stifling the interest of a child. For example, dinosaurs have been very popular with teachers in the 1980s and thanks to the film *Jurassic Park* remain popular today. Clearly, children, too, shared a keen interest in dinosaurs; however, some children suffered "dinosaur overload," by being exposed to dinosaurs at every grade level, often with the same materials.

It is possible that by the time Jim and his friends reach your fourth grade class, they may have studied dinosaurs every year since kindergarten. What was once an interest is now boring. Miscalculating the interests of children with curricular experiences may also add tension to the class and contribute unnecessarily to classroom management problems: bored children are more likely to act up or act out their frustrations than children actively engaged in something they find fun and interesting.

Another dimension of interests is the significant difference to the child between things that are naturally interesting to them and what a teacher does to make something appear interesting. When your children have a natural interest in farm animals, you may have an easy (and fun) time getting your "big city" kids to learn about life in Farmer Brown's barn. If you are planning to teach in a farming community where children have experienced farms and barns since birth, they may have a greater interest in things beyond the barnyard. In this case, if you intend to teach about barns, you will have to make the barn and its contents appear more interesting than they are at first glance.

> **Consider This:** *What happens when interests of children conflict with the interests of adults?*

With both groups of children you will be teaching about barns; however, within the latter group motivation will have to be created, whereas the first group will be stimulated on its own. The difference between creating interest for something and using a child's natural interest is something that every elementary teacher eventually comes to understand. What is critical for teachers is developing that keen ability to "read" when a situation calls for stimulating interest and when it does not. The development of this skill comes from understanding interests, observations of children, and practice and experimentation with using interests.

Interests can also be used to introduce or expose children to the unknown. Interests can become a bridge between what is familiar and unfamiliar to the child. For example, children typically have an interest in stories about other children who are of a similar age. To arouse interest in a story about colonial life, you may find a story about a young boy or girl or both. Another tip that helps build interest is to personify these colonial stories (and other stories as well) with real characters or, at least, appealing fictional characters. This is accomplished by giving these distant and disembodied figures names. Thus, the colonial boy and girl become Thomas and Nancy, or if you were studying about Germany, the children who would "take us on our tour" are Fritz and Greta.

Children may have no understanding of or interest in colonial life; however, when told through the eyes of another child, colonial life can suddenly become interesting to them. Same gender or even gender-neutral similarities are not the only connectors you can use. You may tell a story about something all the children have in common, such as sometimes being afraid of phantom monsters that live under their beds. In sum, you really need to search out the interests of children. An interest approach may be suitable as a means to stimulate children; however, because of the ephemeral quality of interest-based curricula ideas, you may want to consider adding to interest-based instruction another approach that provides stability and flexibility in its curricular foundation.

> **Research Question:** *Investigate interests of children in other areas of the world.*

> **Research Questions:** *What's Hot/What's Not? Interview children of different ages. Identify what they call interests, identify old interests and new, and ask reasons for shift, if any. Find last year's Christmas catalog (J. C. Penney, Montgomery Ward) identify what was hot/what is still hot/what is not.*

Needs

In addition to interests and the other characteristics of youth culture, there is another phenomenon about children that will assist you in the classroom: understanding a child's special needs. Needs may be characterized as something a child consistently requires, that is, something that must be satisfied for the child to grow and develop normally according to his or her own capacities. Specific needs range from obvious basic items such as food, water, shelter, and clothing to more subtle, but still vital needs such as warmth, love, and affection.

Needs are persistent, but they are not distributed evenly nor manifested simultaneously among children. While Sonya craves your attention and affection, Beatrice may appear indifferent to you. Likewise, John may suffer from sleep deprivation and appear constantly sleepy, while Yao is "raring to go," bright eyed and alert. The variety and levels of needs are indeed profound and render accurate need assessment difficult. Nevertheless, children cannot ignore needs, and teachers, too, must learn to help children identify and satisfy their needs.

Although interests are quite powerful in and of themselves, children do not maintain interests as they must attend to needs. For example, children can (and do) walk away from an interest, but not a need. The sharpest contrast between interests and needs is that genuine needs continue throughout life and are not affected by the passing of time, by changes in circumstances, or by will or whim. Interests come and go, whereas needs are only temporarily satisfied, like a good meal or a big hug; sooner or later the child will require that need to be met again.

Additionally, a child's needs remain constant; children do not leave their needs at the front door of the school. Although children treat needs differently from interests, a healthy and secure child can easily focus on her own interests, while temporarily ignoring needs. For instance, given the opportunity, children will play their Nintendo set for hours, while ignoring their body's plea (as well as pleas from significant others) for sleep and food. Thus, children rebel against adult attempts to help or compel them to meet their own needs. In such cases, it is as if the child is claiming that the need will have to wait or that the need will take care of itself as the interest must be dealt with first.

This is clearly one of the most critical areas of tension between adults and children.

As discussed earlier, based upon experience, adults perceive an understanding of needs that the child lacks. Years of experience—of doing—have built a cause and effect relationship of needs. That is, adults understand the reasons for meeting needs and the consequences of not having needs met. Adults come to understand that interruption of attention to needs may cause a wide variety of consequences that adversely delay, stunt, or prolong the individual and social development of the child. When viewed from the adult perspective, needs become legitimate when measured against time. If something is truly a need, it will remain a need over time. On the other hand, if a supposed need is discarded, it must not have been a real need, but rather a desire or interest. As applied here, needs are not simply things a child desires such as a Kit-Kat or Butterfinger candy bar, or to be an astronaut or movie star, but rather needs are essential.

An important issue is raised at this point: who decides what needs are critical, essential, and real, and what needs are unnecessary and illusory: the child or the adult? The differences between adult's and child's perceptions of needs that are real versus needs that are actually desires puts the child at a disadvantage. Because children are not capable of applying the logic necessary to counteract the experience of adults, children are left to at least symbolically accept what adults call needs.

Whether or not a child accepts adult versions of needs, because children develop an inclination towards interests (versus needs) that adults have grown unable or unwilling to acknowledge, an impasse is a likely result of the child-adult exchange. Adults cannot understand why children are so "thick-headed" and children cannot understand what all the fuss is about. To reconcile their differences the primary courses of action are: the child concedes to the adult; the adult gives in to the child; or preferably both seek a rapprochement and agree to negotiate.

Despite efforts on the part of well-meaning adults, the notions of conformity, giving in, or rapprochement on the part of the child may still not work. The young child may simply be incapable of reasoning out the adult's argument to meet needs. To the child, if a need is not related to an established interest and the need is not felt by the child, the child may refuse to cooperate with the adult.

In many cases, meeting needs often is beyond the teacher's ability, inclination, means or circumstance. Moreover, school policy and/or community standards may not permit attending to some needs. Basic needs such as food, clothing, shelter, and security may be impossible to address outside of school. For instance, you may realize Davona is not receiving adequate food; however, beyond providing meals at school, you have no power to ensure that she is given more food at home. Despite your personal efforts, you may eventually be compelled to report your observations to authorities; however, they, too, may encounter difficulties in seeing that Davona's parents provide her with adequate food. The same can be said of other needs as well. We may want Randy's father to show affection and attention to him, yet despite our good intentions, we ultimately remain powerless to affect the quality of Randy's home life.

The tensions created between the child and the adult over the meeting of needs and other problems associated with needs present an interesting and challenging invitation for teachers. Teachers know that meeting and satisfying needs are more important to the child's present and long-term well-being and welfare than attending to any ephemeral interest. However, given the nature of needs, how can one teacher adequately help children satisfy needs when they are presented at various levels and at different times?

Given the charge and context of public education, teachers may think it is not possible and may be futile to attempt to satisfy the various needs of every child. Despite our difficulty with addressing children's needs, we must remember children's needs do not disappear at the school door. Although some needs are impossible to attend to and we may fail at attending to others, every child has four needs that every teacher can help children satisfy: to communicate, to build, to think for oneself, and to express oneself.

The foundation of the curricular approach used in this textbook is built upon knowing and applying these four universal needs of children that are not only suitable for attention in schools, but critical for the normal growth of all children. Every child in any circumstance can be reached and can benefit from meeting these needs. Fully discussed in chapter 4, these needs are placed at the heart of the pedagogy developed for the introduction and practice of social studies in elementary schools. We will learn more about the use of these needs as we progress through the text and become engaged in class experiences, readings, and our own reflective thoughts.

A Brief Summary

So far we have discussed several key ideas that provide teachers with a sturdy and vigorous perspective that can assist us to understand and to appreciate the complexity of youth culture. The guiding theme of the chapter has been that children are the same but different. This theme permeates each of the following generalizations that are the foundation of the methodology discussed in this textbook.

Guiding Theme: Children are the Same but Different

- Behaviors, beliefs, and values are important elements of children's personality.
- Children do not view the world as adults view the world.
- Imagination plays a critical part in bridging the gap between a child's world and the adult world.

- Children's interests provide a powerful influence on a child's thoughts and actions; however, interests should be used with caution.
- Children's needs are the strongest and most persistent motivators of human thought and action; when teachers tap into needs they create the greatest opportunity for learning as well as attending to the child's sense of well-being.

Because the foundation of the social studies pedagogy outlined in this textbook centers upon the child and his and her needs, our work as elementary teachers is justified by revealing our keen sense of understanding children. Therefore, before we examine the four universal needs and their use in teaching social studies, we need to establish a firm rationale to underlie our educational efforts.

It is not simply that teachers employ needs (or any other pedagogical idea) to guide instruction because they are convenient and powerful educational tools. As with any educational enterprise you should also consider why a particular approach for social studies might provide excellent educational experiences for children as members of a liberal democratic community. The mission of chapter 3 is to supply some ideas and challenges for you to consider as you think about youth culture and your role as an elementary teacher. Hopefully, this work will produce a sound philosophy or outlook on teaching and learning.

Marking Your Progress (Kit)

1. Topic/Theme _____

   _____

   _____

2. Potential Interests to Explore _____

   _____

   _____

3. Imagination Ideas _____

   _____

   _____

(continued)

Marking Your Progress (Kit)

4. Same, but Different Ideas to Develop _____

_____

_____

Read More about It Special References

There are a number of excellent materials about children and learning that can be put to good use by elementary teachers doing social studies (many of the following are also suggested readings for chapters 3 and 4). The following represent two types of references: general books that cover a wide range of ideas about children and elementary schooling, and those books that specifically address ideas/themes of the synoptic method of social studies. To prove that not everything has to be up-to-date and brand-new, I have included for your review a number of references that are classics.

General References

The following are grouped together as general references on educational psychology, child development, and cognition. These texts are typical of those readily available and used in college/university courses. Each gives strong overview of the field. If you are interested in a particular topic, be sure to check references/sources for specialized information.

Berk, L. (1991). *Child development.* Boston: Allyn & Bacon.
Reed, S. K. (1992). *Cognition.* Pacific Grove, CA: Brooks/Cole.
Sroufe, L. A., Cooper, R. G., & DeHart, G. B. (1992). *Child development: Its nature and course.* New York: McGraw-Hill.
Sprinthall, N. R., & Sprinthall, R. C. (1990). *Educational psychology: A developmental approach.* New York: McGraw-Hill.
Woolfolk, A. E. (1990). *Educational psychology.* Boston: Allyn & Bacon.

The following are considered by many to be among the best general works on child development and theory. Each is often used at the college/university level. A word of caution—these works and the theories described were produced by researchers outside of social studies with no direct consideration of social studies theory and/or practice. Therefore, you should not assume that the theory/practice can simply be lifted from, for example, the works of Piaget and transferred to social studies practice. Nonetheless, these works represent much of the best studies done on children and learning.

Bruner, J. (1966). *Toward a theory of instruction.* New York: Norton.

Bruner, J. (1977). *The process of education.* Cambridge, MA: Harvard University Press.

Dewey, J. (1916). *Democracy and education.* New York: Macmillan.

Erickson, E. (1964). *Childhood and society.* New York: Norton.

Gardner, H. (1983). *Frames of mind: The theory of multiple intelligences.* New York: Basic Books.

Kohlberg, L. (1976). Moral stages and moralization: The cognitive-developmental approach. In *Moral development and behavior,* T. Lickona, ed. New York: Holt, Rinehart & Winston.

Peterson, R. (1986). *The Piaget handbook for teachers and parents, children in the age of discovery, preschool–third grade.* New York: Teachers College Press.

Piaget, J. (1963). *The child's conception of the world.* Patterson, NJ: Littlefield, Adams.

Piaget, J. (1969). *The psychology of the child.* New York: Basic Books.

Rodgers, C. (1983). *Freedom to learn for the eighties.* Columbus: Merrill.

Vygotsky, L. (1978). *Mind in society: The development of higher psychological processes.* Cambridge, MA: Harvard University Press.

Wadsworth, B. (1978). *Piaget for the classroom teacher.* New York: Longman.

Other General References

Ausubel, D., Novak, J., & Hanesian, H. (1978). *Educational psychology: A cognitive approach.* New York: Holt, Rinehart & Winston.

This remains a solid text, easily read and digested, which gives a fine overview of educational psychology. In addition, Ausubel has a number of original contributions that should be of interest.

Bigge, M. L., & Hunt, M. P. (1968). *Psychological foundations of education.* New York: Harper & Row.

Granted the text is dated (it should still be available in most college/university libraries); however, this is one of the best educational psychology texts ever written for the college reader. Insightful and thorough, Bigge and Hunt put together all the main threads of psychology in a readable format. Hunt also is co-author (with Lawrence Metcalf) of Teaching High School Social Studies ([1955] New York: Harper & Row), perhaps the best social studies methods textbook every written.

Healy, J. M. (1991). *Endangered minds: Why children don't think and what we can do about it.* New York: Touchstone.

Prepared by an experienced educational psychologist, this book is a must for elementary teachers. Healy's text not only reflects up-to-date research, but her suggestions to improve education (and to help children) are sound. You may not agree with all Healy has to say, but she surely gives us much to think about.

Lickona, T. (1991). *Educating for character.* New York: Bantam.

This easy to read book presents a compelling case for bringing the values of respect and responsibility into schools, particularly elementary schools. Lickona offers a number of common sense ideas for teachers to consider as they work to create opportunities for children to explore the meanings and applications of such values as courage, honesty, respect and justice. Teachers must read this book.

Smith, R., & Associates. (1990). *Learning to learn across the life span.* San Francisco: Jossey-Bass.

One of the best overviews of current cognitive psychology for teachers, emphasizing theory building, practice, and empowerment of learners to be invested in their own learning. It gives attention to broad aspects of metacognition and includes a special section appropriate for exploration with elementary-age children.

References for Social Studies

Atwood, V. (1986). *Elementary school social studies: Research as a guide to practice.* Washington, DC: National Council for the Social Studies.
  This book contains a general overview of elementary social studies and a special section on learning and instruction.
Gagne, E. (1985). *The cognitive psychology of social learning.* Boston: Little Brown.
  Although not specific for social studies, Ellen Gagne's text has broad implications for the field, especially for elementary-age children.
Pappas, C., Kiefer, B. A., & Levstik, L. (1990). *An integrated language perspective in the elementary school: Theory into action.* New York: Longman.
  This is one of the best holistic approach texts available that specifically demonstrates the whys and hows of subject/analytic integration of language arts with social studies science, art, music, and mathematics. With experienced social studies expert Linda Levstik as co-author you can be certain that social studies is well represented. A first rate text!

3

COMMUNITY AND EDUCATION

In this chapter you wil

- Explore working definitions of liberal and democratic.
- Identify the twin paradoxes of liberal democratic communities.
- Begin to discuss schooling and education with the context of a liberal democratic community.
- Continue to organize your own philosophy of teaching and learning.

By the time you finish this book, it will not be long before you enter a classroom and meet your children for the first time. How exciting! Your own classroom! Between now and that first day of teaching, you may wonder "will I ever be ready?"

In new challenges like the first day of school, self-doubt often merges with confidence creating an internal paradox. This paradox recognizes poise and confidence, on one hand, and insecurity and uncertainty on the other. Although this paradox of confidence and uncertainty is felt by all first-year teachers, your first day of teaching is intensely personal—one that only you will undergo.

Think about It: What are the first days of school like for teachers and children?

For the moment, set aside your feelings of anticipation and anxiety and think about what your children will be feeling. This may be their first class too! Perhaps they have just moved into the district, or maybe this is their first formal experience in a public school. Even if the children are not new to the school or schooling, you must remember that your children may have had only one or two years of schooling experience. Thus, every new grade or level presents fresh challenges and experiences for children and every first day of class presents new challenges and experiences for you as well. While you are feeling the paradox of confidence and uncertainty, so, too, are children in your class.

In American society, the schooling of children is an enormous enterprise, involving millions of children and adults. State laws generally provide for free public education for children between the ages of six and eighteen, typically from kindergarten through grade twelve. Measured by the sheer amount of change, these years are among the most important in the life of any individual. In this thirteen-year span young people pass from childhood to adolescence and finally adulthood. This chapter marks a transition from discussing children as individuals to discussing children within the context of American society, labeled here as the liberal democratic community. The first two chapters were more directly related to you and your experiences (and thus easier to digest and apply), this chapter calls upon your patience and understanding as we leap into possibly a new area of thinking for you—your future responsibilities as an integral member of the community (teacher). Forming the core of the brand of social studies the synoptic method supports, this chapter needs to be read slowly and deliberately. Be sure to ask questions and reflect upon your own experiences as you progress through the following concepts of democratic life and living.

A Plea for Activism

One enduring measurement of civilization is how a community treats its children. In a literal sense children are the future. Compared to adults, children are less able to defend or speak for themselves. For many years, children are entirely dependent on adults for nurturing, nourishment, shelter, and protection. In theory, proper understanding and treatment of children now will later provide lasting and positive effects for the community. However, if we neglect our children we will bring about many unhappy consequences.

> *Follow-up Question: What "changes" do children typically experience between ages 6 and 13?*

Each member of the community must accept, according to their capacities and abilities, the responsibility to prevent present and future generations of children from falling into the abyss of crime, poverty, abuse, vice, mental and physical cruelty, and all that tears at the fabric of humanity. We each must take the challenge and defend the child against a dismal future becoming reality. It is more than in "our best interests" to care for children now, and it is more than being thoroughly humane. The advancement of individuals and social institutions of this democracy rest upon the successful defense of the child against the twin evils of growing apathy and cold neglect.

The primary goal of the social studies methodology contained in this text is to further the case of the child in three forms: to actively engage children in the enlargement of their experiences, to advance the freedom of individuals, and to provide an atmosphere of experimentation that fosters intellectual growth and self-expression. In this effort, the needs of children (as discussed in chapter 2) are placed far ahead of the demands of content objectives that tend to support passive learning over active learning, unreflective citizenship over fostering individual freedom, and stagnating conformity over individual growth and self-expression.

Those who accept the challenge to activate the cause of children make no excuses for the bellicose-like metaphors. In my view, the issue at hand is very serious and the only hope to overcome the staggering odds against children is sincere, decisive, and direct attention. Thus, in a literal sense, you are being enlisted to serve on the front lines of the battle for children.

Community and Its Nature

The focus of this textbook is the development of a liberal democratic perspective, that is, exploring a way to think about liberal democratic community, the expansion of freedom, and liberal democratic teaching. The cornerstone of this perspective is the child. The child, however, does not exist outside of the community; the child is a vital part of the community. To continue building our perspective, it is necessary to understand the nature of community and the role of the child in the community.

The community is fashioned by individuals and defined by the immediate environment together with the environment outside of your home and neighborhood. The community also includes those institutions and individuals that sustain you and your environment.

Loosely constructed, the community is composed of individuals who share political, economic, and social institutions within a geographic area. Additionally, the community is built with language, religion, and other cultural aspects as commonalities. Although language and religion are powerful social forces, many communities, including those of the United States, exist with citizens speaking a number of languages and practicing a wide variety of religions.

> **Think about It:** *Identify the "pillars" of your community, how are these related to the needs of children?*

Since the day you were born you have been influenced by your mother, father, siblings, and other family members. Besides family, other societal institutions and individuals have worked to sustain and influence your life as well. From the food you ate to the clothes you wore to the toys you played with, other aspects of the community became heavily involved in your life. In fact, without the help of doctors, manufacturers, truck drivers, store clerks, and a host of thousands of other people in a wide variety of occupations, you may not have survived to read this book.

> **Consider This:** *Most children watch several hours of television every day. How much are children influenced by television?*

Our collective need for others forms the essence and basis of community. In our modern world, it is no shame to be dependent upon others; a growing majority of humans rely upon a relatively small number of farmers to produce many of the foods we consume every day. In fact, some citizens, babies for example, cannot help being completely dependent upon adults. Dependency in youth is acceptable because children have the capacity to grow and to learn to care for themselves while making a positive contribution to their community.

As discussed earlier, adults can train children to function on their own at a certain level of expectation or they can educate children to function as free thinkers who have no predetermined limits upon their growth. Regardless of training or education, as long as the child and adult live within the community, they will remain dependent on others in some fashion. When this dependency matures into a synergistic relationship where individuals accept responsibility for their actions and the community acknowledges institutional responsibilities towards individuals, it may be said that the community is operating at an optimum level.

The problem with the relationship between individuals and the community is obvious; not everyone acts responsibly, and the community, through its many institutions, does not always properly consider the case of the individual. For a liberal democracy to function at its highest level both the actions of individuals and the actions of the community through its institutions must be carefully and fully integrated. The following sections of this chapter will detail the workings of the special relationship between individuals and the community. Before we begin to examine this relationship, we need to define the terms *liberal* and *democracy*.

Defining Liberal and Democracy

The use of liberal in the term *liberal democracy* is intended to foster and promote the notion of education that lifts the individual from the group. This movement provides/allows the opportunity for learning and practicing free thought and expression. The aim of such education is to increase both the quantity and quality of the individual's base of knowledge and understanding. Here the direct result of a liberal democratic education is to increase opportunities as well as the capacities for individual growth. Learning then, is demonstrated by individuals striving to learn more through education. In other words, we learn to increase our capacity and desire for more learning by internalizing experiential growth. Thus, properly conceived and implemented, education works to free or liberate individuals from ignorance and blind obedience.

Closely related to the term liberal in the use of liberal democracy is the word *democratic*.The foundation of democratic life is centered upon reasoned and free choices made by individuals. In ancient Greece some 2,500 years ago democracy was introduced as an alternative form of government. In this setting, democracy was viewed as a means for individual citizens to have direct control over public matters rather than having one individual such as a king make all decisions. In eighteenth century France, this view of democracy was reconceptualized into a government system called a republic. Instead of individuals becoming directly involved in government, as in a democracy, citizens of a republic participated in government by electing a representative to attend to public matters in their place.

Follow-up Question: *How do governments differ?*

Both democratic and republican forms of government share the notion of "the people rule." The difference between the two forms is measured by the sheer number of citizens. In a large nation of millions of citizens, it is difficult for every citizen to vote on every decision that the government needs to make. Thus, a representative democracy, called a republic makes more sense. In contrast, a country or a town with a small population can have its citizens directly vote on all decisions. When the United States was formed in the 1770s and 1780s, although both direct and indirect methods of government were established and practiced, representative government became the standard.[1]

Notwithstanding the origins of democracy, improvement in the quantity and quality of the individual's ability to think and act not only facilitates the form and function of liberal democracy, but it also improves the quality of life of those living in a liberal democracy. Thus, the terms *liberal* and *democratic* form a close bond, with political and individual dimensions. In this work they are considered as two halves of a whole. Although both liberal and democracy may be distinguished by particular characteristics as well as abstracted individually, this is not to imply a dualistic nature—in practice the two halves are inseparable in construct and operation.

In its ancient Greek, eighteenth century French, and modern American form, two irreducible elements of democracy emerge: a willingness of diverse individuals to unify, and a free and sustained interaction between these diverse individuals. The task of uniting diverse individuals in schools is centered upon the development of liberal democratic experiences. In this setting, it is critical that members of the community, in this case children, are enabled to interact freely—to become a functional part of the community.

Children, like adults, must be willing to buy into liberal democratic ideals and not be forced or pressured to accept these ideals. To compel children or any citizen of a democracy to accept blindly the dictates of rulers runs counter to the principles of liberal democracy. As difficult as it may be, to remain consistent with liberal democratic principles, we (adults) must provide the opportunities for children to accept or modify democracy, even to the point of rejecting the concept of democracy itself. Specifically, when teachers foster the empowerment of a child's unique thought and action abilities, they must stand ready to confirm each child's freedom.

> **Think about It:** *How important is it to accept the feelings and decision of a child?*

Ideals of Liberal Democracy

In a liberal democratic community those who accept their role as educators preparing children for life now (and not as trainers preparing children for adult life) must continually work to identify, foster, and practice those qualities that facilitate the growth of liberal democratic experiences. Because public schools are charged with enrolling every child in their respective districts (only those children who attend recognized alternatives to public schooling are exempt from attendance), educators are challenged to provide an education

---

[1]When the term *democracy* is in the this text, in its political sense, it refers to the form of government where the people rule. Rather than switching back and forth between democracy and republic, I have chosen to use democracy in reference to the government system of the United States.

consistent with the ideals of the community while fostering the development of the emergent citizen.

The ideals of a liberal democratic community can be described in the form of three priorities. First, a liberal democratic community must establish and promote conditions for the pursuit of freedom. The pursuit of freedom is directly related to the expansion of choices, that is, individuals do not have to follow one set pattern, they are free to choose among a variety of directions or choices. Thus, when individuals exercise selection, they are in fact exercising freedom as well. The establishment of a fertile seedbed (formal education in our case) for individuals to exercise freedom, forms the foundation of the liberal democratic community. The formulation and continuation of a liberal democratic community are impossible without this foundation.

The second priority is the rational formulation of responses to two central questions: What is good? and What is right? The question of good is a moral question posed from the standpoint of the individual, where each individual decides what is good for himself or herself. Illustrations of good vary widely from person to person. For example, it is good for Laura to have a warm, safe bed; it is good for Laura's parents to have jobs that provide ample income for food, clothes, and other needs; and it is also good for Laura to have family and friends.

The question of right is also a moral question; however, it is posed from the standpoint of the community, where each citizen decides what is right. Unlike the question of good that seeks the best for an individual, the question of right asks what is best/fair for all citizens. For example, the community may decide that it is right for citizens to pay their share of taxes to support schools, roads, public programs, and government in general; that it is right to pick up your own trash after a picnic in the park; and that it is right to obey traffic rules. Recent racial events in Los Angeles exemplify the concept of good versus right in a most complex and dramatic form. Some members of the community held that right, seeking justice (not rioting or stealing), was more important and of greater value to the community than any individual desire for good (becoming engaged in acts to satisfy self) or the quick need to vent anger. But the issue of good versus right is very complex, especially when race relations are discussed. The events of Los Angeles should raise public consciousness and become a springboard for honest and frank discussions about life in America (perhaps this issue can be raised in your class discussions).

The third priority is the development of a liberal democratic environment characterized by six sustained principles:

1. Provide for open participation on public issues that includes a meaningful voice and role in how the community is governed.
2. Ensure access to information for the purpose of responsible decision making.
3. Acknowledge the diversity of human forms and ideas, including a sensitivity toward various creeds, religious beliefs, opinions, and other personally held convictions.

4. Support equal treatment of all citizens on matters with social implications.
5. Maintain and respect law, property, and human rights.
6. Accept social obligations to reciprocate service and loyalty to the community in exchange for the protection and promotion of individual liberty.

Introducing the Twin Paradoxes of Liberal Democracy

During application of what the community requires (conformity to prevent chaos) versus what liberal democracy stands for (freedom of individuals), conflicts arise. Conflicts between individuals and their natural freedoms, on one hand, and the community and its required conformity, on the other hand, generate the twin paradoxes of liberal democracy. To prepare children for life in a liberal democracy, educators must understand the nature of both liberal democracy as well as the twin paradoxes. In addition, liberal democratic educators must also understand and practice methods of reconciling the competing natures of life embedded in the twin paradoxes.

Twin Paradoxes in Overview

As you look at the twin paradoxes note that the issue of freedom is deliberately characterized as black and white. In life, as you might expect, issues are full of difficult and challenging decisions. As you practice thinking about and working out the paradoxes, consider the value of compromise.

Private Level:	*Freedom*	*versus*	*Conformity*
	(act as you wish)		*(follow rules)*

On this level, you make the decision to follow rules or do as you think best, to act good.

Public Level:	*Individuals*	*versus*	*Community*
	(support freedom for all)		*(support conformity for sake of community)*

On this level, you make the decision to support the freedom of individuals against supporting the needed conformity of the community, to act right.

One function of a liberal democratic community is to promote and defend the freedom of its citizens. For instance, when compulsory school laws were developed, one issue that surfaced was what happens if a child will not go to school or her parents refuse to enroll her in school? Given these laws, parents were compelled (and still are) to enroll their children under threat of jail sentence. Forcing children or parents to do something against their wishes does not sound very democratic. Nevertheless, by law parents do not have the option of deciding whether or not their child will attend school.

On one hand, a liberal democratic community must protect the rights of parents and children to make decisions. Yet on the other hand, adults of the democracy have determined that it is in the best interest of the public that all children between the ages of six and sixteen attend public school or its equivalent.[2] Is forcing unwilling children or reluctant parents to send their children to school ultimately in the best interest of the community? Would it be more democratic to simply let the child or parents decide?

The decision to attend school is one illustration of the conflict between good and right. While it may be good for the parents to make up their own minds regarding school attendance, ultimately law makers have reasoned that it is right that all children attend school despite the wishes of parents. Regardless of who makes the decision, the two competing natures of right and good continue to exist regardless of any direct or indirect action or nonaction on the part of individuals. There will always be some individual parents who think that their children should not attend public schools. Moreover, there will always be a number of children who believe that they should not be forced to attend school. To initiate the child into the community, modern civilizations most likely will always require some type of formal schooling for their young people.

Still we ask is it possible to be free, if one must conform to social rules/laws? How can a liberal democratic community continue to exist if citizens ignore the conventions of the community (compulsory school attendance)? These questions illustrate the nature of a paradox: two competing elements cannot exist or be promoted at the same time without creating a contradiction. Obviously, citizens cannot do anything they wish regardless of the consequences to others and continue to be part of the community. In the case of school attendance, one side must give way to be other: either we compel children to attend schools or their equivalent or the community allows parents or children to make the decision to attend schools or not.

The paradox of the freedom of individuals to choose and the demand of the community for individuals to conform to rules will continue to persist as long as the community and individuals exist. Given this qualification of a paradox, we can only bring two competing sides together and negotiate. Paradoxes are thus not resolved or solved like a problem with a definite answer, but are reconciled through direct engagement of individuals. In this case, representative arguments from the conformity side and the freedom side are brought together for the purpose of harmonizing differences.

Change, Conflict, and the Twin Paradoxes

Because civilized life places individuals and culture in constant flux, conflicts between individuals and the community are inevitable. In addition, other aspects of civilized life, such as institutions, language, economics, politics, and religion are deeply affected by unpredictable change and irresolvable conflict. The sum elements of change and conflict in the community can be described in the form of social paradoxes. Specifically, two central paradoxes can be identified: freedom versus conformity and the individual versus the community. These twin paradoxes emerge simultaneously whenever individuals seek to maintain their freedom while an authority acting as an agent of the community imposes restrictions. For liberal democratic communities, although authority to govern is granted by the people (through majority rule), the tension between freedom and conformity continues to persist.

Think about It: *How healthy is conflict for the community?*

Although this tension is certainly less in liberal democratic communities than in a totalitarian state (where the people have no active voice in government) individuals cannot totally eliminate the tensions that inevitably arise between the respective sides of these paradoxes. Essentially the paradox and the tension continue to persist independently of individual attention and action. Thus, to repeat, tension created by a social paradox can only be lessened through active reconciliation of individuals in the community.

Science and common sense have made it clear that human survival is a social concern. Because we humans are dependent upon one another for both physical and psychological needs, it is in our best interest (for survival) that we work to reconcile differences. Nonetheless, when individuals are placed in a social context, their needs, wants, hopes, and desires often come into conflict with those of other individuals. Because each individual is born physically independent from others, that is, human do not share a collective will or mind, it is inevitable that individuals should possess different experiences and identities despite living in similar circumstances or even within the same families. In a liberal democratic community, public schools, if properly conceived, offer an excellent opportunity to learn and practice liberal democratic principles. In this view, the extension of freedom forms the essence of education.

The conditions that exist for individuals to exercise freedom must be highlighted. In particular, the liberal democratic community can provide conditions for individuals, through the power of reason, to acquire freedom. A liberal democratic community, or any community for that matter, does not literally give freedom to anyone; the community merely creates a fertile environment for freedom. Each individual citizen must actively pursue, and extend his or her own freedom through the enlargement of experience.

The pursuit of freedom is essentially what being liberal is all about. The liberal community and individual make allowances for differences between citizens. Additionally, in a liberal democratic model, both the community and individuals adopt an egalitarian outlook, which is accepting of competing

---

[2]Each state decides the age requirements for school attendance. This age range is merely an example.

or new ideas and seek to extend and improve the condition of all human beings.

The relationship between the community and the individual is close within the liberal democratic model. For the individual to exist and the community to continue to exist, two critical qualifications must be recognized and followed. First, individuals must exercise self-restraint (have personal morals), and second, individuals must obey rules (have social morals). In return for exercising its personal and social morals, the community employs civil laws that protect individuals from those who make unreasonable infringements upon their freedom, as well as when the community itself attempts such restrictions.

Additionally, a liberal democratic community also provides each individual with a voice and role in government. This action is called political freedom. With these conditions met, the community and individual develop a special relationship that is centered in mutual responsibility. In this context, the individual is responsible to the community and the community is responsible to the individual. The health as well as the actual existence of the liberal democratic nation is dependent upon this special relationship. Although democracy has a strong political nature, we must remember that democracy is more than voting or participating in government, democracy is a way of living.

Democratic living embraces the spirit of community, where the public welfare of every citizen is given your highest consideration. Democratic living evokes the consciousness of sacrifice, not only for the sake of family and friends, but also for the sake of the community. Democratic living relies upon each citizen caring for and about other citizens in ways that establish a special trust—a trust that guarantees your freedom as much as it guarantees the freedom of others.

Freedom versus Conformity: Moving from Good to Right

The first of the twin paradoxes is centered upon the conflict between freedom and conformity. In this paradox, individuals seek what is good for themselves; however, they often find that their good conflicts with the constraints of the community. By virtue of the definitions of the community (simply stated as a number of individuals sharing political, economic, and social institutions within a geographic area), individuals (independent thinkers of that community) must relinquish absolute freedom (that allows individuals to do whatever one wishes without regard to others or consequences) to live among other humans. This giving up of absolute freedom is central to the paradox of the individual versus the community and is the antithesis of the freedom side of the paradox (aligned instead to conformity).

With few exceptions, throughout the history of humanity, people have suffered more from the extremes of conformity than from the excesses of freedom. We need only evoke the images of life under the dictate of people like Adolf Hitler of Nazi Germany, Joseph Stalin of the Soviet Union from the 1920s to the 1950s, and Mao Tse-tung of Communist China to illustrate this case. Historians are hard pressed to present accounts of human life where suffering of the people, not the lives of kings or rulers, was a direct result of the extension of freedom. Thus, to individuals, the greater danger emanates from a community where freedom is suppressed and conformity demanded. For this reason, our first inclination must be to tend toward the freedom side of the continuum of the first paradox (selecting good) and to shy away from attempts that gravitate toward conformity (continually doing right).

> *Follow-up Question: What examples or illustrations of freedom versus conformity do you find today?*

The dismal record of human attempts to sustain freedom dictates an action that comes naturally to individuals—to seek what is best for themselves. In a liberal democratic community what is best for the individual is to extend his or her own sense of freedom. Any move toward personal good is directly linked to the extension of individual freedom. For mature individuals, good is relatively easy to distinguish or mark; the good is simply what is best for you.

> *Consider This: What illustrations of personal good might be considered unwanted for the community?*

In the twin paradoxes the good represents freedom and individuals, while the right represents conformity and community. Eventually, to continue to remain part of a group, individuals must exhibit some conformity to group norms (this is called "doing right"). When individuals exhibit this willingness to cooperate with others, they are working to reduce the tensions created by the paradox of the individual versus the community in favor of the community. When individuals refuse to cooperate with others or the dictates of the group, they are attending to the paradox of freedom versus conformity in favor of freedom.

The first paradox from the individual's point of view is not that freedom is lost to the individual, but how much freedom can be obtained? In reverse, the question from a liberal democratic community's position is not that freedom is taken from individuals, but how much conformity is necessary to maintain or hold together a community? The challenge for liberal democratic community is that no final or ultimate answer exists to either of the above questions.

For children this same question (What is good?) is problematic: children may know what they desire, but not really understand what is good. At another level, when individuals live in groups such as families and communities, what is good for one person may not be very good for another. Individuals of a liberal democracy need to continually question whether they are better served by striving toward that which enhances freedom for all citizens (right) or seeking out that which constitutes freedom without regard for the rights/ freedom of others (good).

Think about It: What are the consequences of choosing good over right or right over good for the individual?

Power, Fame and Money

Questions of good and right are heavily laden with values. For many children, good and right are more determined more by what they observe in the world about them than those values observed and practiced in the home, church, or at school. In particular, many children are conditioned as much by powerful media presentations as by peer groups to apply three readily identified values that come to govern thought and behavior: power, fame, and money. From sports heroes to entertainers to drug dealers, children observe the apparent social attention/importance placed on the acquisition and retention of power (the ability to direct others to do what you wish), fame (the apparent thrill and adoration derived from an individual's instant recognition and respect by others), and money (the seemingly inexhaustibility for one to obtain whatever pleases or excites). For example, big movie stars pick their projects, say, do, and wear what they please, are adored by millions of fans, live in luxurious homes, travel about in private jets, and more; all thrilling to many children who are just shaping their own values systems, seeking their own identities.

These highly individualized values are not necessarily bad for the community. Yet, taken alone, that is, when a child's world is directed by these values at the expense of such community-building values as love, work ethic, sharing, cooperation, respect, and responsibility, children may be rendered incapable of appreciating the need to consider the other side of the liberal democratic paradoxes.

As the division between self and community is left unclear or undefined, the potential for children to begin acting in ways that are damaging to the community and others is heightened. When money is the prized value, how one obtains money is not at issue, only that one has money. This attitude, of course, opens the possibility for any number of behaviors that are harmful for the community (robbery, arson, intimidation, sexual abuse, assault and battery, and more). The same is true for the values of power and fame. The means used for acquisition and retention of these values are not problematic. What is disgraceful or unacceptable within peer groups is one's lack of money, fame, and power. The need to closely examine these values as well as to introduce community-centered values that serve to counter-balance the negative aspects of money, fame, and power, strikes at the heart of liberal democratic thought and action.

The Individual versus the Community and Acting Right

Unlike the first paradox where individuals tend toward the freedom side of the continuum and that which is best for themselves, in the second paradox the direction is set decidedly toward the improvement of the welfare of all individuals and that which is best because it works toward the improvement of institutions that serve the community. The selfish nature of people prompts the community to demand right over individual concerns (good) because individuals may reflect elements that are harmful to others.

The contrast between what is good for the individual and what is right for the community highlights a contradiction of terms most difficult to resolve. Indeed, philosophers have grappled with the definition of "the good" for individuals and "the right" for the community for centuries without consensus or resolution. The theory of liberal democratic education, as posed here, deliberately casts aside this eternal debate and reduces the argument to a pragmatic one: the good citizen is one who knows right and strives toward what is perceived to be right. That is, given the choice between good and right, the good citizen intentionally tries to do the right thing despite personal consequences.

In this context being good (and thus acting right) is a matter of social development. Good is recognized in light of its social context and not assessed by its individual or personal aspects. Individuals, as infants, begin with the perception of "the good" as that which satisfies the individual. Eventually, through social interaction with parents, siblings, other family members, peers, the community, and the wider society of communities, individuals come to recognize the good in its social context simply by being told (or observing) what is right.

Furthermore, each individual may be described as good if she is striving more toward rightness than what is perceived as merely good. For example, Toby, who is now fifteen, has been selling drugs in his neighborhood since he was ten years old. Through his earlier experiences, Toby came to understand that selling and using drugs was not right long before he ever started selling them. Not only had he heard this message from his mother, his older sister, his pastor at church, television programs, and his teachers at school, he had witnessed first hand the devastating effects of drug abuse. In addition, Toby made other observations that supported the notion that dealing in drugs was not right. For instance, illegal drugs could not be bought at the corner store, or any store for that matter, you had to hide the drugs from police, and you could not openly bring or use drugs at school or in church.

Consequently, despite knowing that drug selling or using was not accepted by most people, including police, Toby sold drugs. His reasoning was simple: drugs produced a lot of money and money was a good thing to have. Therefore, although he knew it was not right to sell drugs, it was good to have money. Ultimately, for Toby, the good of having money outweighed the "not right" of selling drugs. How do we classify Toby? Is he really acting good?

From an individual perspective, Toby's behavior can be rationalized as good because he is doing good for himself by making money. However, from a societal perspective, his good creates a multitude of bads, from people stealing property to get money to buy his drugs to fostering a violent and vicious culture of despair and hopelessness. In conclusion, Toby's actions are not right, and Toby knows it. Moreover, Toby's actions are not right because they do not serve the long-term interests of the community; rather his actions are destroying the community.

Despite his past, Toby can do the right thing—he can act right by deciding to give up selling drugs. He may also decide to help his community in constructive ways—to help other children turn from drugs, to attend school, to actively participate when political, social, and economic issues are raised—in short, to care for others. In a liberal democracy, these constructive activities are not merely the singular, isolated behaviors of a reformed drug seller, but the actions of one who perceives the community to be the collective home of the people—all the people.

The deciding factor of rightness, then, is not the damage done to the individual, but the damage done to others. The community, therefore, can accept varying degrees of goodness (individuals doing what they want) without social sanctions; however, the community cannot accept or tolerate behaviors that harm other citizens. Individuals, too, in their social interactions are capable of expressing what they feel is in the public's best interest. The central questions of goodness or rightness, however, are not static, but fluid. Therefore, each generation must ultimately decide what constitutes right, how best to obtain it, and how best to maintain it. In the liberal democratic context, the outcome of this process relies upon free public education to provide citizens with the necessary opportunities to learn and practice liberal democratic principles.

Thomas Jefferson, author of the Declaration of Independence and third President of the United States, eloquently declared that there was no happy relationship between ignorance and freedom. To Jefferson, ignorant citizens would never become free. Moreover, to become free and remain free, citizens must embrace and promote education for all citizens. Jefferson's wisdom greatly affected the growth of public education in the early years of our nation's history and continues to exert influence today.

Given the choice between good and right, it is, of course, possible to cloak your true thoughts and actions from others: to give the impression of acceptance of right when in fact you disagree or despise certain rules. But to withhold your true opinion in a liberal democratic community is in effect to forfeit your freedom. All opinions, including those that appear to contradict accepted thought and practice, must be voiced. It is through the dialogue of differing opinion that liberal democracy gains its greatest strength.

Education and the Twin Paradoxes

Following Jefferson's advice, education offers citizens the opportunity to enhance their own freedom and ensure the continuity of the liberal democratic community. Additionally, education provides the occasion to recognize and explore the paradoxes of freedom versus conformity and the individual versus the community as well as to present children the opportunity to practice and explore democracy. In their application to formal education, the twin paradoxes can be described in the form of two sets of questions that act in opposition to one another:

1. How much freedom do individuals require in school curricula that will not thwart the creative energies of students and teachers? [Against] How much conformity must be instilled through instruction to prevent chaos?
2. How do teachers foster and encourage the intellectual, physical, and psychological growth of the individual? [Against] How do teachers instill a sense of social responsibility that favors the welfare of the group over the individual?

Educators in liberal democratic nations need to acknowledge both sets of the above questions in order to plan, organize, present, and assess educational programs. Once responses to these questions are formulated they may be placed on a continuum. In the first paradox, freedom is set in direct opposition to conformity. In the second paradox, the individual is squarely countered by the community. In between extreme versions of freedom and conformity and the individual and the community exist a variety of possibilities. Each possibility represents an attempt to reconcile the paradox.

Schooling, Training, and Education

In one sense, public schools provide experiences that will later enable young people to function as adults. The view of schooling as preparation for adult life places emphasis upon what adults think children need to know and understand to become functional adults. In this model, curricula are designed around adult-like perceptions of the world.

To survive in the adult world, adult models highlight the need for mathematics and literacy skills, science information and abilities, and a sense of historical heritage and geographic awareness. Moreover, adults often add such topics as sex and drug education, consumer economics, international and diversity issues, as well as environmental studies to the list of "musts" for children under the rationale of preventative education.

> *Follow-up Question: What new topics, skills, or subjects are being proposed for elementary schools?*

Information prescribed by adults, however, is troubling. Information-based education is driven by content and its accomplice, objectives. Throughout the history of education, information has been provided to and for students under the guise of subjects or content. Schools, in fact, excel in the delivery of information.

In the effort to school children for the future, adults then supply, manipulate, and transfer this information to young people. Conspicuously, when adults fail to connect adult-centered information curricula to the child's own context of experience, which is typical, children become socially neutered and intellectually inept. Moreover, children are given a handicap that essentially renders them incapable of functioning as free thinkers and actors in a liberal democratic community.

It is not that schooling does not have its place in education. There are any number of things adults purposely teach children that are important—to tie shoes, to write the alphabet, to say thank you, to turn the computer monitor off, and to memorize their address to name a few. However, training children to *act* like liberal democratic citizens appears to violate a primary tenet of liberal democracy—emphasis upon freedom.

Think about It: *What examples of training versus education can you relate to?*

Schooling for citizenship may function as an integral part of a totalitarian society such as socialist China or what existed in the former Soviet Union, but training (as in indoctrination) for citizenship is not easily justified in a liberal democracy. You cannot force or coerce citizens to follow liberal democratic principles and remain a liberal democracy; children (and all citizens) must choose their way of life and government. Is schooling for liberal democratic citizenship, then, wholly inappropriate?

The question reveals the paradoxical nature of public schools. On one hand, schools prepare prescriptive curricula, demand that children attend school, and repress or stifle creativity by defining class size and tracking students. How can schools that demonstrate such authoritarian dispositions and controls serve as catalysts for liberal democracy to be examined, practiced, and acquired? On the other hand, where else in our nation can liberal democratic principles be employed with children on such a large scale than in our educational institutions? One response to this paradox is to engage liberal democratic principles in public schools despite the handicaps or challenge. To do so, teachers need to be able to identify and transform information-based curricula into a program compatible with liberal democratic principles.

Educating Children

There is a significant difference between schooling as training and education. In contrast to schooling, education is more than learning subjects such as math and science, history and language. Education fosters more than the perpetuation of the community, it provides for the growth and improvement of life for all its citizens on one hand, and provides for individual growth on the other. The root of education is not training people to function with selected information for specific, predetermined roles in the community. Rather, education works to empower children through the extension of freedom to continue learning throughout life whether or not the individual continues to study in institutions of higher learning or other formal settings.

Knowledge is the meaningful application of information. The application of information may be activated by adults; however, information is ultimately processed and continued by learners. Two critical outcomes of information application are the growth and capacity to learn and the expansion of opportunities to increase learning. The creation of knowledge is centered within the learner and cannot be imposed. Knowledge generation is decidedly active in nature and has positive long-term consequences. That is, knowledge (transformed information) is better remembered and more functional when actively used. In this view, then, education is the process that facilitates the growth and opportunity of knowledge generation.

Clearly information must be readily available to all citizens. Yet, adults must stand ready to deliver more than passive information to children that retard and limit the potential for growth experiences. Admittedly, unless adults make the effort to educate their children, to pass the "torch" of life and learnings onto the next generation, in time, the community and its institutions will dissipate. In the effort to pass the torch, adults who highlight only that which they perceive to be necessary for adult life often ignore that which is necessary for the child's present life. To ignore the child's present life in favor of his or her future life is to retard potential growth by experience and raise the possibility of unnecessarily stifling learning.

A child's capacity to learn seems limitless, yet as adulthood draws near the capacity to perceive, conceptualize, and verbalize experience becomes mysteriously leveled or deadened. Many young adults have given up the active pursuit of learning (growth by experience). Education as described in this text emphasizes the goal of developing children as learners for life, not learners of adult life.

Follow-up Question: What things do you suppose children know at ages 3, 5, 7, 9, 11, or 13?

Experience as a Learning Base

Given the importance of attending to the present life of children, schooling as the training for adult life is strictly a secondary concern compared to the aim of education as the lifelong expansion for the capacity for growth. Instead of continuing the popular myth that schools need to train children now so that they will become better adults, the theory found in this textbook assists teachers in providing experiences that enable children to become better children in the present. The notion of "better children" conveys a sense of improved quality of democratic life, not that we are to assist children in improving upon their childish or childlike manners. The ideal is to foster the notion that our educational experience continues throughout childhood and extends to adulthood.

There are many different learning strategies and theories. The learning theory emphasized here is based upon providing structured and unstructured experiences to/with/for children. It may be more correct to say that experience-based education is not a learning theory at all, but a theory of instruction with a prediction of learning. One central assumption of learning theory is that children do learn. Nonetheless, in a liberal democratic community where freedom is a central value, and the question of how children learn is hotly debated, it may be in fact more prudent for teachers to simply provide opportunities and experiences that enable children to learn as they will.

> *Learning Theories*
> *Tabula Rasa (Locke)*
> *Behaviorist (Skinner)*
> *Constructivism (Piaget)*
> *Nativism (Plato)*

Consequently, learning, like liberal democratic principles and freedom, is a function of the individual child, not an imposition of the community or its agents in schools. Even if the secret or definitive answer of how human beings learn were known, if it was put to use it could prove harmful to liberal democracy because teachers might be able to manipulate learners to follow a single course of action.

A special emphasis of liberal democratic education is a recognition of the individual and his or her unique characteristics and attributes. This emphasis includes acknowledging the complex nature of learning and its variations among children. The way children learn may be as varied as the way children look, think, and act. Therefore, providing meaningful experiences is the central task of the teacher; however, learning is the central task of the child. As discussed in the following chapter, experience-based education is presented as the most effective approach to attending to the needs of children in a liberal democracy.

A First Step toward Reconciliation of the Twin Paradoxes

To summarize, we have discussed the fact that democracy is more than a form of government. As witnessed in recent years, particularly in Eastern Europe and the former Soviet Union, liberal democratic dispositions and opportunities are appealing. As an ideal, liberal democracy is a dynamic phenomenon that has the potential to unite all human life regardless of differences in race, language, and culture. Yet, liberal democracy is also fragile. Because democracy depends upon a willingness of diverse people to unite as well as a fostering of sustained and open dialogue between individuals of the community, unless children and other new citizens become cognizant of and actively interested in its continuation, democracy can be easily overwhelmed by powerful competing forces. A liberal education is thus the key to the actualization of an intelligent and active citizenry.

The specific responsibility of the teacher in a liberal democracy is to facilitate opportunities for children that work to extend the freedom of each child as they become fully functioning members of the community. To accomplish this goal, the teacher must possess a disciplined liberal democratic disposition that aids children with the identification and practice of that which is right (serve the community). On the other hand, each teacher must also embrace and practice a personal freedom that assists children with the identification and practice of that which is good (serve the individual). By helping children to choose right as well as good, you and your children will be working to reconcile the twin paradoxes of freedom versus conformity and the individual versus community. These important actions work to ensure the present and future of both liberal democracy and the citizens of a liberal democracy.

In making sense of how teachers can apply the paradoxes in classroom settings it may be helpful to recall John Dewey's simile of the pendulum[3] (that teaching children is like the pendulum of a clock). Dewey argued that teaching typically swings between the two extremes of fostering individual growth (freedom side of the paradoxes) and imposing external commands on individuals (control side of the paradoxes). Acknowledging that the notion of a pendulum implies some sort of middle ground as the ideal area for educational harmony, Dewey carefully pointed out that what was really needed in teaching "is a change in the direction of movement." That is, the regularity of the pendulum swinging from one extreme to the other or staying indefinitely to one side or the other, is not helpful. What children need to further or maximize their growth is some sort of flexible educational plan that can be adjusted and applied as needed.

In specifics, when an educational program burdens students with detail and routine that stifles creativity and initiative (control side of paradoxes), the imbalance must be recognized and corrected by a move toward individual freedom of thought and action. By contrast, when an educational program becomes so lax as to squander educational opportunities with unproductive individualized activities (freedom side of paradoxes), the imbalance must be recognized and corrected by a move toward focused and directly supervised or controlled activities.

Teaching activities cannot be a *simultaneous* blending of freedom and imposition; activities are either more freedom-centered or more control-centered. Although you may make decisions as to which sort of experiences you will provide for your children, you cannot determine in advance precisely how your children will respond to these experiences. What you can do is to carefully craft educational activities that allow for variations (moves toward or away from freedom *or* moves toward or away from teacher controls). In essence, the teacher supporting liberal democratic principles must stand pre-

---

[3]John Dewey. (1988). Individuality and Experience. In *The later works of John Dewey*. Carbondale, IL: Southern Illinois University Press. (First published in *Journal of the Barnes Foundation, 2*, January 1926).

pared to "read" the classroom environment, to gauge children's reactions to the experiences, and to factor in whatever other variables are present or can be anticipated in order to decide which side of the paradoxes the teaching experiences should be moved toward.

This chapter is not an easy one to simply sit down, read, and digest; you need time to reflect, to place yourself and your thinking into the context of the sort of school you believe is best for children. Building upon the important responsibilities of educating young people, the following chapter will introduce the elementary teacher as a principal activator of liberal democratic curricula.

Marking Your Progress

1. Topic/theme _____

   _____

   _____

2. Description of community/context for unit _____

   _____

   _____

3. Relationship of community/children to twin paradoxes _____

   _____

   _____

4. Ideas/experiences for incorporating twin paradoxes into your unit ____

   _____

   _____

Read More about It Special References

The questions of what we should teach and to what purpose are old ones. The answers, however, are both old and new: old in the sense that many ideas and strategies have been developed with various populations of children (especially in the past century), and new in the sense that you have not tried these ideas. As you begin your teaching, the following references present a number of ideas that may prove helpful.

Bloom, A. (1987). *The closing of the American mind.* New York: Simon & Schuster.
   One of the most controversial books on education written in the past 20 years. Bloom takes exception to Deweyan thoughts on schooling and democracy; instead he adopts what might be termed a "traditional view of education." Bloom brings the issue of democratic schooling into sharp focus, especially when read in connection with Dewey, Strike, Gutmann, Greene, and Engle and Ochoa.
Dewey, J. (1916). *Democracy and education.* New York: Macmillan.
   Dewey is the standard work for examining the main threads of democracy in the context of schooling. Many of Dewey's theories on education can be traced to his work (together with his wife Alice) with elementary-age children. It contains a number of chapters that should be read by all students majoring in elementary education (chapters 1 to 10, 14, 15, and 22).
Engle, S. H., & Ochoa, A. S. (1988). *Education for democratic citizenship.* New York: Teachers College Press.
   Written from a Deweyan perspective, Engle and Ochoa synthesize the state of social studies teaching within the framework of democracy. Although more directed to a secondary education audience (the text is clear and understandable), Engle and Ochoa offer a number of ideas that are related to the twin paradoxes (particularly the related notion of socialization and countersocialization).
Goodman, J. (1992). *Elementary schooling for critical democracy.* Albany: State University of New York Press.
   Goodman introduces critical pedagogy to elementary teachers. For those unfamiliar with this developing theory of education, this is a tough book to read. Goodman does not continue within the tradition of Dewey, nor does he place his ideas into familiar contexts. This text represents a move toward social reconstruction from a community-first perspective (places groups value over individual).
Greene, M. (1988). *The dialectic of freedom.* New York: Teachers College Press.
   In this highly readable discussion on freedom and schooling, Greene provides a strong overview of critical issues in American education.
Gutmann, A. (1987). *Democratic education.* Princeton: Princeton University Press.
   This book is more than important up-dating of Dewey—Gutmann launches out in new directions that have a direct bearing on elementary schooling. Gutmann envisions an educational plan that is thoroughly holistic (education to progress through life). Read in context with Dewey and Strike.
Miel, A., & Brogan, P. (1957). *More than social studies: A view of social learning in the elementary school.* Englewood Cliffs, NJ: Prentice-Hall.
   Striving to place the potent ideas of pioneer educational theorist, Florence Stratemeyer, into elementary social studies, the focus of Miel and Brogan on children remains timely. This book contains many good teaching suggestions.
Schlesinger, A. M., Jr. (1992). *The disuniting of America.* New York: Norton.
   Written in response to New York State's proposed social studies curriculum, Schlesinger gives his view on the future of a multicultural society. Certain to spark dialogue within different communities, the brief text should also be read and discussed among elementary teachers.

Strike, K. (1991). The moral role of schooling in a liberal democratic society. In *Review of Research in Education,* 17th Yearbook of the American Educational Research Association, ed., Grant G. Washington, DC: American Educational Research Association.
In this superior accounting of liberal democratic theory, Strike incorporates up-to-date scholarship with practice. The text, however, is dense, and some might find it difficult. Read in context with Dewey and Gutmann.

4

TEACHERS AND LEARNING EXPERIENCES

In this chapter you will

- Contemplate applications of holistic freedom for teaching.
- Look for ways to integrate the synoptic method as a teaching/learning model.
- Be introduced to four universal needs of children.
- Begin to practice transforming your teaching ideas into meaningful lesson experiences.

In the 1830s Horace Mann, one of the nation's earliest educational reformers, sought to humanize the treatment of children in public schools. Mann also worked to soften the hard edges of the common school experience then directed by the schoolmaster, the domineering, absolute dictator of American classrooms. Fortunately, Mann and the many educational reformers that followed him did enact needed reforms that affected public school systems.

> *Follow-up Question: What rules of the schoolmaster do you think might still apply for children in schools?*

During the mid to late 1800s, the schoolmaster was replaced with a new educational leader called a teacher. Many of the changes in schools championed the teacher as the center of the educational enterprise. Then, as now, even though children are in our educational thinking, it is the classroom teacher who holds the keys to providing the appropriate environment for learning to take place.

This chapter will explore the potential of the empowered teacher in a liberal democracy and the form and function of holistic freedom and provide an introduction to the four universal needs as an experimental-experience base. The emphasis upon liberal democratic principles does not imply that these principles are detached from the rest of the elementary school curriculum or that liberal democratic principles should dominate all curricula. You must keep in mind the integrative and holistic nature of the approach taken in this text and seek relationships between the social studies described here in the form of liberal democratic principles and other curricular areas of the school.

We have discussed in previous chapters two of the central questions of curricular development: who is to be taught and why. The question of who (children) was the subject of chapter 2; the question of why (to extend the freedom of children under the umbrella of liberal democratic principles) was the subject of chapter 3. Although the who (children) and the why (to extend freedom) have been presented in some detail, we will return to these important elements throughout the remainder of the text.

> *Think about It: Why should children receive public educational opportunities?*

In ancient Greece, education had two basic functions: first, children were to prepare for the world of labor (*askolia*) by learning a trade or occupation, which would provide individuals and their families with everyday needs (earning a living in our day). In its second function, formal school (from the Greek word *skole*) was not designed as preparation for learning a trade, but used to enhance leisure activities. Formal schools offered privileged children (and adults) the opportunity for contemplation or thinking, a chance to sit about and debate the major issues or questions of the day or whatever else seemed appropriate. Although both upper and lower class people shared in amusements such as attending wrestling matches and other sporting events (the Greeks called this activity recreation), ordinary citizens might have viewed leisure activities as useless and unproductive. Nonetheless, by providing time to contemplate and reflect upon life and living, these so-called leisure activities helped to give birth to the concepts of liberal democracy and freedom.

Following in the tradition of the ancient Greeks, in this chapter and those that follow, we turn our attention to the role elementary teachers play in furthering liberal democratic principles in our egalitarian schools. In the liberal democratic model teachers are connected to the questions of how to expand and extend the experiences of children. Teachers need to become sensitive to the use of holistic sense (viewing experience as complete) and analytic sense (recognizing elements within the whole).

This sensitivity becomes functional when education is conceived as a verb, not a noun. That is, the business of education is to activate learning (in every sense of the word) through the expansion of experience. It is the teacher as intellectual leader who energizes the educational enterprise where children not only learn valuable skills and dispositions that may assist their future work life, but also are enabled to practice and explore liberal democratic principles that will enhance their present life.

Teacher as Leader

The teacher is the intellectual leader of the class, not because of any official position, but, as John Dewey wrote, because of the "wider and deeper knowledge and matured experience" a teacher possesses.[1] Teachers have the power to influence and propose learning experiences. Teachers may directly guide learning or deliberately avoid interfering with children learning, thereby permitting children to learn on their own terms. To add to Dewey's teacher, who possesses "wider knowledge and deeper experiences," the liberal democratic teacher is central to the expansion of freedom for the child because the teacher herself is a living example of freedom.

If the teacher is free to chart the course of learning experiences and extends to the child in like manner the notion of free thinking and action, the child will readily observe liberal democratic principles in application. If, however, the teacher is burdened with curricular patterns designed and produced outside

[1]John Dewey, *How We Think*, Lexington, MA: D. C. Heath, 1933, p. 273.

of his or her influence and input, and then fails to question and examine these patterns, he or she becomes a poor conduit for democracy. In this case, then, the child suffers twice; first, by being subjected to an ineffective role model (teacher), and second, by being denied the opportunity to practice liberal democratic principles, especially freedom.

Just as a friendly environment for freedom is the first element to secure in a liberal democratic community, the first element to secure in the liberal democratic school community is the freedom of teachers to select, organize, present, and assess learning experiences for their students. Finally, teachers must accomplish this work without undue pressures, coercions, influences, and other distractions from those outside of the classroom.

The freedom to create is tempered with reason and practicality. In reconciling the twin paradoxes of freedom versus conformity and the individual versus community, the teacher who accepts liberal democratic principles will work to balance the best interests of community against the unfolding abilities of the individual child. In doing so the teacher is engaging the sense of reason and will not follow a course of wild, unexamined freedom.

On the other hand, school districts expect that teachers follow or at least attend to a set of prescribed suggestions or guidelines. The following sections identify the potential tension between exercising academic freedom and following the prescribed course of study and describe how teachers may address it.

Holistic Freedom

To understand the important role of the teacher in a liberal democracy, the notion of holistic freedom requires some description and exemplification. Freedom forms the essence of a liberal democracy; however, freedom is not something any government assigns to its citizens. Each citizen must acquire and expand freedom in his or her own way. The five aspects or levels of holistic freedom are: (1) to have the potential to think independently, (2) to have the capability to act, (3) to act without restraint, (4) to act from choices, and, if desired, (5) to overcome custom and authority in actions.

> *Five Levels of Holistic Freedom*
> *To think independently*
> *To have the capacity to act*
> *To act without restraint*
> *To act from choices*
> *To overcome custom and authority*

Given the five levels of holistic freedom, it is possible for individuals to possess freedom on one level and not another. That is, individuals need not possess freedom in all five degrees to demonstrate freedom. In fact, complete holistic freedom may not be desirable for every individual; full holistic freedom is an ideal, not a goal. Teachers cannot guarantee that children will absorb and exhibit each level of freedom.

The teacher's role is to present experiences and opportunities for children to practice freedom in each degree. Through practice children are enabled to obtain and activate their own level of freedom. The goal, then, is to provide the conditions for freedom to emerge. For children to observe, to conceptualize, and to display liberal democratic principles, teachers as citizens of the community and intellectual leaders of the classroom must be able to recognize and provide situations where application of each level of freedom can be explored and practiced. The experiences of the classroom should result in opportunities for thought and action, as well as acquisition of knowledge.

First Level

What does holistic freedom look like? Although I could not prove that every individual has thoughts, it is probable that every healthy, conscious individual does think. Because thoughts are hidden from public view (and it is impossible to prove that living humans do or do not possess thoughts), one assumption made here is that freedom of thought must be accepted as a given for every individual. Individuals do not have to prove to others (because they literally cannot) that they do think. Therefore, every individual owns the potential for freedom at the first level.

Second Level

In examining the second level of freedom another assumption must also be made because of a lack of empirical evidence, namely, that individuals could act upon their wishes if desired. To qualify for freedom in the second degree, actions can neither be random nor preordained. If you wish to raise your hand and then lower it, the actions are yours to make. We assume that you are not acting out some pre-existing plan (unknown to you) with unseen strings directing your every action. Similarly, we also assume that you are not simply moving your hand up and down without any internal controls. Again, as with the assumption of free thought (first degree of freedom), we cannot prove your hand actions are not preordained or that your actions are simply random; we merely assume that you can act if you want to.

To credit freedom in the second degree, individuals do not (because they cannot) have to verify that they can act. Therefore, like freedom of thought, we assume that freedom of action is possible for every individual. If individuals were not free to act upon their own thoughts, it would be pointless to continue with this definition of freedom.

Third Level

As we pass to the following three levels of freedom, proof of action or nonaction can be detected and qualified. Say, for example, you wanted to cross the street (assuming you possess the ability to think and act as an individual) and are physically or emotionally unable to or prevented from crossing the street, you would not pass the test of freedom in the third degree/level. For freedom to exist at the third level, the individual (and others) must work to reduce natural or human-made barriers that might interfere or halt actions. Although we acknowledge the existence of natural and human-made barriers, if individuals can conquer these barriers, the third qualification of freedom is met.

Fourth Level

If you think it a public responsibility to recycle your plastic and glass goods, have the receptacles for these materials, and have identified the drop-off sites for collection, you have demonstrated freedom in the first three degrees. However, unless you purposely selected the recycling program over alternative methods such as conservation (reusing glass, plates, and eating utensils) or buying only biodegradable materials or a thoughtful combination of these, you have not demonstrated freedom in the fourth degree.

Freedom in the fourth degree requires that all actions are based upon reasoned choice. If you had seriously considered a number of choices (at least two) and consciously chose the recycling program, then you warrant freedom in the fourth degree. Merely selecting one program over another (or none at all) is not enough to rate fourth level freedom; you must consider your choice carefully, answering the questions, "Is this the best/wisest selection?" "What are the consequences of my actions or nonactions?" "What is the most cost-effective method?" If you meet these standards and can rationalize your choice to others, you have reached freedom in the fourth degree.

Fifth Level

The final level of holistic freedom is the most difficult of all to satisfy. It requires that you overcome any and all custom and authority that may frustrate, hinder, or interfere with your thought and action. For example, you may think about going to the movies (first level) and be able to do so (second level). You may also have the transportation, money, and time that will enable you to get to the movies, pay for a ticket, and watch a film (third level). Moreover, you may have considered each of five films offered at the movie house and carefully selected one to watch (fourth level).

Everything may be set, but as you approach the theater you notice that the film is rated NC-17. You are reminded that your religious organization forbids watching films with such ratings. As you exercise your freedom you must now decide to observe the warning of the church or disregard this warning. Although you may have demonstrated each of the first four levels of holistic freedom, at this moment you must determine if you are going to compromise the values associated with your religious upbringing or not. This compromising of attitudes, beliefs, and values can be very distressing. No matter if you elect to watch the film and then deal with or rationalize your values later, or if you stand by your convictions and do not enter the theater, the decision can be difficult because the "correct choice" appears to have been concluded beforehand.

The strong values attached to custom and authority are difficult to defeat. On one hand, you may not want to defeat these values at all, yet, on the other hand, you may be eager to challenge so-called appropriate attitudes, beliefs, and/or values. For example, Alfreda (daughter of an investment banker) may want to invite Cleophus (son of a cab driver) to her birthday party. Although children of different economic classes rarely interact, Alfreda's parents are willing to have Cleophus attend the party. Parents of the other children, however, balk at the mixture of economic classes.

Where some families may not wish to challenge status quo attitudes, others do not see the sense of devaluing a child according to his parent's income. The choice between inviting Cleophus or not may have some serious consequences for Alfreda and her parents. By inviting Cleophus, Alfreda and her parents may be excluded from other social gatherings for violating custom. In contrast, by having Cleophus at the party, Alfreda's parents are reinforcing the spirit of community and free choice. In either event or action, the decision to reach fifth level freedom is strictly accomplished on a personal basis—we cannot dictate actions to Alfreda, her parents, or their guests.

Because a child may not be able to resist his or her own traditions and demonstrate holistic freedom (all five levels), we should not conclude that our efforts in the class are a failure. Furthermore, we should not highlight a child's inability to reach the fifth level of holistic freedom. Teachers must draw a definite line between the fourth and fifth level of holistic freedom.

Parenthetically, although children do need to understand and evaluate their own attitudes, beliefs, and values, they should not be pressured or coerced to change, alter, or abandon these dispositions either through direct or indirect influence despite what your beliefs may be. The teacher can help children identify the line between fourth and fifth level freedoms, but should not determine when, if ever, a child should or should not cross the line toward fifth level freedom.

In a liberal democratic community, teachers should encourage children to pass through the first four levels of holistic freedom guided by their own thought and action. Teachers should provide opportunities to recognize natural and human-made barriers and assist children with the exploration of their own freedom by fostering the need to make reasoned choices. The line between the fourth level of freedom and custom and authority (the fifth level) is one each child must traverse alone. Public education in a liberal democracy is not the forum to ridicule or humiliate a child. Although it may be appropriate to raise questions about the nature and practice of custom and authority, teachers should not permit or condone the circumvention of family, religious, and other firmly held attitudes, beliefs, and values derived from custom and/or authority.

Applying Holistic Freedom to Teachers

How do the five essential elements of holistic freedom apply to elementary teachers? Unfortunately, in many elementary schools, teachers are not free to determine the pedagogical needs of their children, nor are they free to prepare and present experiences outside prescribed curricula. Some administrators and other school and community leaders (not acting in partnership with teachers) have decided ahead of time what will be taught and, in many cases, how. Additionally, some schools simply purchase prepackaged curriculum to accomplish their goals.

When curricula products are predetermined without teachers' input, they tend to reduce all classroom experiences to the same dead level. That is, such curricula become "one-size-fits-all" programs. Because individual differences, special cases, particular needs, and interests are difficult to reproduce in textual materials, teachers must be prepared to recognize problems and inconsistencies by providing viable alternatives. In liberal democratic schools, every teacher must be enabled to exercise all five levels of holistic freedom and, most importantly, provide opportunities for each child to exercise holistic freedom.

As with our first example of holistic freedom, we assume that teachers have the potential to think independently (first level) as well as being capable of acting upon these thoughts (second level). The central purpose of liberal education is to foster independent thought and action. It is inconceivable that during your college education you would practice these liberal dispositions, while during your professional life (as a teacher) these freedoms would be dismantled.

Teacher-proof textual materials that provide little need for teachers to exercise any independent thought (even if they wanted to) were invented more than one hundred years ago. These materials were developed for teachers during a time when typical elementary or common school teachers possessed very little education or experience. Teacher-proof materials (textbooks with complete instructions, pre-prepared worksheets and tests, answer keys, study guides, suggested teaching practices, and more) were designed to ensure some uniformity to compensate for inadequately prepared teachers. At one time, these materials may have served teachers and their students; however, with the levels of professional preservice educational experiences now available, schools that employ teachers simply to follow a fixed program are not merely wasting talent, they are rejecting liberal democratic principles.

Nonetheless, some schools are reluctant to discard teacher-proof materials. Consequently, in order to function as liberal democratic institutions, schools must foster teachers to think and act independently (first and second levels) and empower them to do so.

To reach the third level of holistic freedom, teachers must be prepared to overcome many barriers, for example, drafty windows, inadequate supplies, undernourished children, overcrowded classrooms, or students not being able to read or express themselves. Anything that physically prevents or restricts you from accomplishing your goals for your children is an obstruction. Teachers, because they are directly responsible for classroom experiences, need to identify barriers and design strategies to overcome challenges. Although some obstacles, such as not having sufficient funds to purchase necessary materials may be discouraging, teachers must continue the pursuit of holistic freedom.

To attain third level freedom in the presence of insurmountable problems, creativity, ingenuity, imagination, and resourcefulness must be used. If, for example, you cannot afford a store-bought pinata for your Spanish Day Festival, try enlisting your children to make their own. Remember with a little imagination a simple cardboard box can become a race car, hotel, pirate ship, clubhouse, rocket, jet plane, mountain range, and more. The point of third level freedom for teachers is to work to create a positive environment for children to explore third level freedom. To assist you with the struggle and challenge of overcoming barriers, the sources of free and inexpensive resource materials will be supplied in later chapters.

The fourth level of holistic freedom, often overlooked by teachers, is central to the liberal democratic principle of making informed choices. When teachers debates whether to use something, such as a prepared textbook series, they are not exercising holistic freedom. This sort of selection has only the appearance of choice. If teachers only have the chance to decide to do or not do something, then they are operating with merely an illusion of freedom.

Holistic freedom at the fourth level involves: (1) the existence of or potential for a number of choices and alternatives; (2) a knowledge and understanding of consequences or potential consequences of these choices and alternatives (or at least a prediction of consequences); and (3) a reflective deliberation (completed by the teacher) as to the best selection given conditions, circumstances, participants, projected and/or past record of consequences, and other relevant variables.

Often teachers must act quickly when conditions or situations do not afford time to make reasoned choices. Such selections, based upon impulse or spur of the moment conditions, are healthy and productive because teachers should be flexible enough to react to unplanned and unforeseen teachable moments. Although appropriate at certain times, pragmatic action should be distinguished from fourth level freedom.

On one hand, if you are in a school system that has empowered teachers to think and act independently, you will have opportunities to make teaching-learning decisions in response to unexpected or revealed situations and conditions. On the other hand, in this same school system, you will also have opportunities to select and prepare learning experiences using fourth level freedom. The freedom either to act quickly in response to conditions or to plan experiences using a reflective model appears to satisfy certain aspects of fourth level freedom. However, fourth level freedom also involves a pause for reflection prior to action, in addition to selecting between a number of viable learning experiences and giving a consideration to consequences of actions.

Teachers as well as children often find the fifth level of holistic freedom difficult to attain consistently. Moreover, the desirability of fifth level conquest is often questioned. Acting against "what is always done here" attitudes or "what is accepted practice" does present problems. It is prudent to adopt a cautious attitude toward acting against prevailing custom and authority of schools. Nonetheless, on behalf of children, teachers in liberal democratic schools should be empowered to reject custom and authority if situations warrant such actions.

The move to implement and demonstrate all five levels of holistic freedom is, of course, just as much an ideal for teachers as it is for children. In practice, however, the first four levels of holistic freedom should be a standard for every teacher and child in a liberal democracy. The decision to cross the line between fourth level freedom and fifth level freedom is one every principal should encourage teachers to effect. This is accomplished by providing the conditions for teachers to make choices, not by supplying the choice they must make. In making decisions about curricula (exercising holistic freedom), teachers need to understand and appreciate the importance of developing reflective dispositions (to think deeply and act with conviction).

Developing Reflective Attitudes

As a public servant in a liberal democracy, the teacher's primary responsibility is to provide educational experiences and opportunities. Teachers, as intellectual leaders of the class, need to become reflective about children and the community. In concert with modeling liberal democratic behaviors, particularly enhancing freedom and providing equivalent (same as) and analogous (similar to) experiences for children to explore, the teacher also contributes by assuming a careful and reflective attitude toward method and content. In becoming cautious and reflective about education, teachers are assuming an intellectual role. Teaching is a complex activity with many challenges, concerns, details, and children to deal with. Although you may wonder on some occasions if teaching is more than controlling children, it does indeed have something to do with liberal democratic learning.

As you enter the classroom you will find many things that require your immediate and complete attention. This, however, may be difficult to accomplish with a group of children vying for notice. The immediate problem is not one immediate problem at all, but a bundle of immediate problems. For new teachers (and veterans too) this can be stressful; how do you help everyone at once while you do everything at once? At this point words of advice or suggestions may be comforting, but only daily classroom experience can expedite your discovery of how to balance all the challenges and concerns you will encounter.

Think about It: In a class full of challenges what problem do you handle first?

As outlined in chapter 2, a critical first step toward becoming an effective teacher is to develop (as much as is possible) a working understanding of children and their world. This understanding begins with the notion of perceiving children as the same but different and extends into a special sensitivity toward children's individual and collective needs and interests. In developing a reflective attitude with these dispositions, teachers work to identify youth culture in all its dimensions from family/home life to popular fads.

In brief, teachers may generate information about youth culture from questions they initiate, observations of children in a variety of settings, and other resources such as parents, multimedia sources, and the community in general. Together with the teacher's own predispositions (the variety of behaviors, beliefs, and values the teacher brings to the class), the teacher constructs a tentative outline of children's youth culture. This outline forms a strong foundation for experience-lesson preparation that is both flexible and firm (reconciliation of paradoxes of acceptance and thought and action).

Over time, with greater experience as a base, teachers become skilled in recognizing shifts in youth culture that may affect experience-lesson presentations. Possessing a strong conception of youth culture also benefits the teacher with the facilitation and distribution of power in the classroom, particularly with classroom management. With a good working knowledge and understanding of youth culture, teachers are better able to anticipate challenges and obstacles to learning experiences. Although classroom management is a primary concern for preservice teachers (and I do not mean to dismiss this important issue), it is not a focus of this textbook. We will now direct our attention to content and methodology.

Content and Method

Content and method, also labeled product and process, respectively, are often separated in teacher training. In practice, we learn our content in one class (courses in literature, science, history and so forth) and our method or pedagogy (courses in how to teach literature, science, and social studies) in another. In the reality of the classroom, there is no separation between content and method: content comprises the learning experiences and method is the best, most effective way to present content. Whenever you learn, there is a method connected to this learning. Method is the context of the experience as well as the way you introduced, practiced, and/or grasped content. Therefore, content and method comprise all the experiences we present children; these experiences are more than bits of information to be consumed by children.

For example, using an information-centered approach, Mrs. Nosac would like her children to understand how the Japanese islands were formed (a science focus) and how Japanese people now live on these islands (a social studies focus). The content of the lesson revolves about information connected to islands and their inhabitants. In terms of content, Mrs. Nosac hopes her children will understand two basic ideas: that the earth's surface is not static and stable, but is in some form of constant change; and that people are directly influenced by their environment. These expectations may be labeled informational goals or outcomes.

Having outlined the ideas to be experienced and explored, the question then becomes a two-part task for Mrs. Nosac, "How do I accomplish these goals so that children will comprehend?"—questions of pedagogy and content. Mrs. Nosac could simply tell her children how islands are formed and how people live on islands. She may decide to have the children read about island formation and island life. In addition, Mrs. Nosac could show a film or ask a visitor to talk about islands. Whatever Mrs. Nosac decides, she will be integrating content with method. If her children read a story about islands and demonstrate an understanding of Mrs. Nosac's goals, then this approach was an effective method. If they did not respond well (grasp the significance of the lesson), Mrs. Nosac will have to consider another approach.

Learning about islands and their inhabitants is the focus of Mrs. Nosac's lesson. Although information-centered approaches like this are common in schools across all curricular areas, the notion of information receiving for the sake of receiving information is not consistent with the approach illustrated in this text. To determine the educational value of this lesson we need to ask Mrs. Nosac why she is teaching about islands. That islands are interesting to study, that islands are the next topic to cover, and that a child in the class was born on an island are not sufficient reasons to justify a study of islands in a liberal democratic school. The study of a topic or experiences presented in class must in some manner be connected to liberal democratic principles. If Mrs. Nosac has not made this connection to liberal democratic principles or cannot, she needs to seriously reconsider this lesson, even if it is required in the curriculum.

The liberal democratic class, as outlined in this text, does not consider information giving as a central theme. Information reception is important, but it is only one aspect of content. Content is multidimensional. In addition to information, content is also the practice and acquisition of skills, exploration of and experience with behaviors, beliefs, and values, and more importantly, the exercise of liberal democratic principles. As discussed in chapter 3, liberal democracy demands participatory education, not passive learning. In this view, content must function as a contributor to liberal democratic education.

In contrast to Mrs. Nosac's lesson, Mr. Rodriguez designs his lesson experience in a different manner. Rather than emphasizing information about islands and their inhabitants in lessons in which students are expected to remember (learn) how islands are formed and how people live on islands, Mr. Rodriguez works to satisfy four universal needs of children. That is, Mr. Rodriguez has decided to put the needs of children ahead of the informational outcomes.

Mr. Rodriguez has four central goals for his lesson experiences on the Japanese islands and their inhabitants (tied to the four universal needs). Basically, Mr. Rodriguez sets up the lesson by having the children look at pictures of a variety of land forms. He questions students about those land forms that are surrounded by water (islands). He later suggests that the children build their own islands, using the Japanese islands as models. The children are divided into several groups, each are given books about the Japanese islands as well as the necessary building materials (plaster of Paris or a simple flour and water mix, a large, flat wooden base, paints, twigs, and other embellishing materials as needed). For the children, the task at hand is to reconstruct on the wooden bases the four major islands of Japan; there are no explicit demands for recall of factual information later.

As the children work on this exercise, each group determines how the islands will be built, decorated, and presented. When the children set to work collaboratively, as learning partners, they communicate with one another. In their dialogues, they raise questions about the height of mountains, distances between islands, how cities should be represented, and more. At this point Mr. Rodriguez suggests that a map key or legend may help others to identify the variety of land forms and other characteristics. If necessary (that is, if the children have not already done so), he may also suggest that the children examine some of the textual and related resources for more clues about what details to include on their map-boards. In the end, after much busy work and intensive activity, the boards are displayed, each in their own manner.

Following the display, Mr. Rodriguez asks the students about this experience with paste and paints, twigs, glue, and books. Without explicitly saying so, Mr. Rodriguez has reinforced a number of liberal democratic principles: e.g., exploration of a number of ideas, group responsibility, decision making, respect for others, and free expression. Collaterally, because they were intimately engaged in building model representations of the Japanese islands, his children may also demonstrate a working informational knowledge of these islands as well as their inhabitants. The goals of Mr. Rodriguez's lesson-experiences were connected to satisfying needs of children, not subject matter. These four universal needs are (1) to communicate (working in collaborative groups); (2) to build (make the four Japanese islands); (3) to use thought and action (ask questions, solve problems); and (4) to demonstrate self-expression (individual styles of presentation on a common theme). These needs will be explored in detail in the following section.

In contrast to Mrs. Nosac's informational lesson, in which students may or may not have practiced liberal democratic principles, Mr. Rodriguez intentionally designed his lesson-experience to provide opportunities that enhanced liberal democratic principles through the use of the four universal needs. As a collateral goal (one that was not expected), the children may also assimilate a good deal of information about the four major islands of Japan. Thus, although Mrs. Nosac's and Mr. Rodriguez's children may have arrived at the same informational level independently, Mr. Rodriguez did not set this as a primary goal. Instead, the children were actively involved in an engaging experience where fun and learning were mixed. Mr. Rodriguez assessed his children not by passive pen and pencil tests, but by the children's active involvement in the lesson experience. This approach to lesson experiences is called the synoptic method.

Engaging the Synoptic Method

Education must activate individuals to be participants in the liberal democratic community, not spectators. In this view, passive schooling as information giving or simple training is more compatible to a dictatorship than to a liberal democracy. If a liberal democratic education offers the best opportunity to facilitate a reconciliation of the twin paradoxes with active participants practicing holistic freedom, how should school curricula be patterned? In recognizing the importance of attending to the twin paradoxes of the community in a liberal democratic setting, to engage students on individual as well as societal levels, educators must turn toward an approach that exemplifies liberal democratic ideals. The approach presented in this text and classroom for your consideration is labeled the *synoptic method.*

In brief, the synoptic method is a teaching-learning model that engages the teacher as the principal activator and facilitator of learning experiences. The teacher is empowered to select, identify, approve, suggest, organize, stimulate, guide, and determine learning experiences. This charge specifically involves content and methodology. Using the four universal needs as guides, the synoptic approach toward social studies involves drawing content and materials from the study of human life that help children learn more about themselves as individuals and as individuals within the community.

Any one or more of the social sciences (subject-research area that includes anthropology, economics, political science, psychology, and sociology), the humanities (history, philosophy, and literature), geography, life experiences, and other sources that deal specifically with human life all fall properly within the realm of learning experiences. The subject-research areas are not intended to be final products or ends for children to consume; rather ideas and information from these subject-research fields are means toward ends (practicing and learning liberal democratic principles). When teachers identify potential learning experiences, these experiences are then connected to children in meaningful ways with the four universal needs as signposts.

First, teachers should strive to meet and satisfy the four universal needs of children, not the requirements or ends of subject matter. When one trains children to perform tasks (read stories, answer when called upon, operate machines) freedom is not a central concern. However, when one educates with holistic freedom as a goal and experience as a guide, the four universal needs of children can be met and fulfilled.

Second, the method is rooted in the continuing effort to reconcile the twin paradoxes of freedom versus conformity and the individual versus the community. The aim is that through specially prepared school experiences and activities educators enhance the holistic freedom of individuals and thereby foster harmony in the community. This sense of democratic purpose contrasts sharply with prevailing rationales such as children need to know and understand information because it will be good for them later.

Third, because freedom is a fundamental element of liberal democratic education, children are responsible for their own learning, however defined. In this view, the teacher is held accountable for facilitating experiences where children are managers of their own learning. Specifically, these experiences should mirror those found outside of school (equivalent) or be related or connected in some fashion to outside experiences (analogous).

Lastly, the teachers are empowered to select, plan and organize, present, and assess their own efforts as professionals, not merely parrot curricula preprepared or required by others. Using synopsis in a literal sense, teachers demonstrate their own freedom within conformity by choosing appropriate strategies, experiences, exercises, activities, and content from a variety of sources. This selection must (1) be consistent in meeting the universal needs of children, (2) foster holistic freedom, and (3) facilitate independent learning. As noted in the example of Mr. Rodriguez, the four universal needs are: communication, building, thought and action, and self-expression.

As we develop various learning experiences keyed to the four universal needs, teachers should also consider the potential of experimenting with experiences that highlight the variety of human intelligence. In the past decade, Harvard researcher Howard Gardner has developed a thesis that challenges the traditional perspective that formal education should be focused upon verbal and reasoning tasks. Gardner argues that children possess the potential not only for verbal and reasoning tasks, but for seven different intelligences.[2]

As Gardner notes, although all children are capable of displaying these intelligences, not all children maintain or can demonstrate the same intellectual capacities or abilities. Gardner's work supports the same but different philosophy as described earlier by presenting another powerful conceptual tool for the teacher to use while attending to the four universal needs of children. That is, as we try to capitalize upon satisfying the four universal needs of children, we may also explore the potentials of providing experiences that highlight and extend the seven intelligences of children. The pedagogical merger of providing for needs as you emphasize practice with the seven intelligences presents an exciting educational opportunity for children. As you explore the universal needs, keep in mind the idea of also fostering the expansion of the seven intelligences with each child.

> *Gardner's Seven Intelligences*
> *Linguistic*
> *Logical*
> *Musical*
> *Spatial*
> *Body Kinesthetic*
> *Intrapersonal*
> *Interpersonal*

The Four Universal Needs of Children

Rather than using the prevailing method of behavioral objectives that seek to change or alter a child's behavior focused upon verbal and reasoning skills,

[2]Howard Gardner, *Frames of Mind,* New York: Basic Books, 1983. See also Howard Gardner, *The Unschooled Mind,* New York: Basic Books, 1991. More detailed examples of how some teachers have applied Gardner's theory see *Interdisciplinary Theme-Based Curriculum Report,* Key School Option Program, Indianapolis, 1990.

the four universal needs of children (communication, building, thought and action, and self-expression) are used to attend to real and necessary needs that every child must have met. These four needs were inspired by the work of John Dewey, who championed what were then called child-centered approaches toward teaching from the late 1890s until his death in 1952.

The nature of needs, introduced in chapter 2, implies a sense of urgency and importance. Since children lack sufficient maturity and experience to meet needs independently of adults, we must work to ensure that every child has his or her needs met. As earlier noted, teachers cannot always be sure children's basic needs for food, water, shelter, and clothing are properly attended to. Teachers also cannot always ensure that other needs such as warmth, love, understanding, affection, and attention are met with any sense of regularity.

These four needs can be met for every child in every classroom. Because each teacher can attend to these needs, I have labeled them "the four universal needs." Each of the four universal needs builds off the natural inclinations of children; that is, not only does every child require that these needs be met, but they also naturally desire these needs to be met. Corresponding to each of the needs, every child loves to talk to his friends and family (communication), every child builds abstractions and loves to make things with his hands (building), every child asks questions and seeks answers (thought and action), and every child likes to feel special and appreciated—that his work and ideas have value (self-expression). In practice, the teacher would design experiences and opportunities according to one or more of the four universal needs. Like the twin paradoxes, each of these needs has two dimensions: the social (group) and the psychological (individual).

Communication: The First Need

The first need is communication. In experiences in which children communicate with one another, they can work on conversation and listening skills. With liberal democratic principles as guides (found in chapter 3) children strive to share ideas with one another, give consideration to the thoughts and ideas of others, appreciate toleration, build democratic consensus, and apply holistic freedom. In addition, teachers work with children to increase clarity of expression, stress cooperation, and highlight communication with consideration.

Although communication needs are probably not met independently of the other three universal needs, teachers can design activities where conversation and listening skills are specifically targeted. For example, children could conduct personal interviews where one child would ask questions (and keep a record of the conversation) and the other would give responses about such things as their personal preferences (favorite movie stars, music entertainers, athletes, foods, toys). Later, the recorders might tally up the results and publish the preferences of their third grade class. Perhaps the teacher may stimulate a discussion about the importance of asking people about their preferences (drawing a reference to how business interests often rely heavily on interview or survey reports to design and market products).

Building/Construction: The Second Need

The second need engages the child as a builder of abstract concepts and ideas, such as government and home, as well as a builder of concrete projects, such as Mr. Rodriguez's four islands of Japan. Children love to make things. Construction experiences provide children with excellent opportunities to practice developing as well as testing of ideas, making plans and preparations, carrying out plans, and assessing final products. When coupled with collaborative grouping, children can also practice interpersonal skills (communication need), work to address common problems (thought and action need), and practice evaluating costs and consequences of building projects.

Moreover, construction activities help children understand the process of analysis, that is, the ability to understand the relationships between the various elements used to construct a whole. For instance, when Mr. Rodriguez's children worked on their Japanese islands project, they identified various components of physical geography (gulfs, harbors, mountain ranges, volcanos, shore lines, and more). In addition, the children also worked with a number of elements of human geography, such as urban areas, airports, farms, industrial centers, and more). While building models of Japan, each child will have had the experience of identifying and placing each component in its proper place.

With careful questioning, Mr. Rodriguez could then ask children to make (another construction activity) an analysis of these various components. Using construction as a guide, rather than telling children what the relationships might be (as in the case of Mrs. Nosac's class), children would be better able to discuss potential relationships because they have handled the materials and issues directly. Learning, then, is not dependent upon a child's memorization of information, but is a product of the child's own efforts.

Teachers can also use construction in reverse, that is, deconstruction, designing activities where children take things apart. Children enjoy the pride of construction as well as the fun of deconstruction. One challenge of deconstruction is to ask children to reassemble the dismembered parts into the original whole or, like a ''Mr. Potato Head'' toy, reassemble the parts into new wholes. Either variation (construction or deconstruction) offers opportunities for children to understand the working or operative elements of an abstract idea or real object in both its holistic sense (conceptualization of the whole object or idea) and analytic sense (understanding the various parts and their relationships to each other and to the whole).

Thought and Action: The Third Need

The third universal need concerns thought and action activities in which children practice and explore thinking and doing independently. Founded in liberal democratic philosophy, thought and action seeks to empower individual learners through the introduction and practice of the processes of discovery, inquiry, challenge, exploration, and imagination. Additionally, thought and action highlights the ability to engage in problem solving, decision making, and reflective thinking. As with communication and construction needs, each thought and action element (with the exception of reflection which must be taught) is natural to every child. Put simply, you cannot teach or direct a child to think because thinking is a natural capability—every child thinks with or without our assistance.

Even before language enables children to directly seek answers to their questions, children are curious about their world. Every day each child is confronted with a world that is seemingly confusing, complex, and often (to a child's sensibility) in need of structure. Essentially, children are attempting to find their place in the world with the familiar question "why?" Using thought and action patterns (that each child practices independently), teachers can structure learning experiences that not only help children make sense of their world by thinking and acting with greater proficiency, but also provide children with needed practice with liberal democratic principles. The eight primary individual abilities of thought and action are described as follows.

Discovery

Place children in a new situation, creating and/or stimulating an experience by which they can interpret, react, define, describe, compare-contrast, or explain the event in their own terms, by their own means. For example, during a field trip to a natural history museum where a number of dinosaur skeletons are on display, children begin to voice their observations: "Dinosaurs look funny without their skins on," "These are really BIG," "Look at those long tails!" In another instance, as children build a model of an Iroquois Indian village you might hear, "Building things is fun," "Hey, glue is hard to get out of your hair," and "I didn't know Indians didn't have windows in their homes."

Inquiry

Create or stimulate experiences in which children will pursue answers to questions, search to clarify an issue, and/or seek out information that sheds light on or permits a better understanding of ideas, issues, or questions that are either posed or revealed through the experience. For example, "How come there are no people with the dinosaurs?" "What happened to the dinosaurs, where did they go?" For our other example, "When Indians made a fire in their homes, where did all the smoke go?" "What do these symbols mean?"

Challenge

Develop experiences that cast doubt and/or raise questions about supposed truth and status quo issues with the intention of seeking truth or more honest conclusions. For example, challenge the idea that dinosaurs were all slow moving, cold-blooded creatures. Challenge the idea that Indians were savages without any real sense of government.

Exploration

Provide for experiences in which children can create/generate possibilities, probabilities, alternatives for a particular question, problem, issue, idea (or set of same), or factual data. All ideas/responses are accepted and seriously considered. For example, investigate the many different types of dinosaurs and where they lived. Speculate on the variety of theories on the extinction of dinosaurs. For the Iroquois, How did they live? How did the Indians deal with the Europeans (particularly the French)? What was most important to the Iroquois children?

Imagination

Plan experiences that highlight opportunities for children to create/generate possibilities, alternatives, scenarios without constraint or limit by known laws, rules, beliefs, conventions, or theories. For example, what would the world be like if dinosaurs lived today? For the Indians, build a time-machine and travel back to the 1600s when the Iroquois League was formed. Write a newspaper report of what you found.

Problem Solving

Present a concrete or abstract problem where children work to identify potential and alternative solutions. Additionally, teachers stimulate children to recognize and analyze various consequences of each proposed solution. For example, how do paleontologists reconstruct the lives of the dinosaurs? In what ways can we apply their research methods to our own problems? As the children are building their village, they discover that they do not have enough materials to complete the village according to their original plan. In this discovery they formulate alternatives and make new projections that might help compensate for the lack of materials.

Decision Making

Given a variety of individual choices and alternative possibilities to select from, provide opportunities for children to craft a specific decision or reach a definite conclusion of their own making. This action should include appropriate attention to potential and/or forecasted consequences of the decision or conclusion. In addition, by creating experiences for children to practice how competent and thorough decisions are made, teachers should also help children to practice articulating and documenting their reasons for the decision. For example, decide which dinosaurs were the most successful and identify those characteristics that made them successful. Regarding the European settlers, given a number of choices, what course of action would you propose if you were a member of the Iroquois League and wanted to maintain your independence?

Reflection

Given an issue, decision, problem, or statement, create or stimulate an experience in which children work to determine if a conclusion or action (either developed by the child or given to the child to think about)—as well as the process used to deliver the conclusion or action—represents the best, most ethical, most truthful, and/or logical move. Reflection is literally a pause when you take time to think back upon something. A special focus should be placed upon children learning to develop and support their judgments with conviction based upon data. For example, children think about and respond to the idea that dinosaurs were important to life on earth. Also ask them to think about what happens when a species of creatures becomes extinct, what is the loss to the rest of the animal kingdom (including people)? Did the Iroquois really value democratic principles? Were the teachings of Handsome Lake (an important Seneca Indian of the Iroquois League) helpful to his people?

The above thought and action elements have been distinguished for analysis purposes so that you can readily forecast and design potential analogous and equivalent activities and experiences. You should recognize that in practice many of these abilities actually overlap with one another. For example, in a planned discovery lesson you might ask children to provide their reaction to a traditional ethnic dinner with unfamiliar foods and table manners. After preparing and tasting the different foods, your children may ask questions about the people and their culture (inquiry). Perhaps, decision making (delegation of required roles: who cooks, who cleans, who taste tests foods, who does the needed research) and problem solving (how to properly cook the foods so that they taste as they should) might also be included.

Thought and action experiences are the centerpiece of the synoptic method and represent the most challenging and rewarding assignment of the liberal democratic teacher. Thought and action experiences offer children the opportunity to think independently as well as to act with and upon their own ideas. In addition, they provide the best opportunities for children to practice, learn, and activate the necessary dispositions, skills, and foundations for responsible liberal democratic citizenship.

Role of Acceptance and Responsibility

As critical as thought and action are in liberal democratic curricula, thought and action must be paired with another curricular element in order to achieve and maintain balance. When matched to the twin paradoxes, thought and action falls upon the freedom and the individual sides of each paradox. To emphasize freedom and the individual at the expense of conformity and the community is to throw each continuum out of balance. Therefore, in opposition to thought and action, the use of acceptance and responsibility (representing the conformity and community side of the twin paradoxes) is often a necessity. Acceptance and responsibility are factors in the initiation of the child into the expectations and culture of the community.

Acceptance represents a certain measure of obedience and compliance with rules, laws, and order. That is, the child must come to understand and accept that rules, laws, and order are necessary elements of social life. In concert with acceptance, the child needs to come to recognize that behavior/ actions have consequences. That is, a child's behavior has consequences for which the child must learn to assume responsibility. In many communities, a child assumes the full responsibility for actions when they become 18 years old. Until that time, in many cases, legal responsibility is deferred to parents, guardians, or the state. When viewed in the context of the twin paradoxes, however, children need to learn to both practice and to actually take responsibility for their behaviors/actions.

One way teachers can help children with acceptance and responsibility is to introduce social skills. Social skills include behavior cues such as reinforcing sharing, listening to others, respecting the feelings others, and helping children to verbalize their own feelings. In addition, social skills include guidance in building constructive, non-violent relationships, recognizing problem situations, searching out solutions, and planning for and anticipating obstacles to action. Most importantly, social skills instruction provide ample opportunities for application and transfer of social skills to natural/real life situations. To help social skills "stick," children need to work through and play out social skills among peers, at home, after school with friends, and in other places. Through the use of social skills acquisition, children can come to appreciate the need for acceptance as well as the need to assume responsibility for actions.

Children will resist some acceptance and responsibility experiences at all costs. For the most part, however, although children may not fully understand the why of acceptance and responsibility, they will follow. For instance, rules illustrate an important element of acceptance experiences in elementary schools (as well as the community). While they may not like rules directed toward their behaviors or actions, most children have a strong sense of the value of rules; games, for example, are more fun when rules are known and enforced. More importantly, rules provide a measure of comfort and assurance—stability. Children appear to be more comfortable with rules than without rules.

In another sense the community values uniformity. For example, the Radio City Rockettes dancers are world renowned for their famous "kick-line." These dancers spend many long hours of study and rehearsal to perform exactly the same movements at precisely the same instance. When the Rockettes accomplish their precise moves (all according to a prearranged plan), the audience is pleased. Becoming a professional dancer requires an intensely demanding focus of repetition and compliance. In the Rockettes program, freelance or free form movements are neither encouraged nor rewarded: a high quality of sameness is the expected norm.

The uniformity of rules in sports is another illustration of acceptance. Organized sports (at any level) from baseball to tennis, from football to gymnastics, would hardly be interesting, competitive, or enjoyable to watch or participate in without rules as a foundation. Imagine a basketball game without referees or time clocks? Despite its opposition to freedom, acceptance, as in the case of rules, is necessary for social living. In fact, children quickly come to understand the sanity that rules or acceptance provide.

Acceptance and responsibility, however, presents two curious challenges. First, neither acceptance nor responsibility is natural to the child (children must be trained, told, and often compelled to follow), and second, acceptance and responsibility are not in themselves universal needs (they must be somehow worked or incorporated into your plans to meet the four universal needs). In developmental terms, it makes sense to introduce each child into the culture and life of American society. This introduction is also known as socialization.

No matter how you choose to utilize socialization, you need to consider both acceptance-style and responsibility-style experiences that introduce individuals to the community and its rules, customs, laws, norms, and institutions as well as to provide opportunities for individuals to take responsibility for actions. As discussed in chapter 3, the community cannot function as a liberal democracy without some measure of social control and sense of community. On the other hand, paired with knowledge application, the community cannot function as a liberal democracy without a strong measure of thought and action. Ultimately, thought and action together with acceptance and responsibility experiences enhance the freedom of individuals and facilitates harmony in the community. Acceptance and responsibility and thought and action experiences provide the necessary means to reconcile the twin paradoxes of freedom versus conformity and the individual versus the community.

When appropriate, acceptance and responsibility experiences can be incorporated into any of the four universal needs. Teachers can engage children in construction activities in which they can design and paint wall posters of class and school rules. Teachers can also organize communication activities in which children model appropriate behaviors such as waiting their turn and putting their things away. Teachers usually have no trouble in putting acceptance or responsibility to work in their classrooms. The problem, from a liberal democratic perspective, is that some schools and teachers spend nearly all their class time asking children to conform to and comply with rules without any chance or opportunity to practice and explore holistic freedom. These actions, too, throw any reconciliation of the twin paradoxes out of balance. The key is to apply both acceptance and responsibility and thought and action: to create in practice the idea of a pendulum. If freedom is needed the teacher adjusts activities toward thought and action; if conformity is desired the teacher moves toward acceptance and responsibility activities.

Self-Expression: The Fourth Need

The fourth universal need is self-expression. As critical as communication, construction, and thought and action are to liberal democracy, self-expression is vital to the well-being of the individual child. The need to be recognized as a single individual among a group is basic to every human being. In this spirit, teachers must provide opportunities for each child to highlight her own unique attributes and abilities in an open atmosphere free of criticism in any form. As a special note, perhaps more than the first three universal needs, self-expression offers exciting possibilities for practice and extension of Gardner's seven intelligences.

Self-expression personalizes your work and ideas. Although the suggestions and ideas of others may be helpful, ultimately each child should follow her own guidelines. Teachers, however, are often all too quick to offer suggestions for improvement or other comments that insinuate the child has somehow failed to please. The point of self-expression is that the only critic is the child herself. When a teacher offers a suggestion, the signal to the child may be that something is somehow wrong or incorrect.

Unlike in construction activities where critique is appropriate, teachers need to be careful to accept and praise the child for her self-expression work, despite whatever that work turns out to be. For example, if you design a self-expression lesson experience in which you ask LaToyya to draw a picture of her favorite animal, you must accept whatever she draws without critical comment. If LaToyya puts five legs on her lion instead of four, it is acceptable. If LaToyya colors her lion blue, instead of tan, it is acceptable. The goal of self-expression is to build confidence and self-respect, not demonstrate knowledge and understanding.

Self-expression activities must, however, make some compromises. Although self-confidence and respect are goals, and each child is the final judge of quality, teachers must provide some guidelines for children. As contradictory as it sounds, children require some framework to work within; they need to know the boundaries or limits of each assignment or task. It is not that you simply leave the child to assemble any of the eighty-eight notes on the piano into a tune. You must provide equivalent and analogous practice with the necessary skills and dispositions so that the child can complete or at least attempt the activity. For teachers the key to effective instruction is to work to balance enough instructions, modeling, and foundations with a strong measure of independence so that the child is invested (has ownership) in the activity without being constrained.

Since you are probably more familiar with basing all instructional experiences and activities in objective-type formats, each of the four universal needs will be highlighted with further explanations and examples in the following chapters. I will now briefly review the synoptic method and then we will finally (and formally) be introduced to social studies in the following chapter.

Assessing the Synoptic Method

When using the synoptic method, the teacher is characterized as the selector, preparer, facilitator, activator, and assessor of analogous and equivalent experiences, opportunities, and activities. The teacher ensures that each experience is connected to one or more of the four universal needs of children. Moreover, when children are presented with an experience, the teacher ensures that each child is given the opportunity to take an active and significant part in the experience. During and following each experience, the teacher is responsible for assessing each child to determine (1) if the child understood the purpose and significance of the experience on his or her own accord or through teacher cues and (2) if additional experiences or explanations are necessary to complete understanding-mastery-introduction or other varying degrees of competency.

Understanding and applying the phrase "learn by doing," often erroneously attributed to John Dewey, are essential to activating learners. Just setting children to work on tasks alone or in groups, without inquiring whether or not they understand or can articulate the outcome of their task, is not the goal of experiential learning. As Dewey wrote, doing is only one part of the task; the second, and critical element, is to gain an understanding by undergoing the experience. The undergoing of the experience or activity means that each child comes to some understanding or knowledge (reconstruction of experience) and that the teacher can make an assessment (as much as possible) to the degree to which the child has accomplished the task, skill, or understanding.

A Brief Review

The synoptic method is used in preparing and presenting learning experiences. First, the synoptic method identifies how to facilitate analogous and equivalent experiences for independent learning; second, four universal needs identify the vehicles to guide all experiences; and third, the liberal democratic principles underscore and furnish a rationale for each experience.

In simple terms, the synoptic method supplies the elements of how, what, and why for teaching. Together with a knowledge of youth culture (who, when), we will now round out the synoptic method with an illustration of the social studies formula. The remainder of the textbook will focus upon helping you prepare lesson experiences that attend to each of the four universal needs.

Marking Your Progress

1. Topic/theme _____

   _____

   _____

(continued)

Marking Your Progress

2. Levels of holistic freedom (ideas to use in lesson experience) _____

    _____

    _____

3. Universal needs to incorporate in lesson experiences _____

    _____

    _____

Read More about It Special References

The following texts treat reforms in education, the introduction of philosophy and other more nontraditional approaches to elementary education. The Goodlad texts offer overviews of schooling and teaching. Many of these texts may be incorporated with readings from chapters 2 and 3.

Goodlad, J. (1990). *Teachers for our nation's schools*. San Francisco: Jossey-Bass.
> *In one of the best texts available on schools and education, Goodlad captures the essence of the reform movement of the 1980s, proposing how teachers can (and should) become engaged in treating complex educational problems.*

Oakes, J., & Lipton, M. (1990). *Making the best of schools: A handbook for parents, teachers, and policymakers*. New Haven, CT: Yale University Press.
> *In this no nonsense approach to what are the persistent problems of education, that is highly readable and clearly argued, Oakes and Lipton make a number of helpful suggestions that teachers as well as parents can benefit from. This must be read.*

Plummer, D. (1988). *Planning for thinkers and learners: The early years*. Melbourne, Australia: Australian Reading Association.
> *Prepared by the Australian Reading Association, this brief text presents a number of refreshing ideas about the integration of thinking ideas within elementary curricula. Of special importance is the emphasis on nonsexist materials (excellent bibliography provided).*

Rugg, H., & Shumaker, A. (1928). *The child-centered school*. Yonkers-on-the-Hudson, NY: World Book.
> *This remains the best text on the subject of children and progressive educational techniques. It has lots of interesting ideas about combining art and music with social studies. It may only be available through library-lending/search.*

The following are representative of the efforts of a growing number of educators who are striving (and succeeding) to bring philosophy and democratic approaches into elementary classrooms:

Calkins, L. (1983). *Lessons from a child.* Portsmouth, NH: Heinemann.

Kohl, H. (1984). *Growing minds.* New York: Harper & Row.

Lipman, M., Sharp, A., & Oscanyan, F. (1980). *Philosophy in the classroom.* Lanham, MD: Temple University Press.

Lipman, M. (1988). *Philosophy goes to school.* Philadelphia: Temple University Press.

Sharp, A., & Reed, R. (1992). *Studies in philosophy for children: Harry Stottlemeier's discovery.* Philadelphia: Temple University Press.

Wigginton, E. (1985). *Sometimes a shining moment.* Garden City, NY: Doubleday.

Some of the more helpful recent texts available on social skills include:

Eisler, R. T. (1990). The partnership way and learning new tools for living. San Francisco: Harper.

Fontana, D. (1990). Social skills at work. New York: Routledge.

Gullolla, T., Adams, G., and Montemayor, R., Eds. (1990). Developing social competency in adolescence. Newbury Park: Sage Publishing.

5

A FORMULA FOR SOCIAL STUDIES

In this chapter you will

- Start to work with a formula for improving the organization and presentation of social studies.
- Look for ways to bring elements of the social studies formula into your unit.
- Continue to formulate your own approach to teaching and learning.

Years ago progressive educators quipped "I teach children, not subject matter!" In many educational circles today the reverse seems to be preferred. The trouble with these statements is that the supposed split between children and subject matter contains certain truths and falsehoods.

The crux of the matter is that when we teach children, subject matter is engaged. Similarly, when we specifically teach subject matter, children are engaged. These statements are an enlargement of the tension between content and method discussed earlier—content is always associated with method and method is always associated with content. Thus, like content and method, in teaching subject matter and children, each is always associated with the other.

Up to this point, there has been much discussion about social studies and little concrete evidence or practice with the substance of traditional subject matters of the field. This chapter will introduce a formula for preparing and presenting social studies experiences for children under the umbrella of the synoptic method.

Subject Matter and Social Studies

Present as well as past critics of teacher education have argued that elementary teachers do not graduate with adequate subject matter knowledge. These critics are, of course, correct to some extent—graduating preservice teachers do not possess subject matter knowledge in each of the principal teaching areas at a level comparable to individuals majoring in a specific subject area. When critics, largely from outside of the elementary school and the enterprise of education, claim that "not enough history is taught" or that "children lack geography skills" (essentially criticizing teachers as inadequately prepared), they demonstrate a certain misunderstanding and naiveté of the special nature and role of elementary education. Such critics believe that the way to improve elementary teaching is to increase the academic training of teachers.

What critics do not understand is why most preservice elementary teachers do not specialize in any one subject area of the elementary school curriculum. The condition of nonspecialization is consistent with the nature of elementary curricula in which the education of children is conceived in holistic terms. No doubt within each of the traditional subject areas of social studies, mathematics, language arts, reading, and natural sciences, some scholars and critics of education argue that every teacher should have a strong command of these disciplines. This is a logical position for those devoted to analytic sense. However, even if schools wanted to adopt an analytic position, with so many diverse curricular areas required for certification, elementary teachers would hardly be able to gain an in-depth understanding of more than one academic subject area, if that.

While the analytical division of subject areas into various parts makes sense to scholars and researchers, it does not correspond to the needs, capacities, or preferences of either elementary teachers or their students. Not only is it impractical to expect elementary teachers to possess expert knowledge to teach every curricular division, it is also unreasonable to assume that children will grasp the complexity of these fields even at a rudimentary level.

Because elementary teachers cannot be trained as subject experts in every field (a feat that even few subject matter specialists would attempt), the business of elementary education must be something other than instruction in the various analytic areas of curricula. Instead, the business of elementary education must be directly devoted to its primary purpose: children.

First, because elementary teachers are often charged to teach topics derived from the traditional subject fields, it becomes necessary to identify and provide some practical experience working with subject area knowledge and applications. Second, because teachers in a liberal democracy are charged to further liberal democratic principles, derivatives of certain subject fields may provide an ideal foundation from which to build and experiment with liberal democratic dispositions.

All this points to a central question of teacher education. Given the complexity of each separate field in both its nature and methodologies, as well as its research questions and more, how does one teach about a subject area when one does not possess the competence of an expert in the field? Moreover, how does this teacher provide instruction to children who will probably not become experts in these fields? Do we abandon the effort to teach anything about these fields if we cannot clearly conceive and articulate questions and problems about the field of study? Of course not, these areas should be attended to.

With the complexities and issues of elementary education in mind, it must be understood at the outset that the nature of elementary education differs from that of subject matter specialists. In this spirit, the following presentation is devoted to assisting teachers responsible for social studies in the elementary grades. This brief presentation is not intended as a quick survey of social studies in a foolish attempt to certify you as a subject matter specialist, but rather as an introduction to the appropriate use and function of social studies within a liberal democratic model of education.

Introducing a Formula for Social Studies

Traditionally history and geography form the backbone of social studies in schools. Some elementary teachers tend to cast an academic veil about these subjects—not that they do not appreciate the importance of these subjects, but feel inadequately prepared or unable to teach children. Early in the history of social studies, however, curricular theorists separated academic approaches to these subject areas as used in college and university studies, with related, but distinct, approaches found only in elementary and secondary schools. It was argued that schools were not in business to make "little historians or geographers" or to specifically prepare children for college, but rather to provide a general education in various subjects. In fact, although secondary schools did follow the leads of subject specialists, many curricular theorists intentionally did not prescribe particular subject matter for elementary curricula.

Despite a general neglect for specific subject matter in elementary curricula, history, geography, and other academic studies/subjects/topics have rightfully been represented in some fashion in elementary curricula. The presence or threads of such studies, however, are often either wrongly focused upon some historical treatment or the outmoded expanding horizons approach to the exclusion of additional equally important and necessary elements. Consistent with holistic nature, our social studies considers the wide range of academic subjects and other conditions and contexts associated with human life for inclusion in elementary curricula.

Because we must alter the form and function of history, geography, and other academic studies for use in schools (our business is not to train children specifically for a life of academic study), we will use the terms *time* and *space* to represent ideas found in traditional academic fields of history and geography, respectively. Issues will be used to represent a contemporary view of other academic studies as well as those areas that fall out of the realm of academic studies.

This formula would still be incomplete if it did not include special attention to matters of a conceptual and connecting nature. Rather than attending exclusively to such things as facts, dates, or events, this formula calls for the teacher to identify specific *concepts* and potential *relationships*. Thus the formula reads:

$$\frac{\text{Time } + \text{ Space } + \text{ Issues}}{\text{Concepts } + \text{ Relationships}} = \text{Child's Learning/Outcomes}$$

To use an analogy, think of the teacher putting into her learning experiences elements or ideas that represent each of these five areas. Like a master chef making chicken vegetable soup, if good quality foodstuffs and appropriate cooking techniques are used, the guests will enjoy their soup. If inferior foods, burnt broth, and overcooked vegetables are used, few, if any, guests will enjoy the ruined soup.

Like a good soup, then, effective use of this social studies formula is dependent upon the quality and use of the five components. Quality, however, is not the only issue. If the chef decides to eliminate the chicken, as long as all else remains the same, that does not mean the soup will be spoiled. The elimination of chicken from the soup recipe merely means you no longer have *chicken* vegetable soup—the guests can still enjoy the soup. So it is with social studies, it is not that children cannot enjoy or benefit from the experience if one or two elements are missing from the formula; the point is to inflate the quality of what is presented.

On one hand, if you ignore or dismiss any one or more of the five elements of this formula, you have devalued the full potential of social studies. On the other hand, to misuse one of the social studies components—although you may still have social studies—may affect the quality and potential of that study. For example, to skip geographic considerations when presenting an experience on Norway or to give geography a minor role in this experience causes children to suffer the consequences of your nonaction or inappropriate action.

Rather than having the opportunity to learn in the context of quality instruction, children are deprived of opportunities that would enrich their learning. Consequently, just as it is far more serious when poor quality ingredients are used in the soup than if the chef eliminates one of the ingredients, to merely play lip service to the five elements and not invest your teaching in their use is to rob the child of the great potential benefits of social studies. The aim of our work is to provide experiences that kindle, enhance, and foster a child's learning. If we do not attend to quality teaching, we cannot expect that children will receive the necessary stimulus for quality learning. Thus, the utilization of all five areas of the formula as well as the promotion of quality teaching within each element is our goal.

As with all our teaching responsibilities, our intention is to provide the conditions, experiences, and practice that generate excellent learning. What is the outcome or result of using these various ingredients of this social studies formula? Like a master chef whose intention is to create a smashing meal that is not merely appealing to the eye and filling, but also thoroughly satisfying, our goal is to provide the conditions for superior learning. We must, however, remember that although the chef prepares the experience, he is not the target of the meal, his guests are. Likewise, when the teacher generates experiences, she is not the target of the experience, her children are.

When we integrate this social studies formula along with teaching about liberal democratic principles, holistic freedom, and the four universal needs, the synoptic approach to teaching social studies is thus engaged.

- Social Studies Formula
- Four Universal Needs
- Liberal Democratic Principles
- Twin Paradoxes
- Holistic Freedom

The following sections of this chapter will explain and illustrate the nature and use of each of the formula's components within the synoptic approach.

The following conceptualizations are for the teacher's use, to help organize, prepare, present, and assess experiences and are not intended to be transferred directly to children.

The Element of Time

One of the most engaging ideas of human life is time. From our first conscious moments, and perhaps even before, we have been subjected to time. Time is at once tangible in the sense that it is 3:23 in the afternoon as I type this sentence or that the movie I want to see begins at 8:00 P.M. Time is abstract in the sense that it cannot be held and to be measured we require the assistance of mechanical devices. Although time seemingly can be stopped in a photograph or recording of your favorite song, time defies any human attempt to control or master it. Time is undeniably one of the primary concepts of human life, and all human activities such as work, play, eating, and even sleep are closely associated or predicated on our knowledge of time.

Time is complex and simple, knowable and unknowable. Three issues are raised when we attempt to attend to time in schools: Why is it important to teach about time? Can children grasp the significance and use of time? If time is important and if children are capable of grasping time, how, then, does one teach about time?

As with all five elements of the formula, the importance and comprehension questions are pragmatically assumed; that is, it is important to teach about time and children can learn about time. For our purposes, like the adjustment of other academic subject matters for schools, the philosophical questions and complexities associated with academic treatments of time must also be shifted or in some cases be abandoned altogether. As in any transformation for school use the value or thoroughness of the academic study is not in question; our guide is rooted in other matters. Thus, I will shift the focus from academic questions to a line of reasoning more appropriate for our task at hand.

Consequently, as a beginning point in pragmatic form we shall make two primary assumptions: time is important to teach about, and children are not only capable of comprehending time, they can learn about its form and its function. Clearly each of these assumptions has its critics. Although this textbook may present an opportunity to discuss these assumptions, it will not contribute to this debate other than by raising these initial questions. Consequently, it will be your challenge and responsibility to contemplate and experiment with this theory in order to test its validity according to your use and needs.

Using Time

The primary objective of teaching about time is that children begin to grasp the use of historical perspective. Historical perspective includes the knowledge and use of four basic overlapping concepts: *time, past, change,* and *continuity*.

Through the use of these concepts, historical perspective empowers children to recognize existing patterns of time and to build connections and relationships between these patterns and their own lives. The frame of reference that is constructed with historical perspective also provides a direct and personal contact with others in different places and at different times. Historical perspective brings life to past events, people, objects, and more by helping children realize their place in the sweep of time—that they not only have a present, a past, and perhaps, most importantly, a future, but that their past, present, and future are also connected to others from the past, present, and future. The following section will illustrate how time can be used with children.

Children experience time very early in life. For infants time is divided between eating, sleeping, and waking periods. Each of these segments has a beginning, middle, and end. As the child grows physically and mentally, the notion of day and night is learned. In addition, the child begins to associate certain activities with portions of the day and night.

For example, when baby Debbie wakes in the morning her diaper is changed and she is dressed and fed. Following a few hours of free play, her diaper is changed and she is fed again and laid down for a nap. After napping, from her playpen Debbie is stimulated by vacuum cleaners, television noise, movements of older brothers, and cooking sounds and smells. At some point, she tells her caregivers she has had enough—a third feeding ensues followed by another nap. After this afternoon nap, Debbie is permitted to move about the floor with her other caregiver and her brothers. Eventually by nightfall, she is bathed, dressed for sleep, fed, and laid down for the night's slumber. The repetition of these attractions produces a cycle or rhythm that the child comes to internalize. When the pattern is changed, the child will manifest other behaviors to alert the caregiver to return to the pattern.

By the time Debbie and Jose come to your first grade class, they have experienced time patterns and established cycles and rhythms. There are times to eat, play, listen to tapes, watch TV, take walks, and more. The salient characteristic of these patterns of time is that each event has a beginning, middle, and end. Although children have their own personal clock and calendar, they do not understand the complexities of how adults measure time. How long is ten minutes? What is a week? When will I be old enough to ride a motorcycle? How long is soon?

The transition from personal time (patterns understood by the child) and how time is measured by adults (clock and calendar) constitutes an enormous conceptual leap. With time measurement understood, the notions of past, present, and future can be engaged. The ideas of sequence, continuity, and change can be known and applied. Certainly, stories of past or future human life can be employed without a clear understanding of time measurement or historical perspective. However, knowledge of time measurement places the event, story, or person into a context that can be sequenced—this happened before that, that comes after this, this occurred before I was born and so forth. This sequencing of events, persons, and things, on a linear scale is called chronology. This concept can be illustrated with a time line that helps the child to expand her experience and knowledge of human life.

Time may be divided into two useful categories: relative and absolute. Relative time is probably what children learn first. It does not have exact or precise measurement. "In a little while," "after lunch," and "this evening," are examples of future relative time that do tell us something is going to happen, but not exactly when. Phrases such as "now," "time's up," and "currently" describe present relative time, meaning at this moment. Phrases such as "in olden days," "a long time ago," and "last year" represent the past in relative terms. These tentative statements of time are also known as indefinite time expressions. Although indefinite time expressions are imprecise, through experience children eventually understand the significance of the measurements in pioneer days and before long.

Indefinite time expressions persist in our culture and are used throughout life; however, precise measurements of time are also needed. Although time is not literally holding still, the absolute measure of time attempts to lock or associate a moment to a precise measurement. For example, "the concert will start at 8:30," "I started work at 5:00 P.M.," and "today is August 1" are all time expressions that tell the listener as closely as possible when something will be, was, and is. Absolute time is typically taught with the use of clocks and calendars. For children, however, there is a significant difference between learning about clocks and calendars. Children appear to learn about clock time from larger measurements to smaller—hours, minutes, to seconds. However, children learn about calendar time from the smaller measurements to the larger—days, weeks, months, and years.

One of the earliest experiences with absolute time is to provide children practice with clock and calendar time. The advent and popularity of digital clocks that read out time in numbers has changed the way children learn to tell time. In the past, the practice of using the big hand and little hand to tell time reduced the complexity of time to movement. The child could literally measure the distance between hand movements. This association between the concept of time and actual movement was critical, marking a bridge between the abstract and the concrete.

From learning about time through the movement of the hands of the clock, the child could account for time in a literal sense. Today, for those children whose practical experience has been reduced to digital clocks, time is not measured or anticipated in concrete terms, but in a sequence of abstract numbers. Concepts such as quarter-till, half past the hour, clockwise, and counterclockwise are rendered incomprehensible by digital readouts. That is, while visualizing the clock as a circle or pie-shaped object, the points (hour markers) of 3, 6, 9, and 12 are soon converted to minutes of 15, 30, 45, and 60. To say that it is half past the hour means that the big hand is at the bottom of the clock, that the clock is divided into half. Without knowing any numbers, the child could be able to tell you how much time was left in the hour (another half or when the big hand comes up to the top again).

For digital readouts, no concrete clock can be visualized. That is, the child must be able to convert half past the hour into numbers, to know that 60 is divided into two parts of 30. Because the conversion must take place in the absence of any concrete assistance, telling time is reduced to mathematic calculations. Although it may sound old-fashioned, teaching about absolute time through clocks with big and little hands first and digital readouts second might be more helpful than using digital readouts alone. Examples of both, however, should be displayed and used to assist children with understanding absolute time.

Another method to teach about absolute time is through the use of calendars. By the time our Debbie and Jose attend your class, they may know a number of dates such as their birthdays, favorite holidays, when school begins, and the date the public pool closes. They may also know that days have names like Monday, Tuesday, Wednesday, Thursday, Friday, Saturday, and Sunday. Debbie may associate Tuesday with the day the big garbage truck picks up the family trash. Jose may tell you that Sunday is the day his mother takes him to the park.

Young children may know about weeks and even months; however, many children do not have a firm understanding of calendar time until much later. Consequently, like clocks, calendars can be used as concrete objects that measure the passage of time. Children can make their own calendar and mark off each day. Using a birthday or favorite holiday, children can also learn to count off weeks and even months.

Using Past

The practical use of clocks and calendars teaches about the passage of time. However, children do not easily perceive the passage of time in reverse. That is, although children do grasp the forward movement of time, they often have difficulty imagining that time has a past in addition to a present and future. Despite this perception, the passage or measurement of past time can be realized by young children. The idea that Mom and Dad were once children and that Grandma and Grandpa were the Mom and Dad are abstract concepts to the child. However, with the use of a time-line device, children can grasp the notion of time in all its dimensions (past, present, and future), together with the two other primary concepts of change and continuity.

Continuing with lessons about time, you can select stories of young children from any time period in the past. Stories about children from different lands, times, and cultures have always fascinated children. The past is a concept that possesses a self-contained logic that is easy to demonstrate, but less easy for children to comprehend. Because pictures of Mom and Dad as children exist, and big trees, old movies, and ancient objects in museums can be seen, the accumulated result of the child's own investigation is that these phenomena existed before she did, that something, some time called the past, existed not only in her family and community, but everywhere people live.

Whether or not teachers can accelerate the acquisition of the concept of past, they can certainly raise the consciousness of children by providing examples and illustrations of past life, so that children can examine the lives of other children in different times and places. The awareness that the phenomenon of past is worldwide helps to assist children with the notion that all people everywhere share a common characteristic—we all are connected to a past of one sort or another.

Using Change

As logical as the accumulated observation of past might seem to adults, the idea that something existed before the child, before the present, defies the child's present sense of reality. If the past existed, where did it go? Why did it disappear? How come the people who built the pyramids are gone? What happened to dinosaurs? These questions are not easily answered or explained. That great civilizations such as the Mayan, Roman, and Timbuktu built beautiful buildings and possessed magnificent cultures, but were then destroyed, does not make sense to children. If these cultures were so great, how could they be wiped out? This question leads the teacher (and children) into the third concept of time, the idea of change.

Like time and past, change can be discussed with powerful examples. By the time our Debbie and Jose reach school they will have experienced change. Jose's family had to buy him new sneakers because his old shoes did not fit him anymore. Debbie, too, had to have a new pair of shoes because she had outgrown her last pair. Besides their own growth, Debbie and Jose have watched the trees lose their leaves in the fall, felt cold weather in winter, listened to icicles melt in spring, and smelled summer flowers in the warm sun. Physical growth is a phenomenon that can be measured and understood in simple terms: children, trees, weather, icicles, and flowers change. Like the growth of children and plants, cities, civilizations, and cultures grow and change, but they also may stop growing and disappear. The young mind may be befuddled by thinking about the past, and can become frightened when the full implications of change are understood.

Change has an eerie, uneasy permanence that children often find unpleasant. Although Jose wishes for the day when he can drive his own sports car, he is deeply troubled that his grandmother is gone and that he will never be able to hear her soft and comforting voice reading stories to him. Now that she is twelve, Debbie is happy to have a bedroom of her own, but misses the fun she used to enjoy when she shared her bedroom with her two younger sisters. Although change cannot be predicted with great accuracy, it is inevitable and inescapable. For young children, the prospect of growing up is, however, unquestioningly more exciting than the idea of staying eight forever.

In the history of human life, change has not always been a happy condition with pleasant consequences. For instance, despite all of the great advances in modern life, water, air, and land pollution are now a sad fact of living. The refinement of machines of war, which may have provided a measure of security at one time, has placed human existence at the edge of extinction. Our great cities have magnificent skyscrapers with internal cooling and heating systems unheard of only a few decades ago within walking distance of cardboard shacks where people huddle about an open fire for warmth. Thus, change is not always for the better. Although children need this understanding, they also need to know that change has a positive side—that life without change would become very boring.

Using Continuity

To many the recording of history is the recording of human change. By examining examples of many different types of change, children can better understand themselves and their world. In the course of this examination, children also will notice that as much as they and the world appear to be changing, some things appear to stay the same or progress with certain identifiable rhythms. The idea of a smooth progression or appearance of sameness over any length of time is called *continuity*. Continuity represents a seemingly confused contradiction—although things change, things remain the same. How can change and sameness exist simultaneously?

The change-same phenomenon is similar to our illustration of same, but different in chapter 2. While young people possess the same sorts of behaviors as young people twenty years ago, they also have different behaviors; while all cars are the same in that they have wheels, seats, motors, and run on fuel, they are very different in style, comfort, ride, and price; while you are different in physical size and mental understanding than you were ten years ago, you are the same person nonetheless.

Children can test the paradox of change-same with simple observation. For example, when Debbie watches the leaves of trees turn many brilliant colors in the fall, then drop to the ground (demonstrating that the trees change), she also observes that new leaves return in the spring (proof that the tree is the same—or always functions the same way). When Jose finished drinking his Coca-Cola (emptying the can of soda represents change), he can buy still another at the store whenever he wishes (buying another soda that is exactly like the first illustrates things staying the same).

Looking for the identifying patterns in life as well as in time are comforting to children. Habits, routines, and conventions assure children that all is well, that life is not as cold and hard as change makes it appear. In illustrating or presenting experiences for children to identify patterns of continuity, teachers can apply examples from the present, the past, or even the future. Stories or accountings from any historical period or time can be used. For instance, you may want to present units of experiences centered on housing, tools, foods, or games. In practice, if perspectives of past, present, and future are given, any aspect of human culture can be used to teach continuity.

Achieving Historical Perspective

Although the elements of time, past, change, and continuity stimulate the acquisition of historical perspective, each element illustrates a different lesson. Telling time represents a skill. Knowing about the past develops the context of past, present, and future. Understanding change represents the reality and nature of life. The notion of continuity provides a positive philosophical outlook on living, on being human—that we are not alone, that life continues, that we are a part of a long, ongoing chain of life that reaches as far back as the beginning of the universe and extends indefinitely into the future.

Children do not learn historical perspective like one learns multiplication tables or names of the states. Historical perspective is acquired after many years of experience with and thinking about time, past, change, and continuity. Our task in the elementary school is to introduce the ideas through practical experience that may eventually lead the child (adult) to grasp the nature, application, and significance of historical perspective.

It is important to emphasize that these introductions are not given with the expectation that children will acquire historical perspective by the end of sixth grade, but that the experiences you provide will be used as a foundation for further growth. By now, you may be able to realize that by providing experiences with each of the various elements of time, the quality of the child's first learnings of historical perspective would be raised. Continuing in this spirit, we will now turn to exploring the second component of the social studies formula, space (geographical perspective).

The Element of Space

Over the past few years advocates of teaching geographical dispositions have made great strides in producing excellent curricular materials for schools. Far more than any other group of subject specialists, the advocates of geography have worked successfully to help teachers organize and present geography. In particular, a special joint committee of teachers and scholars identified five major themes of geographic education[1] to assist teachers and children.

The grouping of the element of space into these five fundamental themes— location, place, relationships within places, movement, and regions—provides a superior framework for the geographical element of the social studies formula. In fact, for our social studies formula I could find no other conceptual framework, past or present, that is as pedagogically powerful in theory and practice than these five themes. Consequently, each theme will be discussed here in full.

With the use of a spiraling technique each theme is first introduced in kindergarten, then reintroduced with increasing levels of sophistication

---

[1]The five major themes were developed by the Joint Committee on Geographic Education of the National Council for Geographic Education and the Association of American Geographers.

throughout the child's elementary education. Space concepts can be presented and practiced in any order. Although the individual components of space could be presented independently of other curricular considerations, the themes of space should be presented as fully compatible and integrated partners of the formula.

In brief, space refers to where and how humans live. Although the nature of space (geographic perspective) is present minded, it can be meaningfully applied to the dimensions of past and future. That is, if you were to tell a story about the ancient Egyptians or a futuristic account of a family living on Mars 200 years from now, all of the five space themes could be employed to enhance, enrich, and/or increase the quality of the child's learning experience.

Using Location

Location identifies where on the earth's surface people, places, and any number of other things exist (or did or might exist). Like time, location uses absolute and relative dimensions. Absolute descriptions explain with as much accuracy as possible the precise location of something. To accomplish this geographers use a reference system that divides the earth into imaginary grids and lines known as longitude and latitude.

Some theorists believe the conceptualization of longitude and latitude is far beyond the scope of young children. On the other hand, it may be possible for children to grasp the foundation of these ideas if teachers present absolute location with increasing sophistication and in concrete terms. That is, if reference systems can be made literally on the floor tiles of the classroom (that are usually marked off in grids), boards, and paper or if a game like bingo can be used to illustrate the notion of grid systems, over time and with practice children may not only be able to visualize the world as divided into grids with intersecting lines of longitude and latitude, but also be able to accurately locate places.

If the use of absolute location in formal terms is a long-term goal for children, in that children will develop its use after several years of sustained practice, the application of relative location can be mastered quickly with younger children. Relative location tells the observer where something is in relation to other objects or things. Debbie is standing next to Jose. The shoe store is across the street from the Wal-Mart. The letter is on the table in the living room.

Whereas absolute location is dependent upon the observer knowing only the grid system of longitude and latitude, relative location is dependent upon the observer knowing the objects or landmarks near, with, next to, or around the subject in question. For instance, to have an idea where Debbie is, the observer must first know where Jose is. To know where the shoe store is, the observer must have an idea where the Wal-Mart is located. The same holds true for the letter. The observer must know about the table in the living room as well as where the living room is. Thus, by nature, relative location is understood in concrete, observable terms. If Jose does not know where the landmarks or cues to relative location are, he will not be able to make much sense of the directions or explanations of location.

Therefore, in teaching about relative location, you must be sure to orientate the observer (child) to landmarks and cues. The child must be able to associate the object or place with terms, other objects, and/or visual images that he already possesses. Telling Debbie that England is across the Atlantic Ocean and next to the main body of the European continent will mean nothing if she does not already know (or can quickly understand) where the Atlantic Ocean and the European Continent are found. Moreover, although Debbie may understand that England is across the ocean and next to the mainland of Europe, unless she can put the Atlantic Ocean, Europe, and England in relation to herself (where she is now), all this remains an abstraction—England's true location in relationship to Debbie will remain a mystery to her.

Using Place

The concept of place presents a literal description of both the physical and human characteristics of a particular place, such as the beautiful Alpine region of Austria, the bustling city of Chicago, the sunny beaches of Puerto Rico, or fertile Nile delta in Africa. The description of characteristics of such places not only helps children to distinguish one place from another, but more importantly, the human and physical dimensions of place breathe a special element of life and reality into the great variety of regions throughout the world. With stories, pictures, films, clothing, games, toys, models, maps, posters, and more, children can be magically transported anywhere on earth.

Whereas location tells a child about position, place makes it real. Place has two elements for children to explore: physical and human characteristics. If you can imagine being transported to a street in Innsbruck, Austria, in the middle of January on a bright sunny day . . . what do you see? Look all about you . . . do you see the majestic snow-capped mountains, deep forests of fir trees, houses of stone and wood? What are the people doing? Are they bundled up in warm winter clothes, some perhaps in ski attire? Are there a number of tourists with cameras of all sorts snapping pictures of themselves and the local scenery?

Place requires the observer to make a 360 degree sweep of the location, to describe mountains and plains, peaks and valleys, forests and fields, streams and rivers, snow and ice, natural resources, climate and daily weather, and all else that can be seen or known. The actual appearance (what is tangible and also intangible) yields a physical description of the natural characteristics of place. When you add those characteristics created by human beings, you then have the human element of place.

Human characteristics include such things as describing the houses, clothing, and work of the people, depicting the local language(s) and cultural traits that exist, and including some information about institutions such as schools and local government. You might also want to picture transportation systems, cars, buses, trucks, or even horse carts.

The descriptions of human characteristics such as these provide a rich texture from which children can capture a real sense or picture of the particular place in question—to visualize as much as is possible what the place looks like. When you stimulate a richer and deeper visual image of place with children, providing a context for experiences, you are helping children to generate meaningful understandings of people and our world—to breathe life into the world outside of the child's immediate perception.

Using Relationships within Places

With location and place as a suggested starting point (you can begin with any of the five themes), the next step is to identify and describe actual and potential relationships within places. In particular, when exploring relationships within places, we are interested in answering three questions: (1) How do people depend upon the environment of the place? (2) In what ways do people adapt to the conditions of the local environment? (3) What is the impact of technology on the environment?

Wherever people live, they must interact with their environment. From the clothes they wear to the homes they build, a special relationship is established between people and their environment. Their lives and the lives of their family, friends, and neighbors depend upon all that comprises the space around them. Humans depend upon the environment for basic needs. For example, if Debbie and Jose lived on a island, in what ways do you suppose they would be dependent upon their surroundings? Given that their basic needs would include food, water, air, and land, to continue to live on the island Debbie and Jose probably would eat fish from the ocean, drink water drawn from pure fresh water wells, breathe the island's air, and live in sturdy houses built upon the land.

In this island setting the ocean would affect the lives of the people, influencing their occupations, their homes, recreation activities, industries, transportation systems, and more. The climate (year-round pattern of weather) and weather (daily observations of conditions) of the island would also affect the people. In answer to the second question of relationships, how people adapt to and change the environment is of special interest. The planting of crops, the building of a sea wall, the extension of a landfill into the ocean—all are adaptations to the environment. The crops may be planted to supplement the food supply by making the people less dependent upon fish, the sea wall built to protect the harbor from high seas and heavy weather, and the landfill extended to add needed space for expansion.

Every community adapts to and changes the environment in some way. How has your community been shaped by your environment? In what ways have you and your neighbors changed the environment to better suit the needs of the people? In similar ways, technology also affects the environment.

Communication improvements such as satellites, computers, cable television, and fiberoptics have revolutionized our lives. Technology also includes changes in toys, food packaging, clothing, cars, housing materials, and in thousands of other ways. There are, of course, negative consequences of technology such as smog and ozone depletion.

The goal for relationships within places is to explore the many ways humans use their environment as well as how humans are affected by environment. Dependence, adaptation, and technology are three areas that can be explored throughout the elementary years.[2]

Using Movement

The fourth theme of space is movement. Where relationships within places covers the connection between people and a specific place, movement describes how people interact with other people and places throughout the earth. Some places on earth are heavily populated such as New York City, Mexico City, or Tokyo; others are sparsely populated such as sections of the Northern Territory of Australia or areas of the Kalahari Desert in southern Africa. Perhaps you live in (or have visited) an urban area that is densely populated or maybe you live in the country where your nearest neighbor is more than a mile away. No matter whether you live on a farm, in a large city, on a mountain top, or in a village, you are dependent on or affected by products, information, and ideas that are transported from one place to another.

The transportation of products, information, and ideas is connected to the notion of interdependence (people relying upon or linked to people from other places). To illustrate, what did you have for breakfast this morning? Did you eat a full meal of eggs, toast with butter and grape jelly, milk, or coffee? Did you eat a "healthy" packaged cereal like Total or a quick bowl of Fruity Pebbles? Perhaps you ate a donut, an orange or apple, or even last night's left over pizza. Where do you suppose all these food items and their ingredients came from? You can check the box or bag to identify where the product was manufactured. You might also look for the source of the ingredients, such as sugar or nuts, fruits or salt.

As a class assignment you might have your children identify the source of their breakfast. You could use a large map of the world and have the children mark the sources of products with pins. Then, with yarn or string have the children demonstrate interdependence by tracking the sources to your town. You might also introduce how these products are manufactured, packaged, marketed, and shipped to various places around the globe. You might have a factory or other company near your school that conducts business throughout the United States and the world that might be willing to have you visit, or perhaps a representative could answer questions for your children that further illustrate interdependence.

---

[2]See appendix F for a listing of suggestions for each grade level.

There is more, however, to interdependence than the movement of products from one place to another. Movement and interdependence also include the means of communication from one place to another. Today, communication systems can link people throughout the globe and do so very quickly. You could telephone a friend in Hong Kong, watch a live speech from the Ukraine, send a fax message or document to Brazil, or listen to a radio broadcast from the Philippines all from your home. You could also become part of a computer network such as Bit-net from which you could send messages to other users throughout the world. With modern technology you can communicate with people from places thousands of miles away or across the street.

Communication systems are excellent methods of moving ideas or information from one place to another, but suppose you wanted to travel to Berlin or Los Angeles. Before the use of advanced communication, the only way to move ideas or information from one place to another was to literally carry them. Today, transportation systems can move people and products to even the most remote places on earth. You could drive your car to Los Angeles, fly in a jet, take a train, or you might even go there by ship.

The sheer variety of transportation systems that people use throughout the world can be a fascinating topic. Some systems, such as river barges connecting the ocean to major ports deep within the United States, have been used successfully for many years. A barge carrying a heavy load of steel for a skyscraper in Detroit could leave its harbor in Houston or New Orleans on the Gulf of Mexico and travel the entire distance to Michigan by water.

If you remembered your friend's birthday was tomorrow and wanted to send a present from your home in Pittsburgh to her house in Oklahoma City, it could be mailed through a convenient service such as Federal Express today and arrive in time for the party the next day. The study of movement is not merely the study of the boat or jet that carries the steel or birthday gift, it is the study of all the people connected to shipping or moving products from place to place—from the suppliers of the product, to the workers on the assembly lines, to the shippers and baggage handlers, to truck drivers and jet pilots, to dock workers—literally hundreds, if not thousands, of people connected to moving one product.

The topics of transportation, interdependence, and linkages between one place and another are fundamental to achieving a geographic perspective. There is, however, another aspect or theme to explore that can help children make sense of their world through the study of space.

Using Region

The basic unit of study in geography is the region, how it forms and how it changes. Region identifies a place based upon a description of selected characteristics. Regions can be described in political terms, such as states, nations, provinces, countries, and cities. Thus, Illinois is a region called a state,

Argentina is a region called a nation, Quebec is a region called a province, Dade (Florida) is a region called a county, and Athens is a region called a city.

Regions can also be described by languages/dialects (French, Pennsylvania Dutch), specific landforms (Gobi Desert, Rocky Mountains), income levels and affluence (Park Avenue, New York City), business activities (farmers' market), and recreation activities (beach). Depending upon characteristics one location (a particular spot on the globe) might have a number of regional names. For example, Chicago might be described as a city, part of Illinois (state), part of a county (Cook), part of the United States (nation), and an area of North America (continent). Chicago also contains a number of ethnic groups that live in neighborhoods that can be labeled. In addition, there are business areas, museums, parks, theaters, street designations, and more.

One particular aim of using region is for children to learn to recognize and label regions as well as being able to understand how they are formed and changed. You could help your children organize their classroom into regions according to activities with desk or sit down work areas, learning stations, books and things, toys and play, discovery centers, plants and bugs, and more. You may also want to help children learn about regions with descriptions of the school as a region with other regions such as rest rooms, cafeteria, gym, library, science laboratory, computer room, main office, nurse's room, play yard, and, even the sometimes dreaded principal's office serving as illustrations of regions.

Children might also discover the other regions around the school such as a new mall being built on an old farming area. The new mall means that new buildings, new streets and highways, new underground sewer and phone lines, and new stores are being built. Here children can observe how the new region (large shopping area) is formed as well as how the new region changes the old region (farm land). The possibilities for creating and observing regions in operation and transition are many.

Putting Space into a Geographic Perspective

The overarching goal of exploring the five themes of space is to help children develop and practice geographic perspective. Geographic perspective is a conceptual orientation that combines all of the five themes of space. Within the social studies formula, geographic perspective is not fact driven or memory based. All too often the emphasis of geographic instruction in the elementary grades is to learn about maps. In this process teachers often equate geography as simply map skills—where being able to locate selected items on a map or to memorize particular land forms is standard instruction.

Maps are an important visual representation of geographic concepts, regions, and landforms, but map skills are not the only medium for instruction. In the social studies formula, map skills are tools for learning about and practicing the more powerful concepts of location, place, relationships within places, movement, and region.

As time, past, change, and continuity yield a historical perspective, similarly location, place, relationship within places, movement, and region yield a geographic perspective. Together, the elements of time and space are powerful organizers and facilitators of social studies learning experiences. There is, however, another powerful element of the social studies formula that emerges when time and space are studied—the element of issues.

The Element of Issues

Issues comprise the third element of the social studies formula. The use of issues presents the teacher with a great deal of flexibility. Issues are sometimes spontaneous; that is, issues can and do emerge when children are studying or discussing or making observations about a particular phenomenon. At other times you will be able to plan to explore an issue in advance of instruction. Issues possess three basic features for use in elementary curricula: (1) issues are something important to discuss with children; (2) issues are consequences raised during the course of some action or thought; and (3) issues are a point in question between two or more parties.

Issues as Something Important

The first use of issues concerns anything you or the children decide to talk about. Perhaps a child witnessed a car accident or noticed that the local fire station purchased a new fire engine. Maybe you read in the paper that someone attempted to lure a child into a car. The idea of seeing a car smashed and people hurt, watching the fire station workers wash down the new fire engine, or listening to a frightening story about an attempted abduction presents opportunities to talk about the concerns of children as well as things that concern children.

Debbie might be troubled about the car accident and wants to talk about it with you and the other children. You might think it important to remind the children about strangers. The car crash invites a spontaneous lesson, one you did not have time to prepare ahead of class (or whatever sets the children to discuss). The crash might be an opportunity to talk about the safety features of a car, the science of action-reaction, or what to do in case of emergencies. One idea is to take the child's concern seriously and turn the issue that is raised by the child into a learning experience for everyone. The other idea is to bring your concerns or those of other adults to children for their consideration and discussion.

The initial difference between the two is that the issue raised by the child is felt by the child; that is, Debbie thinks the issue of car accidents is important. The issue of child abduction raised by you is felt by the adult; that is, it is important to you to inform children about. Keeping this difference in mind, remember that issues raised by you may not be understood or have value to children. On the other hand, not every issue raised by children will be suitable or appropriate for class exploration and discussion.

Issues that Emerge

The second use of issues concerns those that emerge during class or when children are reading, studying, practicing, and/or playing. In general, issues can materialize from any activity. For instance, perhaps Debbie was completing a project about American presidents. One of Debbie's observations was that there were no female presidents of the United States. From this observation, Debbie concluded that women were not permitted to become president. According to Debbie's research, this may be a valid generalization; however, Debbie also noted that the Constitution does not bar women from any political office, particularly the presidency. The issue that emerged from Debbie's observation was why in the course of 200 years, no woman was ever elected president or even vice-president.

Having raised the issue of women as president, Debbie's fifth grade classmates could explore any number of questions such as why women have not been elected to high political office, what is the role of women in government, and what happens in elections. During this investigation or discussion, Jose may also note that no Hispanics or Native or African Americans have ever served as president. Jose, then, raised a similar issue, asking why individuals from particular cultural groups have not experienced political success at the highest levels of American government.

Issues also may be questions, problems, inconsistencies, misunderstandings, or anything else that is perplexing about the subject or experience or activity at hand. This use of issues, then, is very difficult to predict and plan for—you may not discover what the child finds troubling until the child identifies the problem.

On the other hand, your own experience working with children may help you identify issues that consistently emerged with children. That is, in advance of your study of the ocean and its uses, you may plan for questions and problems that children eventually raise as important issues. For example, drift nets are used by fishing boats and their crews to catch large numbers of fish in a short period of time—making drift nets very profitable. Drift nets are designed to literally drift upon the upper thirty feet of the ocean's surface (they can be adjusted). Because nets are made of light weight but durable, plastic, fishing boats can drop nets that cover a large area, typically many miles long.

One issue that emerges from the use of drift nets is that when the nets are used for catching tuna, for example, the nets do not discriminate between tuna and other fish, animals, or sea birds, catching any creature that falls or swims within their reach. Jose may call the class's attention to the consequences of drift net fishing, explaining that when tuna are caught, dolphins, seals, birds, and more are also caught and killed. The price of the tuna, then, includes the death of creatures not intended to be harvested. When the consequences of drift net use become known, children invariably raise the issue of ethics—Jose may ask "Is this the right thing to do?"

The issue of drift nets is, however, complex. It is not as simple as demanding that fishing crews stop using these nets—if that is the opinion of the children—because fishing crews and their families depend upon catching fish as their source of income. If they did not have the nets, they would not catch enough to support their families. This perspective raises new issues to explore, such as what rights do individuals have to earn their own living, how much influence should the government have over industries, what are the values of the oceans and the life they support, and/or what alternatives exist or could be created to support the ocean creatures, while supporting the fishing crews? (Refer to chapter 3, the paradox of the individual versus society.)

For the teacher, knowing that a particular topic or experience will raise issues among children is important. Having this knowledge, then, you can anticipate discussions, inquiry assignments, questions, and other projects. The ability to plan in advance to discuss emergent issues, is an alternative to simply standing up in front of the children and telling them why you think issue X is important to know.

Issues that Involve Disputes and Differences

The third use of issues involves a dispute or difference between two or more individuals or groups of individuals. Disputes or differences may also occur between individuals/groups and institutions, individuals/groups and circumstances, or even individuals/groups and nature. On a personal level, for example, Debbie promised Jose that she would bring him a Butterfinger candy if he would take her hall duty today. Jose agreed and showed up for duty that afternoon. After standing duty for just a few minutes, however, Jose was sent to the gym by Mrs. Cason to watch an unannounced special assembly. The next day Jose wanted his Butterfinger and Debbie refused, explaining that Jose did not complete his bargain. As you might expect, issues were raised. Should Debbie hand over the Butterfinger? Should Jose take the hall duty on another day? Is it appropriate for Debbie to bargain with another child over her responsibility?

If this disagreement surfaced in your class, what could you do? Of course, you could decide to ignore the issue and let Debbie and Jose resolve their own dispute. However, you might consider exploring the nature of keeping a promise or following through on our agreements, the value of services, or the importance of understanding the expectations of others. Thus, on a personal level, disputes between children offer a number of teaching opportunities and experiences to explore children's feelings, behaviors, values, and beliefs.

At another level, disputes, disagreements, or conflicts that individuals or groups of individuals experience offer the opportunity to explore how issues have been dealt with in the past. How did other people handle disputes or problems? You might also want to present issues of the present and perhaps the future. Finding examples of how individuals overcame problems can be very inspiring, especially if you can find stories of how children resolved differences or solved problems. You should also look for stories of how children are presently working on a problem.

Typically issues used within the social studies formula draw upon concerns, problems, and disputes from such overlapping areas as citizenship or law, culture, the environment, current events, global concerns, technology, economics, ethics, and future studies. In practice, however, issues can emerge or be raised from any number of sources. The resolution or reconciliation of conflict, differences, and disputes presents opportunities for children to practice dealing with problems.

Sources for Issues

One prime source for issues is the media. For example, a few years ago three young whales were trapped in an Alaskan inlet. Winter was imminent and the entire inlet where the whales had traveled was soon to be frozen solid—only a few small open holes remained in the frozen inlet for the whales. Since whales are mammals and breath air, it was certain that they would not be able to hold their breath long enough as they swam under the ice to reach the ocean many miles away. There was no doubt among the experts that without help the whales were certain to die. The reports and pictures of this story soon captured the hearts and minds of people everywhere, particularly children.

When the news of the trapped whales made all the national television and radio networks, thousands were fascinated and deeply troubled. Children were moved to send money and their sincere encouragement and prayers to the whales and those who were to free them. Even the Soviet Union sent ice-breaking equipment to free the whales. Nonetheless, as the ice covered over more and more of the few remaining holes, the situation was fast becoming desperate. Children wondered, "What's going to happen?" "Why can't they free the whales?" "Can't we do more to help?" The story continued in the papers and on television for days; daily reports and pictures were relayed through all the news organizations. The whales were even named by the rescue crews. Then, happily, at least two of the whales eventually were led to the open ocean and freed (the third went under the ice and its fate was unknown).

The story had captured the attention of children and, incidently, a number of issues were raised. Many teachers took advantage of the opportunity to address these issues. The story was a current event, a real life adventure that was unfolding literally before their eyes. If children became interested in following a news story, teachers could capitalize upon this phenomenon by pointing out the value and importance of tracking things that affect our lives. The story was also an account of the environment and teachers could raise issues about the plight of whales and other sea life, as well as all endangered species.

The story raised the attention of people throughout the world, thus making it a global concern. Children could identify how some events and situations transcend nationalities and require the care and attention of people through-out the world. The story also raised a number of ethical questions. For instance, supposedly the freeing of the two whales cost approximately $600,000. Given the condition of some human beings who live in cardboard boxes and eat out of garbage cans and others who are starving to death, were the lives of two wayward whales worth that much time, money, and media attention?

One event, the whales being trapped under the Alaskan ice, then, raised four general issues that could be divided into a number of possibilities. Care-fully cultivated, issues provide direct opportunities for children to learn the values of attending to such logical operations as definitions, explanations, descriptions, examples, compare-contrast situations, alternatives, conclusions, references, and other sources when discussing or exploring them. Teachers need to be mindful of this search for clarity and understanding. An important part of using issues is that children have experiences that not only inform, but also assist them with their communication and socialization skills.

Whether or not the issues were raised by or emerged with the whale story, children were provided with opportunities to practice logical operations such as definitions (What is an ice breaker?), alternatives (people often need to consider any number of potential solutions before finding one that works), and references (books on whales) to illustrate, explain, and contextualize issues. The use of logical operations, then, helps children to clarify and gain a better grasp or understanding of issues.

Teachers, nonetheless, need to decide what issues raised by children will be discussed and explored in class as well as to decide what issues they will introduce through planned experiences. In brief, as the intellectual leader of the class, you need to determine what issues merit or warrant class time and attention.

The Element of Concepts

The fourth part of the social studies formula involves the use of concepts. Concepts are mental constructions that are either inductively built by individ-uals or deductively introduced, defined, and illustrated for us by others. Deduc-tive or social concepts are often conveyed (transferred) from one individual's mind to another through words or speech. Language, then, is the vehicle through which objects, experiences, and ideas are given labels. These labels are called concepts.

For example, we share the idea that a creature with four legs and a tail that is domesticated, barks, and occasionally chases cats around the neighbor-hood can be described by the word *dog*. When enough people come to under-stand that this description matches the word dog, we have a social concept (a mental construction that is understood and accepted by others). In reviewing the above sentence that begins with "For example, we share the idea . . .," you will find that each of these words is a mental construction. For you to understand what is meant by the term *dog*, you need to understand the words given in the description. Thus, if you know what share, idea, creature, legs, tail, domesticated, barks, chase, cats, and neighborhood mean, as well as understand the context in which these words are used and have observed examples of creatures that match the meanings of these words, then you will understand the word *dog*.

By the time children attend formal school, they know about and can use thousands of concepts. Some of these mental constructions are derived from contact with other people; some, however, are constructed and given labels independently of others. Children, then, may know about fire trucks, giant condor birds, waterfalls, and zoos by watching and hearing descriptions from the Discovery Channel or other television programming such as Sesame Street or Reading Rainbow. In addition, they may have made observations or experienced things like an electric shock, the smell of fresh strawberries, or a warm feeling from giving a gift to a friend independent of any explanations.

In this case, when Jose received the shock, smelled the strawberries, and experienced the warm feeling, he was not able to connect these experiences with words (concepts) that he was familiar with—to him, these events had no antecedents. Unless he was told or asked someone what these experiences were, Jose is left to define and categorize these experiences into his own concepts.

Formal school is a place where concepts can be introduced and discovered and where concepts can be built and refined with experiences. For Jose and his classmates, school, then, is a place where they are exposed to any number of concepts as well as a place where they can practice using concepts. The benefit of exposure to concepts in schools is that unlike the streets or playgrounds, schools offered a controlled and protected environment for children—a place where experiences can be enriching, where experiences can be explored, and where children can grow mentally and physically without penalty. With special care and consideration, our task is to single out those concepts that we wish children to explore and experience. Three key thoughts should be considered with either concept building or concept introduction:

1. The concept should be within the experience of the child as much as is possible, provide opportunities that connect the child to the concept—avoid pure abstractions.
2. The concept should be used in its context(s)—avoid defining or explaining concepts that are removed from where and how they are actually used.
3. Once introduced or revealed, the concept should be used and explored (where appropriate) throughout the elementary grades and beyond—avoid treating concepts as something children experience once and do not need to revisit.

Building Concepts

Whenever children construct concepts from their experiences, teachers should remember that building concepts takes time and considerable patience—not only for children, but for you too. It is not that children do not know how to construct concepts (they have been building concepts successfully since birth), what is important to remember is that they may not have had sufficient experience to understand the concept you want them to grasp and use. Consequently, rather than telling a child about a concept, you may consider helping the child build concepts from carefully predetermined and planned experiences and examples.

For example, rather than telling children about the concept environment, or simply giving a definition and description of the word, in addition to showing pictures, watching filmstrips, and reading books, you might want to prepare a number of experiences that would engage children to develop the concept on their own. This approach is called inductive concept formation. Although the teacher is manipulating the examples and experiences, he is not telling children or giving answers.

The basic process of inductive teaching is:

1. to provide examples for children to observe, handle, play with, take apart, and study.
2. to help children look for similarities and differences.
3. to help children to verbalize common characteristics and functions.
4. to ask children to describe and label their ideas.
5. to ask children to state relationships or connections to other concepts within their experience.
6. to ask children to generate new examples from their descriptions or definition of the concept.

Providing opportunities for children to build their own concepts with these guidelines is time consuming. However, inductive concept formation gives the child ownership and first hand experience with the development of the concept—the concept is not something the teacher simply told them about. Every time teachers provide children with opportunities to build concepts, they are reinforcing the child's ability to construct them own understanding of experience within the context of society. Nonetheless, due to conditions, circumstances, and other curricular and practical needs, it may be appropriate to highlight concepts for children.

Introducing Concepts

Introducing concepts to children is nothing new—children have been given concepts (new words) from parents, siblings, television, and many other sources. The quality of these conceptualizations, however, may be uneven and incomplete. Consequently, introducing concepts presents opportunities for children to gain a greater and more complete understanding of them.

For example, when Debbie hears a new phrase on television such as a sock commercial that claims "you get more socks for the money," she may understand what socks are and that money is used to buy socks, but has no idea what "more socks for the money" means. The concept represented in the commercial is rooted in economics, if you with to be a thrifty shopper, to extend your purchasing power, then buy Burlington socks. To Debbie, however, the economic concept may be lost to her and all that remains is that Debbie remembers the name of the brand of socks. Perhaps this is enough for advertising—to sell socks—but not for concept attainment.

The alternative to inductive concept development is deductive concept attainment. Deductive concept attainment is teacher-centered. The basic process of concept attainment is as follows:

1. State the name of the concept.
2. Provide a description and definition of the concept.
3. Illustrate the concept with examples from a variety of sources and contexts.
4. Highlight the major attributes of the concept.
5. Repeat a clear definition of the concept.
6. Ask students to generate new examples that match your definition and description of the concept.

This direct style of concept attainment can be as effective as the indirect process of concept development. You need to be aware of the benefits of each approach, as well as any potential consequences. But more importantly, you need to practice working with each style by looking for opportunities to integrate each within your lesson experiences.

The Element of Relationships

The final part of the social studies formula is the most critical. No matter what you do or do not do, the child will always generate an outcome from using the social studies formula. The quality of this outcome (as discussed earlier) depends in part on the quality of the instruction and experience. Despite how much quality instruction is given—that you are careful to include excellent examples and experiences with time, space, issues, and concepts—unless the child makes the connection from the presented experiences to his own experience, the exercise may be lost, a failure.

Relationships, then, are those connections from the experiences of life and school to the internal or private world of the child. The discovery of a relationship is like a light bulb turning on in the child's head—the "ah, I understand" phenomenon of learning that is so very difficult for children and teachers to capture and reproduce. To the child, the learner, relationships make sense and viable use of what is experienced.

Relationships reflect our individual and social schemata, they are the way we identify, classify, compare-contrast, analyze, assess, reflect, and do all the logical operations necessary to understand our world as individuals and as members of a group, community, or society. Unless we are able to help children translate their experiences to relationships (either directly or indirectly), and to place things into contexts and with meanings, then our jobs as teachers may be reduced to nothing more than occupying the time of children.

You might be familiar with the phrase "learn by doing" often attributed to the educational theorist John Dewey. What this phrase is understood to mean is that children (people) grasp, comprehend, and master something when they are actively engaged in the learning experience. As far as Dewey was concerned, however, this is not the complete story. Just because a child is doing something—taking an active part of the experience—it does not follow that the child is learning. That is, if Jose was actively engaged in building a model tyrannosaurus rex, we cannot assume that he understands what this creature is or was, or how it lived or how it died. Moreover, we cannot assume that Jose understands how to construct model dinosaurs or has any knowledge of scale. According to a Deweyan view, building a model dinosaur is simply one experience for Jose unless Jose, another child, or the teacher helps him understand the nature of the experience. The second, and most neglected part of Dewey's theory of experience, is the undergoing of experience. That is, experience has two parts: the active doing element and the active undergoing element. The undergoing of experience provides the understanding or connection from previous experiences to the new experience. Undergoing is the expansion of the child's mental schemata, the enlargement of meaningful experience.

To Jose, undergoing means that he understands the learning, that he is able to make connections to other experiences, and that he is able to verbalize his understanding to others. Active doing, then, is not sufficient for learning, the child must come to an understanding on his own, be led to an understanding by another, or simply be told. Nonetheless, the teacher as the intellectual leader of the class is responsible for ascertaining the level and degree of understanding, to answer the question, "Does the child understand?"

Brief Summary

The social studies formula contains five integrated elements. At one level, the exploration of time, space, and issues informs and provides perspectives to, with, and for children. At another level, concepts and relationships are used to make sense of experience, to connect meaning and understanding from experience, and to assist children with their own learning. Combined, the two levels of the formula present a powerful tool for helping children to build meaningful experiences with social studies. Given this final theoretical construction, we are now ready to integrate the social studies formula with the four universal needs and liberal democratic principles.

The following chapter will highlight and illustrate the synoptic approach to social studies, using the formula, universal needs, and liberal democratic principles as our guides.

Marking Your Progress

1. Topic/theme _____

   _____

   _____

2. Ideas for incorporating time into your unit _____

   _____

   _____

3. Ideas for incorporating space into your unit _____

   _____

   _____

4. Ideas for incorporating concepts into your unit _____

   _____

   _____

5. Ideas for incorporating issues into your unit _____

   _____

   _____

6. Ideas for incorporating relationships into your unit _____

   _____

   _____

Read More about It Special References

For social studies, the amount of content available for teachers or children to choose from is literally staggering. One of the first sources to be consulted is your local school district or state social studies curriculum. In many states class content is mandated; in others content is suggested. The synoptic method can be applied whether or not social studies content is mandated or suggested. You simply begin with the content as the basis of meeting the four universal needs. There will be many opportunities to add to prepared curricula, or perhaps you will be in a school district that permits its teachers to construct their own curricula.

Regardless of whether you are handed a curriculum or not, social studies content can be overwhelming. The following references are not meant to oversimplify a very complex field of study, nor are these references the only sources available. Rather, the following are offered as helpful suggestions on what to teach about, to what ends, and, perhaps, more importantly at this point, how to go about it.

Within the synoptic method your task is to identify appropriate content, skills, values, attitudes, and beliefs found within these sources and use them to help children meet the four universal needs. Note: Most of the following begin social studies from a content-centered perspective (typically defined by the subjects history, geography, and civics). You will need to identify and detach appropriate concepts, issues, and relationship as appropriate for your needs-based curricula.

Atwood, V. (1986). *Elementary social studies: Research as a guide to practice.* Washington, DC: National Council for the Social Studies.
  This is a handy overview of appropriate elementary social studies topics, designed to complement analytic, not synoptic, approaches to social studies. Nonetheless, the text is helpful.
Bradley Commission on History in Schools. (1988). *Building a history curriculum: Guidelines for teaching history in schools.*
  This brief booklet outlines a complete history-centered program for schools, kindergarten through twelfth grade. The Commission, however, takes a decidedly content-centered approach to schooling.
California State Department of Education. (1988). *History-social science framework.* Sacramento, CA: California State Department of Education.
  During the 1980s/1990s era of school reform, California was the first state to break with the tradition of the expanding horizons approach to social studies (see chapter 7). Houghton Mifflin was the first major publisher to produce a social studies series expressly designed to follow the California suggested requirements for kindergarten through eighth grade (see Houghton Mifflin's Social Studies Series [1991]).
Davis, K. (1991). *Don't know much about history: Everything you need to know about American history, but never learned.* New York: Avon.
  An inexpensive accounting of American history for the novice reader. Easily read and digested. Helpful for planning a full year of experiences in which chronology is important.
Demko, G. (1992). *Why in the world: Adventures in geography.* New York: Doubleday/Anchor Books.

This book is strictly for teachers wanting to know more about geography. The book is not merely educational, it is fun and entertaining.

Grant, N. (1992). *The great atlas of discovery.* New York: Alfred A. Knopf.

A wonderful resource that focuses on major discoveries of Western civilization (also includes Chinese, Muslim/Arab accounts).

Hirsch, E. D., Jr. (1991). *What your 1st grader needs to know.* New York: Doubleday. (Note: this is the first of six volumes covering each of the first six grades.)

Out of his cultural literacy research, Hirsch has turned his attentions to preparing materials suitable for teachers and parents of elementary age children. While debates about what should be taught to children are heatedly discussed in the media, school board meetings, and more, Hirsch has developed his Core Knowledge Series *(first grade through sixth) to clearly identify what he thinks literate young Americans should know. While the project is not necessarily endorsed here, Hirsch remains one of the few authors to put together grade-appropriate listings of knowledge. All elementary teachers should be aware of what is being suggested in these texts. As with all proposed materials, these guidelines should be used with caution. Incidently, Hirsch suggests only content, he does not provide any ideas on the thornier issue of how to teach content or how teachers can help children remember details or information (if that is what is meant by being literate).*

National Geographic Society. (1992). *Story of America.* Washington, DC: National Geographic Society.

Well respected for their excellent maps, the National Geographic Society weaves story into maps that help history come alive for children (and adults) in this beautiful single volume history of the United States.

Natoli, S., ed. (1988). *Strengthening geography in the social studies.* Washington, DC: National Council for the Social Studies.

This is an excellent policy statement and guide for the introduction and placing of geography in schools. Although directed more to the secondary curriculum, the text should be used to assist elementary teachers in their own geography education.

Quigley, C. N., & Buchanan, J., Jr. (1991). *Civitas: A framework for civic education.* Calabasas, CA: Center for Civic Education.

In what might be the most comprehensive text of social studies content, Civitas *neatly outlines knowledge important for young citizens. Heavily invested in historical, government, and sociological themes,* Civitas *will be most helpful for teachers who might require a quick summary. This text is not suitable for elementary age children. Again, as with the Hirsch texts, no real pedagogical helps are offered.*

The Random House Children's Encyclopedia. (1991). New York: Random House.

The single best comprehensive dictionary available for children is fully illustrated (all color) and stuffed with readily usable material/information that should be very helpful for teachers as well as children. It is a must for every classroom.

Sowell, T. (1981). *Ethnic America: A history.* New York: Basic Books.

This is one of the best books about race and ethnicity for the general readers (not suitable for children).

The Unfolding River. (1992). London: Quarto Publishing.

This fascinating fold-out book (measures over seven feet, fully extended) with full-color illustrations provides a rarely seen holistic view that traces the path of a river from the mountains to the sea. It highlights the complexity of life dependent upon the flow of the river and is an excellent resource for the classroom.

Tye, K. (1991). *Global education: From thought to action.* Alexandria, VA: Association for Supervision and Curriculum Development.

An important contribution to social studies education, this book is a general policy statement, rather than a guide to action in the elementary school. It contains helpful information and references.

The World Book Encyclopedia. (1993). Chicago: World Book

Without question this is the most thorough encyclopedia for elementary age children available today. Readable (4th grade and up), interesting (all ages), and informative, the World Book *contains hundreds of articles appropriate for elementary social studies. The encyclopedia is a must for every classroom.*

Winston, B. J. (1986). *Map and globe skills: K–8 teaching guide.* National Council for Geographic Education.

The best single source on the five geographic themes for elementary schools, this is a must for every teacher who wishes to bring geography skills to elementary age children. Order your copy from the National Council for Geographic Education, Leonard 16A, Indiana University of Pennsylvania, Indiana, PA 15705 (cost $5).

Zinn, H. (1980). *A people's history of the United States.* New York: Harper Perennial.

A thoroughly different accounting of American history than is typically available in standard United States history texts, this book is strictly for teachers developing materials/ lessons.

6

APPLYING THE SYNOPTIC METHOD

In this chapter you will

- Apply your knowledge of the synoptic method to transform your topic, teaching kit, and lesson ideas into specific lesson experiences for children.
- Organize your lesson experiences into meaningful units for teaching and learning.
- Assess your lesson planning and unit construction efforts.
- If time and conditions permit, share your lesson experiences with peers.

At the start of your social studies experience you began constructing a working teaching kit. Between the first chapter and this point you have been introduced to a holistically centered philosophy of teaching called the synoptic method.

The Synoptic Method

The synoptic method incorporates three overlapping ideas: (1) meeting the four universal needs of children; (2) practicing citizenship skills and developing the dispositions of liberal democracy through acceptance and thought and action; and (3) enriching experiences through the five components of the social studies formula.

Underlying these three ideas/applications are knowledge about youth culture, community, education, learning, and most important, the expansion of liberal democratic principles. The idea of holistic implies a sense of interconnectedness, that all of these variables are vital to consider when teaching.

In application, the synoptic method places the treatment of needs—within the context of liberal democratic principles—ahead of teaching content. That is, content-focused teaching targets bits and pieces of information for learning, such as knowing the names of each president, the Great Lakes, or the seven continents. In contrast, a synoptic teacher might use teaching about continents as a means to satisfy children's needs and to allow them to practice liberal democratic principles. In this method, learning the names and locations of the continents becomes secondary. Synoptic teachers are more concerned that children have positive quality experiences that satisfy the universal needs and provide practice with liberal democratic principles; synoptic teachers do not become preoccupied with children learning factual information.

I hope you have given the idea of applying the synoptic method a good deal of thought and are now ready to activate your teaching ideas. However, just working with the concept and explanation of the synoptic method may not be enough for you to start teaching. In addition to theory, many teachers appreciate examples that demonstrate the mechanics of putting together teaching experiences that conform to the synoptic method.

There is, however, a danger with presenting models in which teachers or children have no input. For example, every time we demonstrate something to and for a child we take away the potential for individual discovery and creativity—where the child can take pride in the idea that "I did it all by myself!" On the other hand, by providing examples and demonstrations we may stimulate a child's sense of creativity and boost self confidence, generating a "Hey, I can do that, that looks like fun!"

As with your lesson experiences, here, too, your developing ability to use or discover your creative skills may remain untested if you rely too heavily upon the examples. For this reason, keep in mind that the following are merely examples and suggestions of how teachers might wish to engage the synoptic method. Remember that holistic teaching fosters and empowers teachers to apply their skills and knowledge, but holistic teaching also implies that teachers will help children to initiate their own learning experiences. Therefore, although suggestions are presented here for you to explore as you prepare your lesson experiences, keep in mind that as you begin teaching in schools you should help children to construct their own lesson experiences as well.

Four Basic Lesson Considerations

In chapter 1 a model for planning, organizing, presenting, and assessing lesson experiences was briefly introduced. These four components—necessary for all synoptic lessons/units—represent decisions that teachers need to make before, during, and following teaching experiences. You may think of these four steps as questions for you to answer. These questions are briefly noted here.

Planning

What preparations, decisions, and materials need to be considered and/or secured in advance of the lesson experiences? Given initial choices, note other possible teaching alternatives, other selections of materials, ideas, and topics that might be used.

Planning for experiences focuses upon identification of potential actions and choices that teachers and children need to make. In addition to needs, teachers will consider what particular interests to cultivate, how practice in holistic freedom might be engaged, and what other considerations/challenges need to be worked out before instruction can begin.

Organization

After a preliminary direction of experiences is worked out, exactly how will the experience be presented to children? Will you focus on acceptance or thought and action? What will be the nature and sequence of activities?

In organizing experiences, teachers and students decide on a course of action. That is, given the possibilities, what will be done, what will be used, how will it be used, and when (sequences established) are other decisions made. These decisions are committed to paper (lesson plan).

Presentation

As the lesson experience begins, what adjustments need to be made for conditions found on instructional day? Are ongoing adjustments needed? What is the initial response of children? What are your feelings about the lesson?

In presenting experiences, teachers work to apply ideas found on paper (as well as those made at the point of instruction) to actual class conditions with children—to breathe life into inert lesson and unit plans. Any adjustments that can be made immediately you do, other refinements or changes might have to wait until the lesson is completed. The presentation is critical because it represents proof and confirmation of your judgment. Although educational miscalculations are frequent, you, too, can benefit just as much from your overestimates (and underestimates) of children as you can from your successes. Regardless of outcome, you must continue to strive to make the best informed decisions you are capable of.

Assessment

Following the lesson, take time to ask yourself: Did the lesson/unit work? Did the children benefit from the experience? What problems or concerns were raised by children or by other observers? How might you improve the experience for the children?

In assessing experiences, teachers review the lesson itself and children's accomplishments. Teachers also consider whatever problems or concerns that were raised either by the children, other observers, or themselves as well as any issues that emerged from the experience. Given answers to these questions, the teacher needs to consider his or her role in the lesson, noting whatever future adjustments that may be made to increase teaching effectiveness as well as to increase opportunities for children's learning.

Four Needs as the Central Focus of Instruction

The overriding principle of lesson planning in the synoptic method is for teachers to have a working understanding of the four universal needs of children. These needs provide the central framework for all synoptic lessons. Specifically, each lesson experience is designed to satisfy a child's need for communication, building, thought and action, and/or self-expression. Although not every experience will include each need (some do however), the four universal needs should be addressed in each unit or subject of work. Within these experiences, teachers create opportunities for children to practice citizenship and develop liberal democratic dispositions through acceptance and thought and action.

Units

Synoptic teachers begin lesson planning after gaining a sense of the depth and range of a particular broadly defined subject (as presented in your teaching kit). Operating with the supposition that teachers cannot teach about things they have little understanding of, synoptic teachers use information culled from their teaching kits to identify potential individual lessons and patterns or collections of lessons. This collection of lessons is typically called a unit or module. Units incorporate both acceptance and thought and action activities that may be centered on ideas/concepts/topics, themes, projects, or questions.

Rationale for Unit Construction

As will be explained in chapter 7, many elementary teachers use a standard social studies textbook for instruction. Although social studies textbooks such as the recent Houghton Mifflin *Social Studies Series* (see appendix F for scope and sequence) provide interesting and innovative ways to teach about social studies, textbooks are prepared for the average child. Moreover, textbooks, particularly social studies texts, are closely examined for political correctness; that is, authors and publishers hope to appeal to the widest audience and are very careful to avoid offending anyone. Such textbook construction by committee may not serve your children very well. Consequently, while our classrooms are composed of many children with different interests, needs, capacities, abilities, and backgrounds, the standard textbook does not (and cannot) take into account your particular children. When textbooks reduce all instruction to the same level, the textbook's effectiveness suffers.

The second reason standard textbooks should be avoided as the primary means of social studies instruction is that teachers are left out of the planning and organization of lessons and learning experiences. As discussed and reinforced throughout this book, teachers are the intellectual leaders of the class. As professionals (because you know your children and the context of learning better than anyone else), they (you) need to have a strong measure of control and empowerment over what is and what is not taught. To place teachers in situations in which they have little to no curricular input mitigates against the principles of the synoptic method and liberal democratic goals.

One alternative to teacher-proof textbooks is the use of unit construction. Unit construction combines flexibility and freedom; you can select topics for the year as you see fit, tailor individual learning activities as needs be, and restructure, fine-tune, or reject units according to results (measured by you). All primary learning experiences can be directly attended to by the teacher; individual learners benefit best when particular needs can be targeted by teachers. In planning for your school year, you can begin collecting ideas and materials (build teaching kits) to store away in a folder or file drawer to retrieve when needed. As your career progresses you can add to and subtract from your existing teaching kits as needed and even create new teaching kits. The following section presents some ideas to consider as you begin to shape your unit.

Sample Ideas for Units

Idea/concept/topic—a focus on a single thought, issue, subject, or idea: "Recycling," "Japanese Origami," "Endangered Animals"

Theme—a connection of related topics, ideas, events, practices, or processes: "Wagons West!," "Life in the Middle Ages," "Holidays around the World"

Project—use of process and product, all activities necessary to complete a construction venture: "Making Paper," "A Trip to Mars," "Building a Pirate Ship"

Question—seek explanation, answer, reason for some event, phenomenon, action, condition, or issue. "What's a President?," "Who Discovered America?"

At first glance the notion of dividing materials, skills, and ideas into discrete units may appear more analytic than holistic. Indeed, in subject or content-centered teaching, content dictates the sort of learning experiences found in units. In synoptic teaching, however, the unit is not considered apart from the context of the lesson experience or the child. Content-centered teaching puts content first, and then calls upon children to find the context and relate the meaning of the unit to that of other units or their own life experiences.

In contrast, synoptic teachers view the child as an integral part of the context of the unit experiences in which units are related segments of greater wholes that teachers and children work to understand. Because teachers are the intellectual leaders of the class, it is their role to foster, stimulate, and/or guide children to and through learning experiences. Therefore, although both content-centered teaching and synoptic experiences use units, the design and purpose of teaching units are quite distinct.

Duration and Sequence

Units can be designed for children to experience for a brief period of time (two to three days) to much longer periods (one month or more). Additionally, units may be broken into parts that are covered over consecutive days (for example, twenty to thirty minutes a day for five days), completed in full (spend an entire school day or a significant portion of one on the same topic for one day or longer), or used as a "holiday" approach (a twenty-minute lesson, once a month over the course of six months).

You may even decide to mix these time frames in your unit. For example, you may introduce "American Indians of the Eastern Woodlands" for twenty minutes a day for four days, then celebrate a different Indian group with a similar four-day session in each of the next three months. You might begin with a full week of experiences called "A Festival of Cultures," that feature ways of life in Asian, African, South American, and European nations, then prepare ten thirty-minute lessons for the next two weeks that highlight selected cultures and people from these areas.

Finally, the matching of experiences to roughly defined time frames (twenty minutes a day, two weeks, full day) is extremely valuable in lesson planning. Although we cannot predict exactly how long children will need for a particular activity, timed periods can help teachers (and children) to sequence a number of experiences over days, weeks, and months. When conditions or situations permit, teachers can take advantage of preparing lesson experiences well in advance of instruction (typically called long-term planning). Where long-term planning might not be advisable, teachers can adapt by putting lessons together using short-term planning techniques (deciding upon lesson experiences or units to be implemented within a matter of days or weeks). All three types of lesson planning (long-term, short-term, and spontaneous) can be adapted to the resources of your teaching kit.

Ideally, teachers should cultivate skills with both long-term and short-term planning (remembering that lessons and/or units are always subject to revision). Despite expert planning, however, sometimes unexpected golden opportunities for learning present themselves right in the middle of our best laid plans. For example, when an important news story breaks in the world, teachers should be ready to help children understand what is happening when children begin to talk about such headlines as "Berlin Wall Falls—Germany Reunited," "Challenger Space Capsule Explodes," or "Gulf War Begins." Local events should be covered as well. Children might be concerned or interested with local issues such as "School Strike Threatens," "Citizens Must Boil Water," "New Zoo to Open."

Unless we are flexible enough to drop whatever we are doing and workup some activity to seize the moment, the chance for a valuable learning experience may be lost. Although "off-the-cuff" lessons do not involve sitting down weeks or months in advance of instruction to put together a lesson, spontaneous lessons do involve a good deal of thought on your part and may be just as valuable to children as our units prepared weeks in advance. The ability and creativity necessary to construct lessons—sometimes literally on the spot—is a skill that you need to practice and cultivate in your teaching.

Activating Lesson Experiences

In planning lesson experiences for children, one way to help you focus lesson experiences on children (and not content) is to identify an individual lesson by activities. The device used to highlight activities is called a *teaching map*. A teaching map presents a brief overview of what children will be doing during a given time frame, not what children should be able to do as a result of the activity. The differences between these two statements (emphasizing children doing versus what children should be able to do after the fact) helps to illustrate whether or not a lesson is child-centered or content-centered.

Using these two statements then, typically behaviorists begin lesson preparation with specific content in mind. Using this content-centered approach, these teachers designate curricula from math, science, the language arts, social studies, etc., that children should learn about. With the identified content in hand, teachers then devise lessons that will guide children to reproduce the content or to apply particular skills with the content. In this manner, teachers use behavioral objectives to predict what cognitive abilities or skills a child will have by the end of an experience. Thus, for example, "given the reading, the child will be able to identify the four main characters of the story with 100% accuracy."

The focus of this activity is on the adult prediction that child will be able to "identify the main characters of the story." What happens, however, if, after reading the story, a child cannot do this? Perhaps Kathryn believes that only one character is significant and, while Kathryn correctly recognizes one of the predicted main characters, say she did not think the other three were very important, what then? Is Kathryn wrong?

Predicting how children should act or think or that a child should be able to demonstrate a particular skill or recall a piece of information is important to many teachers. Nonetheless, holistic, child-centered teachers do not view teaching in terms of suspect predictable behaviors or outcomes. Holistic teachers who apply the synoptic method begin instruction planning with the four universal needs in mind, not content. It is this application of using children's needs as the foundation of lessons that makes the synoptic method uniquely child-centered.

In preparing your teaching map, then, using the four universal needs as guides, you map out activities/experiences that will specifically engage children with meeting their four universal needs. Content is applied not as an end product, but as a vehicle to satisfy the needs of children. However, as you work to meet needs, collaterally, children may also learn about content.

For example, returning to the example of Kathryn and the story, a synoptic teacher might design an experience in which Kathryn and her classmates draw illustrations about the story. In satisfying Kathryn's and her classmates' need for self-expression (drawing their own pictures), need for thought and action (interpreting the story line into pictures), and need for communication (collaborating with classmates, sharing crayons, deciding upon duties, cutting, pasting, etc.), Kathryn and her friends may also be able to describe or identify the main characters of the story.

In fact, in a discussion following the activity, if different teams of children set about the same task of illustrating the story for class presentations, the teacher could ask for comparisons, contrasts, and explanations for choices, as well as other questions about the various visual interpretations of the story. In this collective and shared discussion of what the story was all about, the main characters of the story will be revealed. Although agreement as to which characters are significant and which are not may not be reached, the point is that the teacher has engaged children in an activity in which they are in charge of their own learning. True, the teacher may instigate or create the learning environment or context, but the children determine the learning.

Thus, whereas the behaviorist teacher tests to see if children can name the main characters (which the teacher has established before the child completes the reading), the synoptic teacher prepares a need-based experience in which the main characters emerge through guided activity. Although the results of the behaviorist treatment and the synoptic experience may turn out to be the same (children identify main characters), the behaviorist application reinforces a passive model where the child is dependent upon a teacher's predicted answer, as opposed to the synoptic experience where the children are free to discover their own answer(s).

The question for you to investigate as you begin teaching is which approach will provide the most benefits for the child in terms of developing his and her own sense of well-being as well as fostering individual learning (metacognition). Although one resolution is presented in this textbook for your consideration (to become a synoptic teacher), as you enter the classroom you may want to experiment with both behaviorist and synoptic models to discover what works for you and your children. In helping you to gain a better sense of and practice with the synoptic method, challenge yourself to think about how the following ideas and examples might apply to your own lesson ideas.

Synoptic Lesson Plans

One of the most common devices used in teaching today is the lesson plan. Ideally, lesson plans outline—sometimes in great detail—what is to be taught and how. Why do teachers need to write out lesson plans? Lesson plans are a written record of your teaching. Although lesson plans require precious time to prepare, they are worth having as both a record of your work (for your principal to review and for legal reasons), and as a means to help you keep tract of your own teaching activities.

For some teachers, lesson plans organize lesson experiences that help them to pace and improve teaching efforts. For others, lesson plans save them from having to reprepare lessons for future classes. In effect, lesson plans serve as a living memory of past teaching efforts that may be recalled or activated quickly.

Lesson plans come in many different formats, for many different purposes. Some principals demand that all teachers use the same format; others do not. For example, many schools use the Madaline Hunter program or some other system that prescribes exactly what a teacher should put in a lesson plan. Other principals, however, allow teachers to prepare plans according to their own style of teaching. When you begin teaching, you might want to consider the "when in Rome, do as the Romans" theory. If your principal is familiar with child-centered/holistic approaches, you should not have much difficulty adjusting your synoptic lessons to the school format or, if need be, even to create your own plans. However, if your principal is neither familiar with or does not endorse child-centered/holistic teaching, you may not be able to practice your synoptic teaching, let alone write your own synoptic lesson plans.

The question of teacher empowerment is moot in a school that does not permit teachers to be empowered and a discussion of how to prepare your own plans might be pointless. However, we will continue to operate with the hopeful prospect that your future principal and fellow colleagues will not only be receptive to child-centered/holistic teaching, but will enthusiastically support your efforts to effect synoptic teaching.

An Overview of a Sample Synoptic Lesson Plan Format

What, then, does a synoptic lesson plan look like? The answer is as you might expect—a synoptic lesson plan is what you decide it will be. Although you may be happy to have this freedom to do what you think is right, the question may still linger: Yes, I'm free to decide, but, still what should a synoptic lesson plan look like?

Major Components of Synoptic Lesson Plans

The components of a synoptic lesson plan are:

Needs addressed
Acceptance or thought and action
Activity/purpose of experience
Sequence of activities
Elements of social studies formula applied
Assessment of children
Materials/resources needed

Needs Addressed, Acceptance or Thought and Action
Early in the plan you should identify what needs will be addressed. In addition, you need to decide if the lesson experience will focus on acceptance or thought and action methods, or any combination of the two. (Review chapter 4 for descriptions of acceptance [generally telling children information] and thought and action [foster the growth of independent thinking and learning]).

The decision of what needs to emphasize can be determined by the following rules.

1. Whenever you have children working together communication can be applied.
2. If you want children to practice planning, designing, and execution according to some known model, construction can be applied.

3. If you would like your children to work on their independent, critical thinking-learning skills, thought and action can be applied.
4. Finally, if you desire to create opportunities for children to express themselves without criticism (from you), self-expression can be applied.

Although combinations of the four needs emerge with most experiences—communication with thought and action, self-expression with thought and action, communication with construction—teachers should be aware of the different aspects and characteristics of each of the four needs. For example, if the children were to plan a trip to Russia, all four of the needs could be engaged. As the children discuss how they would get to Russia, how long they would stay, and where they would visit, communication needs are addressed. When the children make their passports, and do pretrip reports on necessary shots, papers to be prepared, clothes and other personal items to bring, construction needs are addressed. When Russia became the destination country and a host of questions are posed for the children or raised by the children themselves to investigate (inquiry), thought and action needs are addressed. Finally, as the children write a play about their trip, draw pictures, or share a diary of the wonders they encountered in Russia, self-expression needs are addressed.

As you think about this example, you may see many other variations that capitalize on thought and action ideas ranging from discovery to reflection. Thought and action contains a number of promising possibilities for children to make decisions, generate ideas, explore, solve problems, and more. The potential lesson variations are limited only to your imagination and that of your children.

Activity/Experience

Following the needs and acceptance/thought and action decisions, you should clearly describe the main activity of the lesson. Try to capture the essence or nature of the individual or class experience in a brief statement containing action verbs. Incidently, when building a unit, these statements (declarations) of individual lessons can be used for your teaching map. The following are examples of individual lesson activities. Today we will

Build medieval castles
Explore Japanese culture
Visit a New England seaport village
Cook and eat a full course traditional Irish dinner
Develop the concept of work ethic
Draw a map of your neighborhood
Talk about our favorite books

Each of these statements suggests that at least one universal need is being applied. When we say that the children will draw a map of the community, a host of questions and decisions should flood the teacher and children's minds. What kind of map will it be? How big? Can everyone make their own map? Should we make several group maps or perhaps one giant classroom map? What materials should we use? How will we gather enough information about the community to complete a map? What plans have to be made? What tasks need to be done? Who will do these tasks? What will we do with this map?

For the map lesson, the teacher instigates but does not direct the activity. The teacher is responsible for helping children direct their own learning. The synoptic teacher enlists children to pose questions, make choices, organize plans, and begin work. The room should become a flurry of activity—children moving about, reading resource materials, checking equipment, drawing blueprints, forming groups, developing ideas, discussing options, planning information excursions and more. Children love activities; your role is to keep the excitement and momentum going.

Sequence of Activities

With all the busy children in motion, it is often helpful for you to keep an eye on the flow of the activity. To assist you, write down a suggested sequence of events that outlines the main actions of the lesson—what do we do first, second, and so forth. Include here any ideas or actions the children or you will have to consider or become engaged in. Additionally, any other information on readings, use of materials, and other special considerations should be noted. Although you may have to alter the plan as you see fit during a lesson, the sequence of activities helps you and the children to stay on a relatively even pace. The sequence should to be detailed enough for you to follow, but not so detailed as to limit or prevent variation if necessary.

Elements of the Social Studies Formula

As conceived in this textbook, the social studies formula is designed to help children not only to understand more about a topic, but also to enjoy the experiences more. Therefore, recalling the soup analogy of chapter 5, the social studies formula is suggested as a seasoning that adds flavor and texture to the soup (activity); the formula itself should not be the only thing on the plate. The main course of the lesson experience is the activity and the needs being attended to.

Before, as well as during, the lesson you may want to consider ways to enhance the lesson with elements of the social studies formula. If you take that trip to Russia, bring in some globes and maps. Identify where you are and how far away Russia is. Have the children note the various countries and different land forms you will pass on your imaginary trip. Russia is a very large country with vast resources; however, the nation depends upon a number of countries for its needs—bring in some books with charts and graphs that describe Russia and its trading partners.

Look for ways to introduce historical information, too. Children can build time-lines to the past, read stories about Russian children, stage folktales, write stories about Czars and Czarinas, and more. In addition, watch for major concepts to integrate into the lesson as well as selected issues to introduce and discuss with children. Good sources for concepts and issues are newspapers, major news magazines, and television programs that might help bring Russia and its people into focus for your children. You may also want to write to the Russian Embassy for information about developing pen pals with Russian children (see appendix C).

Assessment

Assessment has been traditionally and continues to be an important part of teaching and learning. However, because synoptic teachers emphasize activities/experiences that are based upon the four universal needs, formal assessment of children appears inconsistent with child-centered/holistic teaching. Furthermore, because synoptic teachers have an intimate knowledge of their own children, they should be able to gain a strong sense of the achievements and learnings of their children without formal testing.

Synoptic teachers create experiences and facilitate activities that work to satisfy children's needs. This action naturally activates a child's mental and physical abilities, special talents, and imagination. Assessment given under these conditions is not used to merely determine or demonstrate learning or knowledge acquisition, but to improve the actual conditions for potential learning experiences. Because synoptic lessons are based on needs satisfaction and not content attainment, standardized and criterion-referenced tests, as well as other forms of summative and formative evaluations are not particularly helpful, or even appropriate.

Despite the philosophical inconsistencies between synoptic assessment and more traditional methods, teachers should work to ascertain the child's level of understanding/learning, the degree to which a child can apply a particular skill, and any other useful piece of assessment information. However, this assessment information should be gathered only if the information may prove helpful to either enhance teaching or further learning opportunities.

Given this setting, assessment information is valuable because it documents your teaching efforts and it helps both teachers and children realize what has been understood and perhaps learned. Also assessment information can reveal what connections (relationships), if any, were made from the child to the activity, what was fun and interesting, what skills need practice, what experiences were valuable, and whatever collateral information was learned. In short, assessment tells us what happened as a result of children being exposed to a particular activity or experience so that we can improve or enhance future teaching experiences.

Recently, a special publication of the Association for Supervision and Curriculum Development (ASCD)[1] suggested that teachers should explore new and innovative ways to assess children. According to ASCD, the core of assessment

---

[1]See Vito Perrone, ed. (1991). *Expanding student assessment.* Alexandria, VA: Association for Supervision and Curriculum Development.

begins with a teacher's daily, weekly, and monthly observations. As discussed in chapter 3 on youth culture, teachers should become skilled in recognizing whatever interests, attitudes, beliefs, and values a child may hold. In addition, teachers should note particular skills, abilities, and other outward characteristics of their children. Observations make use of a number of different instruments such as written anecdotal logs, rating lists, and other checklist forms that assist teachers and children.

Another example of assessment is a performance sample that represents what a child has actually accomplished. These samples include items such as creative writing, written documents, role playing, speeches, and personal interviews. Other performance samples would include group or individual projects, staged plays, art work, completed readings, video and audio recordings, and other specific assignments. As with observations, performance samples can be reported by checklists, rating sheets, daily logs or diaries, actual demonstrations, and other various projects.

In finding new ways to help children learn, ASCD suggests two assessment practices that provide many interesting possibilities for synoptic teaching. The first technique (ASCD calls these *attitudes*) involves teachers, with informal keeping track assessments that describe what each child is doing or has done. Keeping track assessments ask, What activities have children been involved in? What books has a child been reading? Which children have not yet finished the activities? (ASCD, p. 29)

The second ASCD idea calls for teachers to assess children by "finding out" or figuring out what is going on: What did the child mean? What do you suppose the children got from that story (Versus did they get the main idea)? (ASCD, p. 30).

In sum, ASCD suggests that new assessment techniques move away from standardized testing and move toward assessments that:

- are ongoing and cumulative
- use open-ended formats
- draw upon a variety of settings
- are theory-referenced
- are teacher-mediated. (ASCD, p. 31)

Because there is little prospect of designing and implementing effective assessment instruments within a university methods course (typically we have no children to practice with), many of your assessment skills will have to be crafted while you are student teaching and later refined when you become a classroom teacher. Consequently, although we may presently lack the opportunity to practice on children, we still can develop our skills in designing assessment instruments that keep track of and find out about children's accomplishments through observations and performance samples.

Materials/Resources

The final section of the lesson plan should include some information about the resources and materials needed for the activities, as well as whatever resources were used to prepare the lesson experience. Much of this information can be taken directly from your teaching kit (refer to chapter 1 for details).

You might want to include information on specific books or readings you completed, as well as any other information that helped you put together the lesson. This record of your background work can be used for later lessons, as well as a springboard to other teaching ideas. References to resources and materials used in the lesson not only help you keep track of what will be needed for the activity/experience, but also are useful for planning.

Summary

For the synoptic method to work for you, you will need to take time to practice your synoptic teaching. In the methods classroom, you have worked to develop dispositions and skills that prepare you and facilitate your role as an elementary teacher responsible for nurturing young citizens of a liberal democracy. You have also begun to practice your developing teaching techniques.

As you make the transition to the elementary school, it is hoped that you will have both the desire and opportunity to continue to practice at your synoptic craft. Practice doesn't always make perfect, but determined practice is critical to successful teaching. The following chapter presents an overview of the current state of social studies. As you will see, activating the synoptic method in elementary schools may be a real challenge no matter what methodologies or content is used. However, although putting together all the elements of the synoptic method takes commitment and hard work, this "journey of a thousand miles" will be well worth the effort if you can help just one child to build a meaningful relationships between themselves and to the world.

Marking Your Progress

Synoptic Method

Teaching Matrix

Topic _____

ACC/THOUGHT-ACTION	SS FORMULA	ASSESSMENT

1. Needs

(continued)

Marking Your Progress

Communication

Construction

Thought and Action

Self-Expression

2. Use the matrix to
    Identify which needs are applied
    Note acceptance and thought and action experiences
    Highlight particular elements of social studies formula
    Indicate assessment techniques

A Lesson Plan Checklist

1. Goals/purpose
2. Brief overview of lesson
3. Nature of experience
    telling, watching, showing, doing (activity), questioning, going (outdoors/field trip), individual work, group project
4. Motivation
    interests of children, problem/dilemma/puzzle, novel object/artifact, reward, competition
5. Sequence of activity (what comes first, second, etc.)
6. Actual children's activities
    listening, working in groups, construction, self-expression, drawing and art work, free time, watching, telling, reading, observation, writing, thought and action activities
7. Things to reinforce time-on-task/motivation
    praise, rewards (stars, candy, privileges), acknowledgment of achievement, letters to parents/guardians, fun time
8. Assessment of children
    real assessment techniques, informal and formal observations/assessment, self-assessment, oral tests, pen and pencil tests
9. Materials needed
    teaching kit, writing materials, books, records and tapes, pictures, charts, and other visual aids, building tools, special equipment, historical and other important objects/artifacts, miscellaneous items

This is not a thorough list, you are encouraged to add (or subtract) from the list as needed.

Read More about It Special References

The actual construction of synoptic lessons will vary from teacher to teacher based upon the special needs/interests of children and/or curricular requirements of your local district. In fact, many schools proscribe the lesson plan. The following references contain many excellent ideas for the teaching of social studies. At this point, however, of particular interest will be references on interdisciplinary design, technology, assessment, and curriculum planning.

Banks, J., & Banks, C. A. (1989). *Multicultural education: Issues and perspectives.* Boston: Allyn and Bacon.

> *No social studies curriculum could be complete without special attention and understanding of multicultural education, gender studies, and exceptional learner themes. Banks and Banks offer the most comprehensive accounting of these topics and more for social studies teachers. The text is not for elementary children; however, Banks and Banks have brought together a number of excellent essays that should be read and digested by all elementary teachers before they begin curricula construction.*

Budin, H., Kendall, D., & Lengel, J. (1986). *Using computers in the social studies.* New York: Teachers College Press.

> *There are many guides to using computers in elementary classes, but few specifically attend to social studies. Although dated in terms of technology, this brief, readable text provides a number of helpful suggestions for both experienced computer operators and novices.*

Egan, K. (1990). *Romantic understanding.* New York: Routledge.

Egan, K. (1986). *Teaching as story telling.* Chicago: University of Chicago Press.

> *Egan presents an interesting and innovative way of helping children not only enjoy, but learn about social studies themes, especially history. Elementary teachers will also appreciate that Egan explores the development of rationality and imagination. These texts should prove very helpful in lesson preparation and design.*

Gall, M. D., Gall, J., Jacobsen, D. R., & Bullock, T. (1990). *Tools for learning: A guide to teaching study skills.* Alexandria, VA: Association for Supervision and Curriculum Development.

> *One element of teaching often neglected by teachers is how to help children learn, to study better and more effectively. This ASCD text offers a number of practical suggestions that can be applied to elementary age children.*

Jacobs, H. H., ed. (1989). *Interdisciplinary curriculum design and implementation.* Alexandria, VA: Association for Supervision and Curriculum Development.

> *This is an excellent source for those who are seeking to forge a meaningful relationship between discrete disciplines and children. As is typical of ASCD publications, the discussions are state-of-the-art and thorough.*

Key School. (1990). *Connections, animal patterns, changes in time and space.* Indianapolis: Indianapolis Public Schools.

Key School. (1990). *Working in harmony.* Indianapolis: Indianapolis Public Schools.

> *These publications represent practical applications of Howard Garner's theory of seven intelligences. Developed and tested by elementary teachers, these texts contain actual lesson plans (with detailed instructions) divided by themes and by grade.*

Massialas, B. G., & Cox, C. B. (1966). *Inquiry in social studies.* New York: McGraw-Hill.

> *At one time inquiry-style teaching was the most talked about method of teaching social studies. This text, which should be available in libraries or through interlibrary loan, is representative of the best thinking and application of inquiry for social studies. As in*

most social studies texts, Massialas and Cox have directed their efforts primarily for secondary students; however, elementary teachers should be able to adapt lessons for children.

National Council for the Social Studies. (1990). *Social studies curriculum planning resources*. Dubuque, IA: Kendall/Hunt.

This must for all elementary teachers is the state-of-the-art text on social studies curriculum planning. Contains major policy statements of the NCSS (the professional teachers' organization devoted solely to social studies in schools), including a special section on early childhood and elementary school children. An excellent source with many first-rate references.

Perrone, V., ed. (1991). *Expanding student assessment*. Alexandria, VA: Association for Supervision and Curriculum Development.

Perrone has put together a number of well-written essays that tackle the thorny question of how do teachers honestly assess the progress and achievement of children. This brief text is a must for elementary teachers seeking to break out of the routine of pen-and-pencil rote testing.

Routman, R. (1991). *Invitations*. Portsmouth, NH: Heinemann.

An excellent overview of holistic teaching, complete with an extensive teacher resource list (fully annotated).

Slavin, R. E. (1990). *Cooperative learning*. Boston: Allyn and Bacon.

More than any single researcher of the past twenty years, Slavin has done more to revive the notion of effective teaching through small group. This text clearly explains how teachers can use small groups techniques with children. In addition, Slavin reviews research projects that illustrate to what degree cooperative learning promotes student achievement.

Social Studies Curriculum Resource Handbook. (1992). Millwood, NY: Kraus International.

Although directed to student-centered teaching, synoptic teachers will find the many annotated references very helpful; a must for school library.

Social studies in British Columbia. (1991). Technical report of the 1989 Social Studies Assessment. Assessment, Examinations and Reporting Branch, Ministry of Education (Canada).

A good overview of standard assessment practice with numerous examples based upon a study of over 100,000 students in grades four, seven, and ten. Elementary teachers should be able to adapt many of the assessment examples to the synoptic method.

7

SOCIAL STUDIES AND SCHOOLS

In this chapter you will

- Compare and contrast your work with the synoptic method with prevailing methods and dispositions found in many elementary schools.
- Assess the merits and shortcomings of the synoptic method approach to social studies.
- Reflect upon your developing philosophy of teaching and learning.
- Begin preparing for your opportunity to help children learn to become more valued and productive citizens.

When you first learned you were required to take a social studies course to obtain your certification or when you decided to read this book to become more familiar with social studies, what thoughts came to mind? Typically, people associate elementary social studies with the study of specific topics in history and geography, while others might add civics or government to this brief list.

Although we have explored the use of the social studies formula, to many people social studies is simply important dates, famous people, and key events in the history of the world and the United States. Social studies is also the names of states, location of countries, and other geographic terms. Additionally, social studies might mean activities such as book reports on Eleanor Roosevelt or Susan B. Anthony, memorization of the last names of every president, and naming the continents. Perhaps you may have discovered by now that this description of social studies is far too narrow and confined to serve a liberal democracy.

Despite the potential of the brand of social studies fostered by the synoptic method, the situation in many schools is to rely exclusively on the rote memorization of facts from topics in history and geography. In sum, the reality is that most social studies teaching is subject/content-centered, not child-holistic centered. As discussed in chapter 3, in practice the focus of most schools is placed upon presenting prepackaged materials to passive learners.

What Children and Teachers Tell Us about Social Studies

To gain a sense of the state of social studies education in American elementary schools, this chapter will present research findings that reveal attitudes of both children and teachers toward social studies and a sampling of national, state, and local social studies curricular patterns. In addition, a brief historical perspective of the beginnings of social studies will also be presented.

The purpose of this discussion is to give an overview of the type of expectations and requirements typically found with the teaching of social studies in elementary schools. Although child-centered and holistic models have been in use for many years, as you will see these models are far from the accepted norm. In chapter 3 you were challenged to explore the synoptic method as a means to activate a child-centered, holistic curriculum. As you review the state of social studies, perhaps you will not only see the potential for the synoptic method, but also come to recognize some of the challenges associated with activating a new method of teaching.

Before we examine the existing patterns of social studies in elementary schools and their historical antecedents, we will first identify and describe what children and teachers think about social studies. In addition, we shall look at how social studies is currently presented in elementary schools.

Some Children's Views on Social Studies

What do children think of the prevailing brand of social studies? You may want to begin answering this question with your own experiences. Given your past experiences, how do you feel about social studies? Was social studies your favorite or least favorite subject in school? Do you remember social studies in your elementary school experiences? What activities did you do? What experiences did you have? Were they positive? Did your friends like social studies? And finally, what about your teachers? Could you tell if they enjoyed presenting social studies experiences?

As a beginning elementary teacher (or an elementary teacher beginning a new approach toward social studies), these are important questions. When you return to the elementary class, this time you will be sitting in the teacher's chair. It will be your responsibility to present meaningful experiences. When your children leave your class, will they take happy, pleasant, and useful experiences with them? Will they be able to say your efforts made a difference in their lives? Will they say social studies was fun and interesting?

In recent years some educational researchers have sought to document children's attitudes toward social studies. One group of researchers reported two basic results, one negative and one positive: children generally do not like social studies experiences that are unchallenging and render the learner passive; however, children generally do like social studies when a variety of experiences that activate learners. Children who did not like social studies revealed to researchers that:

1. Young people do not feel social studies is a particularly valuable or interesting part of the school curriculum.
2. English, mathematics, and reading were more important than social studies.
3. Social studies is not perceived as being a particularly enjoyable subject.
4. Many students find social studies content to be uninteresting because the information is too far removed from their own experiences, too detailed for clear understanding, or repeats information learned earlier.

5. The most frequent comment (from children who thought social studies was uninteresting) was that social studies was boring.[1]

Adding to this list, another researcher claimed,

One of the things we know—and sometimes wish we didn't—is that social studies usually ranks as the subject children like least (or hate most). To make matters worse, they do not see it as useful. . . . [S]ocial studies . . . is apt to be regarded as an unnecessary evil—as something students could just as readily do without.[2]

Given statements like these, Carole Hahn, a careful and thoughtful writer on social studies, lamented that social studies in elementary schools (using a medical analogy) was "not well, especially in the primary grades."[3] Because so many elementary schools (particularly in the lower grades) offer little social studies instruction, Hahn's observation may be an understatement of actual conditions. As a self-check, how do these results compare to your attitudes toward social studies? Did you remember your elementary social studies as

- unimportant?
- uninteresting?
- less important than English, mathematics, and reading?
- not enjoyable?
- too far removed from your own experiences?
- too boring?

What do you suppose children think about social studies today at your local elementary school? During your visits to schools you may want to use the above items as guides to ask children to characterize their social studies experiences and attitudes. It might be interesting (as well as helpful) to find out if these research results match your personal attitudes (and remembrances) toward social studies as well as the attitudes of your local elementary children.

You should not be too surprised if you find that social studies is not a favorite among most children. As you ask yourself and others questions about social studies, you may also begin to speculate about elementary teachers' views of social studies.

---

[1]"Why Kids Don't Like Social Studies," Mark C. Schug, Robert Todd, and R. Berry, *Social Education*, 48, no. 5 (May 1984): 382–87.

[2]David A. Welton, "What we Know About Teaching Elementary Social Studies," *Social Education*, 45, no. 3 (March 1981): 191.

[3]Carole L. Hahn, "The Status of the Social Studies in the Public Schools of the United States: Another Look," *Social Education*, 49, no. 3 (March 1985): 220.

Some Teachers' Views on Social Studies

What do teachers think about social studies? If a good proportion of children say they do not like social studies, do you suppose teachers might hold similar attitudes? Do you think your elementary teachers liked social studies? Similar to studies on student perceptions on social studies, educational researchers have also sought to discover the perceptions elementary teachers hold toward social studies.

Two basic patterns of social studies emerge with elementary schools, those associated with kindergarten through third grade and those found in fourth through sixth grades. Apparently the division between third and fourth grade is directly related to subject offerings. Typically many states require state history to be presented in fourth grade, while most states do not mandate any specific social studies for kindergarten through third grade. Within these two divisions (kindergarten through third grade and fourth through sixth grades) attitudes toward social studies vary. In the lower grades one researcher found that social studies is "known as 'afternoon time': that is, [social studies] is taken up after lunch or close to dismissal, when the serious work is over." Continuing, this researcher noted,

> *One teacher told me that she was sorry I was visiting in the afternoon: "We do academics in the morning when children are fresh." Social studies is known as "bump time": the [subject] that gets dropped if there is an extra assembly or an early school closing or some other interfering event.*[4]

In 1977, a social studies researcher reported that elementary teachers "were backing away from social studies."[5] This perception was later confirmed in a major study of public schools conducted by John Goodlad, which revealed that significantly more time was devoted to language arts and math than to social studies.[6] Two other reports of social studies offered similar data and one found that social studies "was literally fighting for existence" in kindergarten through third grade.[7]

In a related research finding, some teachers have reported greater confidence and felt more qualified teaching mathematics or language arts than teaching social studies.[8] Covering a wide range of recent social studies research, including teacher beliefs about social studies, student thinking in social studies,

[4]David Jenness, *Making Sense of Social Studies* (New York: Macmillan, 1990): 382.

[5]Richard Gross, "The Status of Social Studies in the Public Schools of the United States: Facts and Impressions of a National Survey," *Social Education*, 41, No. 3 (March 1977): 194–205.

[6]John Goodlad, *A Place Called School* (New York: McGraw-Hill, 1984).

[7]Irving Morrissett, et al., and James Shaver, et al. as reported in Virginia Atwood, *Elementary Social Studies: Research As a Guide to Practice*, Bulletin 79 (Washington, DC: National Council for the Social Studies, 1986): 2–6.

[8]Mary Van Eslinger and Douglas P. Superka, "Teachers," in Irving Morrissett, ed., *Social Studies in the 1980s* (Alexandria, VA: Association for Supervision and Curriculum Development, 1982): 52–53.

and conceptions of planning in social studies, another source that supports these data is the *Handbook of Research on Social Studies Teaching and Learning.*[9]

The general picture that these reports suggest is that teachers do not perceive social studies to be as important as other subject areas. What about you? Of the four academic areas (science, mathematics, language arts, and social studies) which is your favorite? Which do you feel most confident to teach? Which do you think your children will like the most? How would you rank order experiences? Which subject areas do you feel most confident to teach?

If you believe that each subject area is important and that you are competent to teach any one or all of these, these questions may seem strange. Yet, as you begin teaching, you will find that available time, effort, motivation, and opportunity may strain your initial idealism to present meaningful experiences which reflect each emphasis area. For elementary teachers under the pressure of time and other constraints, the issue is then raised (especially for kindergarten through third grade teachers): What should I devote my energies toward? Just as was suggested with children's attitudes, you may find it enlightening to ask some elementary teachers what they think about this issue—what they hold to be of value.

How Social Studies Is Presented in Elementary Schools

Throughout this century, the principal methods of instruction in elementary social studies can be characterized by four techniques:[10]

- lecture
- recitation
- textbook readings
- completing worksheets

Given your own experiences, you may not find these data surprising. However, you may find it surprising that one group of researchers found that "as much as 90 percent of classroom instruction is structured by instructional materials, especially textbook."[11] In a related study, researchers confirmed that 90 percent of teaching time in social studies was centered around curriculum materials, while at least 60 percent of class time was spent on printed materials (textbooks).[12]

[9]James P. Shaver, ed. *Handbook of Research on Social Studies Teaching and Learning* (New York: Macmillan, 1991).

[10]Goodlad, 213.

[11]Arthur Woodward, David L. Elliott, and Kathleen Carter Nagel, "Beyond Textbooks in Elementary Social Studies," *Social Education*, 50, No. 1 (January 1986): 51.

[12]Data reported in Douglas P. Superka, Sharryl Hawke, and Irving Morrissett, "The Current and Future Status of the Social Studies," *Social Education*, 44, no. 5 (May 1980): 366.

John Goodlad's study also revealed that kindergarten through third grade teachers taught social studies 25 minutes per day, whereas in grades four through six teachers spent approximately 46 minutes per day.[13] During "social studies" time, researchers found that teachers frequently relied upon lecture and discussion, approximately one-quarter of the teachers said they lectured daily (including kindergarten through third grade teachers) and roughly 60 percent of the teachers said they used discussions daily.[14]

When teachers lectured, researchers found that fact information learning was highlighted and expected. Moreover, teachers did not emphasize independent thinking, experience-based curricula, or participation; children were intentionally required to accept whatever was taught without question.[15] These same researchers also found that when teachers did hold discussions, discussions were typically large group and dominated by teachers. In addition, teachers did not develop lessons according to children's interests, but used external motivations such as grades and teacher approval—"doing one's lessons is the thing that is done in school."[16]

In sum, when engaged in social studies, children typically are listening to their teacher talk to them, reading their text materials aloud or to themselves, completing worksheets or workbooks in small groups or alone, and taking quizzes. No doubt there are teachers (and classrooms) where exciting and dynamic social studies take place; however, from what research is available such experiences are not commonplace.[17]

Given available research on attitudes of children and teachers on typical instructional practices and emphases, perhaps confirmed by your own research on these topics, we are not left wondering why children and teachers do not like social studies. If teachers are to persist teaching social studies regardless of children's dissatisfaction or even their own, clearly the continuation of mindless lecture, discussion, worksheets formats, based upon irrelevant and unconnected fact information methods determined outside of any meaningful consideration of children's needs must be seriously reconsidered and adjusted or abandoned outright.

As you are challenged to enlist in the battle for children, in a related sense, your next enlistment is to become engaged in the battle to eject uninteresting, uninspired, and ill-suited social studies curricula from elementary schools, beginning with your classroom. In this spirit, the following studies are presented for your discussion and reflection.

---

[13]Goodlad, 199.

[14]Superka et al., 367.

[15]James Shaver et al. "The Status of Social Studies Education: Impressions from Three NSF Studies," *Social Education*, 43, no. 2 (February 1979): 151.

[16]Shaver et al., 151.

[17]Nathalie J. Gehrke, Michael S. Knapp, and Kenneth A. Sirotnik, "In Search of the School Curriculum," in Gerald Grant, ed. *Review of Research in Education*, 18th Yearbook of the American Educational Research Association (1992).

What Researchers Tell Us about the Potential and Promise of Social Studies

What is the research base for elementary social studies? This question is part of a policy statement issued in 1990 by the National Council for the Social Studies (NCSS) Task Force on Early Childhood/Elementary Education. A necessary component of any sound educational idea or program is a solid research base; that is, the proposed (or ongoing) idea or program has been tested (and retested) with some measure of success. Admittedly, the synoptic method was founded on a theory or philosophical base, not an empirical research base. Yet you yourself (through this course and textbook) are currently testing the synoptic method and, perhaps, when you begin teaching you will continue to test the synoptic method.

Despite its ultimate source, the synoptic method is related to research in the field of education and social studies, not merely as a reaction to the reported dismal condition of social studies, but also in response to other reported data. The NCSS task force prepared a brief listing of research data that are directly and indirectly connected to the aims and proposals of the synoptic method. Given this connection, it is appropriate that these data be summarized here. Although these data are grouped according to prevailing patterns, they do provide important underpinnings and applications for use with the synoptic method (Table 7-1).

Another excellent source for identifying promising research related to elementary social studies is the massive *Handbook of Research on Social Studies Teaching and Learning* (see footnote 9). The *Handbook* provides an accurate and thorough overview of a number of social studies topics, issues, and concerns, as well as a picture of social studies in general. One distinct message that the *Handbook* repeats through its many chapters is that although social studies research can be valuable, not enough social studies research is being attempted, completed, and disseminated for practical classroom application.

The Dominant Social Studies Pattern

So far we have looked at how children and teachers feel about social studies, the prevailing practices, and the promise of research for social studies in the elementary grades. We turn next to existing patterns of social studies in elementary schools and their historical antecedents. Remember that this sampling of a national social studies curriculum is not presented as an endorsement to follow, but merely as an overview of curricula to reflect upon. The NCSS suggests the focuses shown in Table 7-2 for applications of democratic beliefs and values.

What do existing social studies curricula emphasize? In general, social studies follows a pattern of topics or themes that have become known as the

TABLE 7-1   Research Data Applied to the Synoptic Method

- Young children who are active participants in a highly structured and sequential series of geographic inquiries can learn complex analytic processes and concepts of geography (Crabtree 1974; GENIP Committee on K–6 Geography 1987; Muessig 1987).

- Evidence indicates that children do possess complex spatial information and can abstract information from map symbols (Hewes 1982; Hatcher 1983; Park and James 1983; Liben, Moore, and Golbeck 1982).

- Children can learn cardinal directions as early as kindergarten (Lanegran, Snowfield, and Laurent 1970).

- The type of discourse used in history teaching appears to influence student interest. Children who encountered historical data in the form of biography and historical fiction exhibited interest in and enthusiasm for history and for further investigation in more traditional sources (Levstik 1986).

- Historical and geographical understanding may not be linked to the developmental patterns associated with acquiring physical time concepts (Kennedy 1983).

- Children are more open to diversity in the early elementary years than in later years (Stone 1986). A fourth grader, for instance, is more likely to express interest in studying and visiting foreign countries than an eighth grader.

- Positive self-concepts, important in positively perceiving and judging social interactions, also form during these crucial early years (Stanley 1985, 77). Particular classroom environments seem to influence the ways children develop these interactions. Teachers who appear to enjoy teaching, who include student-to-student interaction, shared decision making, and positive student-to-teacher interactions, foster more positive self-concepts in their pupils.

- As early as kindergarten, students engage in citizenship education, both covert and overt (Edwards 1986).

- Political feelings, evaluations, and attachments form well before the child learns the relevant supporting information (Greenstein 1969, 72).

- By eighth grade, children have already acquired basic orientations, and political socialization is generally well advanced by the end of elementary school (Hess and Torney 1967, 220).

- By the eighth grade, children have developed a sense of the need for consensus and majority rule in the democratic process. They have not recognized the role of debate, disagreement, and conflict in the operation of a democratic political system (Hess and Torney 1967, 216).

- A developed sense of justice and law appears to be requisite to democratic citizenship (Kohlberg 1976, 213). Particular types of classroom environments, including discussions in which students must actively think and communicate about another's reasoning, appear to facilitate this type of growth (Berkowitz 1981; Berkowitz and Gibbs 1983).

- By age seven, children have formulated fairly accurate conceptions of work, wants, and scarcity and evidence the capability of developing a method for making decisions (Armento 1986).

(Continued)

TABLE 7-1 *(Continued)*

- Pictures and other concretizing tools can greatly benefit children with learning disabilities and those who have not enjoyed a broad variety of experience (Armento 1986).

- Interest in and analysis of racial and ethnic differences begin early. Between the ages of six and nine, children begin to identify their own racial group as "better than the outgroup" (Semaj 1980, 76).

- Acquisition of concepts about racial and ethnic groups is complex, but there is evidence that early, planned, and structured activities can result in improving positive attitudes in children (Katz 1976, 234).

- Elementary age children are already well aware of societal attitudes toward different groups (e.g., housing patterns, dating, and marriage mores). Research also indicates that elementary children can think critically about these patterns where they have sufficient experience and active involvement in discussion and inquiry (Ragan and McAulay 1973).

Reproduced with permission from the National Council for the Social Studies Task Force on Early Childhood/Elementary Education. (1990). *Social studies curriculum planning resources,* 79–800.

"expanding horizons" or "expanding communities" model.[18] Typically a study begins with the individual (self) in kindergarten, shifts to groups (family-home) in first grade, and extends to larger groups (neighborhood, community, region, and state) in second through fourth grades, and eventually extends outward to the nation and world beyond in fifth and sixth grades. Much of the content of this elementary social studies sequence emphasizes information and facts, not children's needs.

Throughout the United States elementary schools have purchased textbook series that follow the expanding horizons model.[19] Although major publishers use this basic scope (the breadth content and skills to be taught and to what degree) and sequence (when taught), none acknowledge the source or development of expanding horizons. If the expanding horizons model does indeed dominate elementary schools, what is its source? Who were/are its advocates? Why does it persist?

Social Studies in Perspective

To begin to gain a sense of expanding horizons, we first need to discover some details about the origins of social studies. Social studies was developed during the early part of the twentieth century by a group of progressive educational

---

[18]Jere Brophy (1992), "The Defacto National Curriculum in U.S. Elementary Social Studies: Critique of a representative example," *Journal of Curriculum Studies* 24(5):401–447.

[19]A selected list of major publishers of social studies series for elementary grades include Harcourt Brace Jovanovich, Houghton Mifflin, Macmillan, McGraw-Hill, and Silver, Burdett and Ginn.

TABLE 7-2   Illustrative Examples of Applications of Democratic Beliefs and Values

Grade	Central Focus	Democratic Rights, Freedoms, Responsibilities, or Beliefs Addressed	Illustrations of Opportunities
K	Awareness of self in a social setting	1. Right to security 2. Right to equal opportunity 3. Respect for others' rights 4. Honesty	1. Explore how rules make a room safe for everyone. 2. Every child is scheduled to be a leader for a day. 3. Focus on common courtesies; e.g., when someone speaks, one should listen. 4. The teacher reinforces honesty as exhibited by children.
1	The individual in primary social groups	1. Impartiality 2. Freedom of worship 3. Consideration for others	1. When an altercation is reported, the teacher tries to find out exactly what happened before taking action. 2. Stress that each family decides whether or not or how to worship. 3. Everyone has a right to a turn.
2	Meeting basic needs in nearby social groups	1. Respect for property 2. Respect for laws 3. Value personal integrity	1. Discuss vandalism in neighborhoods. 2. Laws protect the safety of people. 3. Explore the importance of keeping promises.
3	Sharing earth space with others	1. Pursuing individual and group goals 2. Government works for the common good	1. Goods are exchanged with other places to meet the needs of the people. 2. Government is concerned about the unemployed and works to reduce unemployment.
4	Human life in varied environments	1. Respect for the rights of others 2. Respect for different ways of living	1. Respect the right of individuals from other cultures to have different values. 2. Appreciate that life-styles of people in other places are different from ours.
5	People of the Americas	1. Freedom to worship 2. Right of privacy 3. Freedom of assembly	1. People came to the Americas because of religious persecution. 2. A home cannot be searched without a warrant except under most unusual circumstances. 3. Laws may not prohibit people from getting together in groups for any lawful purpose.
6	People and cultures	1. Governments respect and protect individual freedoms	1. Compare the record of various governments in protecting individual freedoms.

(Continued)

TABLE 7-2 *(Continued)*

Grade	Central Focus	Democratic Rights, Freedoms, Responsibilities, or Beliefs Addressed	Illustrations of Opportunities
		2. Right to life 3. Right to justice	2. Study societies in which individual human rights are not respected. 3. Examine various types of judicial systems.
7	A changing world of many nations	1. Freedom to participate in the political process 2. Right to equality of opportunity 3. Use of government to guarantee civil liberties	1. Discuss the anticolonial movement in parts of the world. 2. Discuss social class systems in various parts of the world. 3. Debate the status of civil liberties in developing nations.
8	Building a strong and free nation	1. Right to liberty 2. Participation in the democratic process 3. Freedom of expression	1. Discuss the injustices of slavery. 2. Analyze the voting record of Americans and particularly that of young people. 3. Study the debates and compromises reached in the development of the Constitution.

Reproduced with permission from the National Council for the Social Studies Task Force on Early Childhood Elementary Education. (1990). Social studies curriculum planning resources, 33.

thinkers who were responding to a number of pressing social conditions. Additionally, these thinkers were attempting to identify curricula that would further liberal democratic principles. By the beginning of the century, rapid urbanization, industrialization, and immigration placed enormous pressures on American society. Many thoughtful men and women believed that education held the key for maintaining the democratic character of the United States amid all the hustle and bustle of urban and industrial change.

In addition to preserving democracy, the education of American youth was viewed as a necessary part of individual and national progress. Thus, for America to retain and expand its form of democracy and make individual, social, political, cultural, and economic advances, educating young people (all young people) became a top priority.

One cannot stay the same and change at the same time. As identified in chapter 2, during the turn of the century this paradoxical nature of same/change created a number of challenges for educators. Progressive educational thinkers had the challenge of same/change in mind when they developed the first prototype social studies program between 1913 and 1916 for grades seven through twelve. These thinkers believed their program was flexible enough to build a meaningful foundation in liberal democratic principles as well as to respond to the rapid changes in society.

The initial social studies program was written by the National Education Association's Committee on the Social Studies. This committee of public school teachers, college professors, and government officials wrote three reports for schools between 1913 and 1916. The intention of the committee was to open the forum for a public debate on curricular issues; however, World War I interrupted their work.

During the war years democratic debate was sharply curtailed; consequently, what became the last report of the social studies committee was not revisited nor revised after 1916. This was unfortunate for schools because many teachers and administrators were uncertain how to interpret the social studies conceptualization of foundational curricula (on the conformity and society sides on the twin paradoxes) and experimental curricula (on the freedom and individual sides of the twin paradoxes). One result of this uncertainty was that by 1924, only eight years after the report was published, middle and secondary schools had fallen into a pattern one educator called "a confusion of tongues."

Thus, although the early social studies practitioners cultivated a conceptualization of their field, by the early 1920s the lack of a clear, universally accepted definition of social studies came to plague the field in the upper grades. Even the formulation of the National Council for the Social Studies in 1921, which sought to harmonize curricular misunderstandings with this new school program, could not remedy the chaos. Since the 1920s each generation of social studies practitioners has labored to understand just what social studies is. In fact, despite as much as fifteen to sixteen years of formal schooling, as you began this book, you, too, may have possessed only a vague sense of what social studies was all about.

The vague sense of definition (not conceptualization) is directly related to what the original formulators of social studies had in mind when the emphasis area was invented in the first two decades of the twentieth century. Rather than spell out exactly what every teacher should teach and exactly what every student should learn (in definition form), the early social studies writers developed an experimental program of citizenship education for educators to consider that worked to directly engage children in learning. That is, the conceptualization was flexible enough that each school district and classroom teacher could decide what was best to teach and how. On the other hand, the definition or explicit content of social studies was intentionally left vague.

By design the prototype social studies program attended to both traditional and experimental themes. In practice teachers might present social studies curricula that focused upon a predetermined curriculum drawn from such subjects as United States history and geography, while other elements of social studies were determined and worked upon experimentally by children and teachers. Unhappily, since the 1920s, the outcome of this flexible nature has generated a number of competing definitions of social studies. In practical terms, the experimental part of the prototype program (conceptualization) was lost while the traditional focus remained (need for explicit definition).

Operationally, school powers continued to dictate curricula in a preexisting, predetermined form, without the sense of the enterprise of experiment. Rather than providing for at least some elements of dynamic programs, responsive to local conditions, curricula tended to become fixed. As teachers failed to critique their own curricular efforts and those imposed upon them, the result was that schools institutionalized a dogmatic, static curriculum.

Instead of viewing social studies in the conceptualization that its originators intended (experimental and localized), practitioners since the early 1920s have sought to define a social studies ideal in the literal sense. Ironically, the original prototype program goal was that each school worked toward its own ideal. As applied to schools, one major tenet of liberal democracy is that teachers not accept one curriculum or practice of social studies education, but explore any number of examples with the intention of selecting the best social studies education in the context of their own schools (teachers and children included).

In theory, the 1916 social studies report described the importance of needs and interest as a foundation for teaching and advocated integrated approaches with subject matter. In practice, however, the separation of social studies into discrete subjects such as history, geography, and civics (using analytic sense) became standardized for grades seven through twelve. Consequently, while some major educational writers, such as Harold Rugg, fought to keep integrated curricula and needs and interests as part of the social studies in the 1920s and 1930s (using holistic sense), others continued to conceive public schools as places populated by little adults who would absorb information and dispositions from prearranged lessons in history, geography, and civics (using analytic sense). Although not included in school reform at the middle school and secondary levels, elementary schools eventually became involved in the controversy as social studies entered the lower grades.

Evolution of Social Studies in Elementary Schools

The original social studies program ignored elementary school curricula. In fact, the 1916 report did not include any curricular specifics for the elementary grades. Where the social studies conceptualization entered middle and secondary schools through the dissemination of the 1916 social studies report, social studies for the elementary grades entered the schools in piecemeal fashion over the next three decades.

At the turn of the century, elementary school curricula were influenced by five primary ideas espoused by Francis Wayland Parker, G. Stanley Hall, Edward Thorndike, the Herbartarians, and John Dewey. Parker opened a school in Quincy, Massachusetts, where instruction was informal, subject matter was blended, activities were stressed, and scheduling was flexible. Parker's ideas were in sharp contrast to the prevailing common school where teaching was formal, subjects were clearly defined, activities were not approved of, and scheduling of the school day was strictly adhered to. Parker, who some called "the father of the progressive movement," illustrated that schools did not have to be places of drudgery (Table 7-3).

Hall, however, took child-centered study in a different direction. Hall

TABLE 7-3   **The Elementary School Curriculum of the Francis W. Parker School**

Grade One

Central Theme—The Immediate Environment
  The city environment
    Shelter: building brush, snow, and brick play houses.
    Foods: visits to farm, store, market, garden.
    Planting the garden in the spring.
    Cooking.
    Clothing: materials, where obtained; making luncheon cloth, doll-bed outfit, etc.
    Occupations of the family in the city environment.
  Study of tree people and cave people: their shelter, food, etc.
  Study of Eskimos: their shelter, food, etc.
  Other activities
    Care of animals, doves, aquaria.
    Garden: gathering corn, planting seeds.
    Cooking: making jelly, cereals, butter, cocoa, pop-overs, etc.
    Social experiences: parties, birthdays, special days, morning exercises.
  Subjects as needed—Reading, dramatization, phonics, writing, number, arts, music,
    handwork, physical education.

Grade Two

Central Theme—Four Industrial Activities in the Immediate Environment
  Harvesting.
  Milling: garden work, threshing, winnowing, gathering seeds.
  Cloth making: weaving, dyeing; study of Indian life; study of shepherd life.
  Care of a flock of chickens: feeding; gathering eggs; caring for baby chicks.
  Subjects as needed—Reading, literature, oral expression, writing, spelling, number,
    art, music, physical education, to meet certain minimum essentials. There is no
    classification of subject matter in grades one and two.

Grade Three

Central Theme—The Story of the Growth of Chicago
  History—Tracing the growth of Chicago from days of French explorers to the present.
  Geography—Study of early and present-day Chicago.
  Science and nature study of local environment—Study of swamp life, birds, trees,
    lighting and water systems of early and present city; collecting an aquarium;
    gardening activities.
  Literature, oral expression, composition, painting and drawing, clay and other
    handwork—As they contribute to the central theme and also to the development
    of certain minimum essentials.
  Mathematics—Minimum essentials. Correlation with central theme wherever
    possible.
  A miniature grocery store is conducted sometimes with toy money and toy
    products.
  Use of check book and school bank for supplies.
  Other activities and studies—French, German, classroom housekeeping, music, and
    physical education.

(Continued)

TABLE 7-3 *(Continued)*

Grade Four

Central Theme—The Study of Greek Life
   History—The history of Greek life as represented in the story of the *Odyssey.*
   Nature study and geography—Gardening; caring for grade pets—animals and birds; one field trip each month and collections made on each; writing a physical geography of the local
area. One class made a *Travel Book* from a study of world geography. Another class made a *History of Time-Keeping Devices.*
   Literature—Palmer's translation of the *Odyssey;* Greek stories and poems; other literature.
   Art and handwork in connection with Greek studies and science activities.
   Reading, composition, mathematics—Minimum essentials.
      Have regular periods for study of each.
      For mathematics—daily use of required measurements; conducting a real store with real
         supplies.
   French, German.
   Other activities to develop habits and attitudes—Class committees to care for business, order, etc.; lunchroom etiquette; class post-office box for exchange of letters; two mothers' meetings planned and held by the class; half hour a week for individual interests—collections, handwork, games, toy making, etc.

Grade Five

Central Theme—Colonial History (Bravery, Adventure, Exploration, Invention)
   History—Early colonial history. Events leading to discovery of America. Struggles between French and Indians.
   Geography—Study of North America as setting for its history: routes of explorers; industries; the change from home to factory system.
   Science and nature study—Correlations with geography and history.
      Weekly excursions to local points, developing a study of Chicago.
      Nature study of local bird, plant, and animal life.
   Literature—Stories correlated with history and geography: adventure stories—*Messer Marco Polo,* etc.; Christmas stories; last unit of year—Robin Hood legends and ballads.
   Art, clay modeling, handwork (in wood, clay, metal—three months each) in connection with history and geography interests.
   Composition, mathematics, French, German, music, physical education—Minimum essentials in each and as needed.
   Social habits—Through social units and life of the school.

Grade Six

Central Theme—History of the United States from the Colonial Times to the Present (Transportation, Westward Expansion, Immigration)
   History—Territorial growth and westward expansion of United States.
   Geography—Geological foundations of geography of North America.
   Science—Correlated with geography two thirds of year. Remainder of year devoted to bird study.
   Hygiene—Series of health talks lasting through the year.

TABLE 7-3   (*Continued*)

Home economics—Girls only.
Art and handwork—Correlates with history and geography interests; railroads, bridges, boats, constructed in miniature.
Literature—Sigurd; *Iliad;* stories and poems of American life.
Minimum essentials in composition, mathematics, French, German, music, and physical education.

The Whole School

Central Theme—The Social Motive
Morning exercises—Each class responsible in turn.
The Parker Fair—Held in the fall; each class contributes product of gardening and other activities.
Thanksgiving baskets for poor.
Santa Claus toy shop—Making toys for poor children.
Gardening—There are class and individual gardens, but the whole garden is considered a school affair.
The Parker Weekly—Paper published by the students.
Spring Field Day.
Other activities—Class parties; mothers' days; special days; Easter Bazaar; summer vacation activities.

This outline of the Francis W. Parker School curriculum is a condensation of the curriculum published in pamphlet form by the Francis W. Parker School (1926–1927).

believed that you needed to observe children to determine their curricular needs. Hall introduced the notion of laissez-faire or let the child alone for the elementary grades. Essentially, Hall's theory of education evolved into no recognizable patterns of schooling. No schedules were set, no course or subject work was expected or demanded; in brief, teachers were not to direct the learning of children. To the many observers of such schools, the daily activities of children appeared to resemble chaos and anarchy, rather than school. The foundation of laissez-faire education eventually grew into the Progressive Education Association, chartered in 1919 (to be discussed in the following sections).

The third individual who helped shape early elementary curricula was Edward Thorndike. Thorndike found that when children learned, it appeared that they were more successful when teachers associated the past experiences of the child to new experiences. Thus, if you wish to facilitate learning, teachers needed to expose children to familiar ideas/objects, then introduce new ideas/objects. This concept, which Thorndike drew from his testing of children, was introduced earlier by a group of educators called the Herbartarians (after the Herbart), who introduced the ideas of concentration and cultural epochs.

The Theory of Concentration and Cultural Epochs

At the turn of the century a group of educators known as the Herbartarians believed the subject-centered curricula did not serve the pedagogical needs of children. Rather than dividing the curriculum into segments (analytic sense), these educators took the radical position that school subjects should be concentrated into an organic whole, that is, one single area of study. Today this concept is called holistic education.

Within the notion of concentrating subjects, the theory of cultural epochs emerged. For the elementary grades, the origins of the standard curricular schema self, home, neighborhood, community, state, nation, world, follows a pattern championed by Herbartarians. Building on the notion that all children, like civilizations, pass through a series of stages (called cultural epochs) from barbarism to civilization, the Herbartarians stressed the importance of moving from the known to the unknown, from the familiar to the unfamiliar. In theory and practice, it made sense to begin with the immediate environment of the child and expand outward in ever larger circles.

According to the cultural epoch theory each child was born without any prior knowledge or disposition to culture and civilized life. To teach children, then, you had to follow the child's natural development through these stages. For the elementary grades the plan of study for social studies included fairy tales from the Grimm Brothers in the first year, Robinson Crusoe in the second year, other mythical and heroic tales in the third year, and the study of history in following years. These studies were to follow the stages that each child passes through. Each child was at first intuitive and receptive. In this stage mythical and heroic tales are suited to the child. In the middle stage, imagination and reality begin to merge and the child is well adapted to studying primitive man and the beginnings of civilization. In the last stage, the child begins to understand freedom and social and political development. Here the formal study of history can begin.

The growing child-centered movement simply did not embrace cultural epochs. The theory did not foster the growth of the individual child (that the child-centered group favored), nor, for that matter, any social aims (that Dewey supported). Within ten years of its introduction, the cultural epoch theory went the way of the dinosaur and was extinct by 1907.

Despite the Herbartarians' failure to move into the mainstream of elementary education, the notion of grading school curricula according to the perceptions of the child (which the Herbartarians claimed went through these three stages) survived in the form of developing curricula with the intent of moving from the known to the unknown, the near to the remote. In essence, this concept was the basis for Hanna's expanding horizons; however, unlike Hanna's theory, no social responsibility was attached to the cultural epoch theory.

Beginnings of the Child-Centered Movement and the Influence of John Dewey

Social studies for the upper grades was founded with social action in mind where students worked with a common goals/community spirit. However, social studies for elementary grades, founded in the child-centered movement, was designed to enhance the freedom of individuals. The difference between the upper grades and the lower grades, again illustrates a distinct split between the twin paradoxes (see chapter 3). The upper grade social studies emphasized the conforming individual and the elementary grade social studies came to foster the free individual.

The child-centered movement was first popularized through the work of G. Stanley Hall and the efforts of John Dewey. The idea that children should be directly involved in their own learning and curricular decisions was a new, radical idea compared to the conventions of the 1890s. Dewey and his wife Alice, together with their friends and neighbors opened the Chicago Laboratory School in 1896. Like Parker, Dewey abandoned school subjects, like history, math, and science, as well as traditional school furniture with bolted down individual desks, among other conventional elements. Despite the predictions from many visitors and critics that Dewey's experiment was doomed to scholastic chaos and failure, Dewey was able to develop one of the most important educational theories of the twentieth century.

Dewey and his wife remained at the experimental school until 1904. At this point, from his new position at Columbia University, Dewey spent much of the rest of his career rationalizing his own experience with child-centered education. Dewey's attention to the needs and interests of children and to activating learners with democratic thinking profoundly influenced social studies at both the elementary and secondary levels. Dewey's writings reveal that he clearly understood the complexity of the twin paradoxes.

Some devoted child-centered educators, however, did not appreciate, accept, or attend to the twin paradoxes. Instead, this dedicated group of educators emphasized freedom and the individual exclusively. Thus, two major strands of the child-centered movement emerged: Dewey's socially responsible individual and what eventually became the Progressive Education Association's platform, the wholly free-acting child.

Progressive Education Association

Educators of the Progressive Education Association (PEA) defined freedom in a laissez-faire sense (let the child alone). Teachers were not to define objectives or goals, control learning experiences, or provide direct guidance to or for children. In a sense, these new progressive schools became the direct opposites of traditional schools with their fixed or rigid curricula as well as those schools that modeled the 1916 conceptualization of social studies. Moreover, the progressive schools ignored social issues—essentially rejecting the conformity and society side of the twin paradoxes.

The seven principles of the PEA listed below were all concentrated upon the child:

- freedom to develop naturally

- interest, the motive of all work
- the teacher a guide, not a taskmaster
- scientific study of pupil development
- greater attention to all that affects physical development
- cooperation between school and home to meet the needs of the child's life
- the progressive school: a leader in educational movements[20]

Many critics called for more social responsibility in the child-centered movement of the PEA; however, the association remained committed to the above principles. The conspicuous and persistent absence of social responsibility in progressive theory and policy prompted Dewey (who the progressives claimed as their leader) to remove himself from the movement in the early 1930s.

While the emphasis upon the freedom supported by the PEA was welcome to some extent, when the Great Depression of the 1930s moved the nation at the edge of economic and social devastation, the child-centered movement failed (at least the laissez-faire model did). Without teaching plans, clear direction, defined goals, or any real emphasis upon social responsibility, the whole system of progressive education eventually collapsed amid the social and economic demands of the 1930s and 1940s.

Influence of Paul Hanna

In the midst and wake of the collapse of the progressive movement in the elementary grades, Paul Hanna reasserted the role of structure in the lower grades with his "expanding communities of men" textbooks. The action that began with the Herbartarians in the 1890s eventually replaced the traditional discrete subject approaches centered in history and geography and established the curricular features of self, home, community, etc. as the dominant social studies curriculum.

First introduced in the early 1930s, Hanna's ideas and the many textbooks that copied his model brought attention to both sides of the twin paradoxes. Still, the expanding communities idea typically stressed the importance of socialization over the need to develop the individual. Thus, the model was biased toward the conformity and society side of the twin paradoxes. In opposition, the earlier child-centered movement of the PEA favored freedom and the individual sides of the twin paradoxes.

The expanding communities idea embraced two philosophically based movements: the scientific management model and the social reconstruction model. The scientific management model identified (predetermined) through so-called empirical research, curricular materials, and practices suitable for

---

[20]"A Statement of Principles of Progressive Education, 1924," *Progressive Education*, 1, no. 2 (April 1924).

elementary children. Once developed and tested, the curriculum (in the form of textbooks) could be given to students throughout the country to yield certain measurable results. The results or outcomes of this predetermined curriculum could be checked against standardized tests and other measurements. Tests results, then, identified those schools (and children) falling behind the normal standards and indicated remedial instruction.

The model of social reconstruction arose during the Great Depression in the hope of building a new world through education. Educators such as George Counts sought to reconstruct prevailing education systems and reconstruct in their place a society more in tune with social responsibility and heightened social consciousness. In sum, the social reconstructionists failed to gain much of a foothold on curricular policy control, and subsequently, were defeated by the more potent scientific management model.

Given World War II, the Cold War, and the literal hysteria over democratic citizenship during the 1950s, the socialization styled expanding communities model became entrenched in elementary social studies curricula. Although social studies researchers such as Hilda Taba (discovery learning and concept formation), Florence Stratemeyer (persistent life situations), and Alice Miel (democratic citizenship) offered attractive alternatives to expanding communities, Hanna's pattern was only briefly challenged in the upper elementary grades during the 1960s with humanistic approaches such as the failed "Man: A Course of Study" program. Recently a new round of challenges has emerged with the push for more history- and geography-centered curricula in kindergarten through grade twelve. Nonetheless, despite much attention given to reforming social studies, the expanding communities model persists as the dominant curricular pattern of social studies.

A Past Model of Elementary Scope and Sequence through the Use of Questions

Table 7-4 shows a curriculum used in Virginia circa 1935, which focused on the use of questions.

A Current Model of Elementary Scope and Sequence Emphasizing Content

Table 7-5 shows a current curriculum emphasizing content.

Over the past 30 years, the curious mix of social studies ideas has merged into two competing approaches. The first advocates integrating subject matter, fostering freedom, and basing curricula upon children's needs and interests. The second relies heavily upon prepackaged, discrete topics determined by adults, and presented in linear, step-by-step fashion. When measured by the twin paradoxes, the child-centered school of the PEA championed freedom and

TABLE 7-4   Curriculum Used in Virginia circa 1935

Grade I Home and School Life	Grade II Community Life	Grade III Adaptation of Life to Environmental Forces of Nature
How do we protect and maintain life and health in our home and school?	How do we in the community protect our life, health, and property? How do animal and plant life help people in our community and how are they protected?	How do people, plants, and animals in communities with physical environments markedly different from ours protect themselves from forces of nature?
How do the things we make and grow help us?	What do we do in our community to produce goods and services?	How do environmental forces of nature affect the goods produced in different communities?
How does our family provide itself with food, clothing, and shelter?	How do we use the goods and services provided in our community?	Why can communities markedly different from ours furnish us with goods we cannot produce?
How do members of our family travel from place to place?	How does our community provide for transportation and communication?	How does the physical environment affect transportation and communication?
How can we have an enjoyable time at home and at school?	How does our community provide for recreation?	How does the physical environment influence types of recreation?
What can we do to make our home and school more beautiful and pleasant?	What do we do to make our community attractive?	How do people in communities markedly different from ours express their artistic impulses?
		How do people in different communities express their religious tendencies?
		How do people in different communities provide education?

A Curriculum Guide, state of Virginia, circa 1935

the individual, ignoring conformity and society. Hanna's expanding horizons, however, emphasized conformity and society at the expense of freedom and the individual. To date, few theories of elementary social studies have sought to embrace both sides of the twin paradoxes. This is the unique contribution of the synoptic method experiment.

For children and teachers, this confusion of incompatible theory generated

Table 7-4

Grade IV Adaptation of Life to Advancing Physical Frontiers	Grade V Effects of Inventions and Discoveries upon our Living	Grade VI Effects of Machine Production upon Our Living
How does frontier living affect the protection of life, property, and natural resources?	How do inventions and discoveries alter our ways of protecting and conserving life, property, and natural resources?	How does machine production lead to the conservation and to the waste of life, property, and natural resources?
How does frontier living modify and how has it been modified by the production and distribution of goods and services?	How do inventions and discoveries affect the variety and availability of goods?	How does machine production increase the quantity and variety and change the quality of goods?
How does frontier living restrict the consumption of goods and services?	How is the consumption of goods and services influenced by discoveries and inventions?	How does machine production of standardized goods influence the choice and use of goods?
How do ways of transportation and communication serve to advance frontiers?	How do inventions and discoveries improve our means of transportation and communication?	How does machine production affect transportation and communication?
How is recreation influenced by frontier living?	How do inventions and discoveries influence recreation?	How does machine production influence recreation?
How are music, literature, and art affected by frontier living?	How do inventions and discoveries affect our art, music, and literature?	How does machine production modify art, literature, music, and architecture?
How is religion affected by frontier living?	How do discoveries influence the spread of religion?	How does the church function as a means of social control?
How is education influenced by frontier living?	How do inventions and discoveries influence education?	How does machine production influence education?

a number of unwelcome outcomes for social studies in the elementary grades (as found in the attitudes of children and teachers toward social studies). At present a number of educators and theorists have worked to fashion social studies education that includes elementary grades into a nationwide predetermined curriculum centered exclusively in the subject of history (with an analytic model). Using the debatable claim that children do not possess enough knowledge of history and geography information, such educators hold that all social studies instruction should begin and end with the learning of informa-

TABLE 7-5 Outline of Social Studies Content

Kindergarten	*Grade 3*	*Grade 5*
Tools for learning about the world: maps, photos, globe	Tools for learning about the world: maps, photos, graphs, time lines, diagrams, tables	Tools for learning about the world: maps, graphs, photos, time lines, diagrams, tables
The individual and others	How to study a particular community	Ways of learning about the past
Living in a family	Representative communities in the United States	Chronological history of the United States
Going to school	Cities, towns, and suburbs	An overview of the geography of the United States
Changes in seasons, animals, people	Farms and ranches	Geography of:
Need for food, clothing, shelter	Fishing communities	New England states
Need for rules	Need for rules	Middle Atlantic states
Different places to live	Communication	Southeast states
		South Central states
Grade 1		North Central states
	Grade 4	Mountain West states
Tools for learning about the world: maps and photos		Pacific states
The individual and the family	Tools for learning about the world: maps, photos, time lines, diagrams, tables	History and geography of Canada and Latin America
Needs of families:	Forest regions in Washington state, Hawaii, and Puerto Rico, Soviet Union, and Amazon Basins	
Food		*Grade 6*
Clothes		
Shelter	Desert regions in southwestern United States, Africa, Arabian Peninsula	Tools for learning about the world: maps, photos, graphs, time lines, diagrams, tables
Families in neighborhoods		
Living in the United States	Plains regions in central and coastal United States, China, Kenya, and Australia	Beginnings of Western Civilization:
		Mesopotamia and Ancient Egypt
Grade 2		Ancient Greece
	Mountain regions in Colorado, West Virginia, Switzerland	Ancient Rome and the Roman Empire
Tools for learning about the world: maps, photos, graphs		Geography and history of:
Setting for communities: the earth, North America, the United States	Interdependence of regions	Western Europe
	Materials for learning about one's own state	Eastern Europe and Soviet Union
Large and small communities made up of neighborhoods		Middle East and North Africa
Community services		Africa south of the Sahara
Different kinds of work in communities		South Asia, East Asia, and Australia
Rule in communities		
Communities long ago in our country		
Celebrating holidays in communities		

Reproduced with permission from Ellis, A. K. (1991). *Teaching and learning elementary social studies,* 8. Boston: Allyn and Bacon.

tion such as facts, dates, persons, events, and more drawn from American, European, and world history topics.

Other thoughtful educators have resisted this move, urging practitioners to teach social studies exclusively through critical thinking or value/moral clarification. Still others insist that cooperative learning, reflective thinking, decision making, multicultural education, and other related themes are treated as central to the development of citizens. In fact, both the history core curriculum and such ideas as issue-centered education (among the others listed earlier) share the goal of producing liberal democratic citizens. On careful examination, although all these strands of thought have merit and deserve to be explored further, none corresponds to the inaugural social studies approach of promoting stable, conserving programs in a flexible, fluid, experimental context (holistic model).

One of the most interesting challenges to the existing expanding horizons curriculum has been recently launched by Houghton Mifflin. This innovative social studies series based on a history-centered curriculum combines a sound research base and practical suggestions. Because this curriculum (adopted statewide in California) is the first major elementary social studies plan to come along in 30 years to differ from expanding environments, the Houghton Mifflin scope and sequence warrants our careful attention (Table 7-6) (see appendix F for full scope and sequence).

Toward the Future of Social Studies

What recent social studies curricular advocates have sharply misunderstood or ignored about the beginnings of social studies is that social studies presented in one set fashion against or excluding another is inherently undemocratic and unsuited for educating children in a liberal democracy. The originators of social studies worked to develop an elastic social studies model, not program, that could benefit every school, including elementary schools.

The legacy of the first social studies model has been its greatest strength and greatest weakness. The social studies as crafted by its formulators was supple and easily adapted to any school. Over time, this flexibility has generated a multitude of social studies curricula that for one reason or another have become rather fixed and immovable instead of becoming dynamic programs.

The notion of flexibility is a strength, but the expansion of rigid programs is not a desired result. In practice, because information and its use changes over time, fixed or rigid programs based upon information must be eventually overhauled. Rigid programs are typically changed only when the need for change is great—when textbooks become painfully outdated. Instead of using a flexible program that is in itself a continual process of renewal, principals and teachers begin every round of reform by supporting a similar (updated,

TABLE 7-6   Houghton Mifflin *Social Studies Series* Themes by Year and Grade

Kindergarten	The World I See (Individuals and Families)
Grade 1	I Know a Place (Communities and Families)
Grade 2	Some People I Know (Historical Themes and Families)
Grade 3	From Sea to Shining Sea (Environment and Historical Themes, Focus on Others)
Grade 4	This Is My Country (Contemporary United States and Geography)
Grade 5	America Will Be (United States History and Geography: Beginnings to Civil War)
Grade 6	A Message From Ancient Days (World History and Geography: Ancient Civilizations)
Grade 7	Across the Centuries (World History and Geography: Middle Ages to Enlightenment)
Grade 8	A More Perfect Union (United States History and Geography: Revolution to Early Modern Times)

Reproduced with permission from Houghton Mifflin *Social Studies Series*.

of course) information-centered curriculum that will one day have to be rewritten. This process of replacing one information-centered program with another is both time consuming and wasteful. Using flexibility as a guiding conceptualization, the synoptic approach toward social studies works to eliminate typical five-year reformations.

Summary

Is there something wrong with social studies? The answer is yes!

- Is it a wrong emphasis? Perhaps.
- Is it unmotivated children or teachers? Perhaps.
- Is it too much emphasis upon facts? Perhaps.
- Is it an incomplete or outdated theoretical foundation? Perhaps.
- Is it all this and more? Perhaps.

The basis of the theory found in the synoptic method does not rest upon the faults, shortcomings, or misunderstandings of the work and efforts of others, no matter how great or small. Instead, the foundation of synoptic theory rests upon a firm conviction that liberal democratic principles and attending to the needs of children are valuable and, as such, should permeate all social studies.

If research (including your own) demonstrates that present (and past) curricular efforts in elementary social studies leaves more than something to be desired, then a window of opportunity exists for other conceptualizations to enter our thinking and practice. It is not so much that another model is better, but that other conceptualizations may be more conducive for education in a liberal democratic community. Experimentation and exploration of various ideas should guide your curricular efforts, not blind obedience to admittedly unsuccessful models.

Educational patterns can change, but they will only change if committed individuals take direct action. By using the synoptic method, by integrating the social studies formula within the context of supporting a liberal democratic community, we are working to reform ineffective elementary social studies models. But more importantly, we are working to improve the lives and opportunities of children. One of the most important goals of a community should be to attend to the welfare of its children. Indeed, throughout the world from large urban centers to small towns, villages, or tribes of people, one of the most critical measures of humanity is the time and attention placed on children. Where we expect the community to share in promoting healthy environments for children, together with parents and guardians, teachers are directly responsible for creating positive, nurturing environments where productive, happy, and healthy learning experiences can occur. Teachers should also contribute to the growing possibilities of each child, to care for every single individual, to leave no child unattended, unwanted, or unloved.

Thus, the challenge is made, "become a great teacher." As a teacher you can have a positive effect on the todays and tomorrows of every child you teach. However, in the effort to extend the frontiers of teaching and learning, you must first involve yourself in the battle for children and in the battle for community. The struggles and confrontations in teaching will be many, difficulties and frustrations will shadow your steps, but the joy of watching a young person discover the world makes all the efforts worth it. I cannot think of a more noble endeavor than to join the company of caring, involved, and dedicated individuals who proudly call themselves teachers.

At the beginning of our journey you were challenged to explore new ideas, to experiment with new thoughts, to practice new skills and abilities, and to develop new perspectives. How far have you come? How far do you have to go to become the teacher you want to be? If you decide to march to a different drummer, I wish you good luck and peace. If you have not yet decided to continue the edventure, I urge you to take time to reconsider. If you are willing to join the effort, I eagerly welcome you. Whatever the case, whatever your decision, I appreciate your efforts. If you can, when you reach the classroom, please let me know how you and your children are doing.

Marking Your Progress

1. Make comparisons between your elementary program (as well you remember) or where you will probably be teaching and present practice in the field of social studies. _____

    _____

    _____

2. Reflecting upon your experience with the synoptic method, and other experiences related to elementary schooling, outline your personal philosophy of education (including your approach to teaching, learning, and children). _____

    _____

    _____

    _____

    _____

    _____

Note: To measure your own growth, you may wish to express the differences (if any) between what you believe now and how you once thought about teaching, learning, and children.

Read More about It Special References

As you have read, the field of social studies is diverse and often broadly defined. The following references can help you place social studies in the context of elementary schools, provide an overview of the history of social studies teaching, and introduce other promising practices in elementary social studies for your consideration.

Gagnon, P., Ed. (1989). *Historical literacy: The case for history in American education.* New

York: Macmillan.

Prepared under the auspices of the Bradley Commission on History in Schools, Gagnon and associates present a compelling case for the study of history in schools, especially at the elementary level. The authors are sympathetic to other social studies areas, but decidedly center all social studies instruction on history.

Gifford, B. R. (1988). *History in schools: What should we teach?* New York: Macmillan.

Although the title implies that particular information on what should be taught will be discussed, the text is actually another plea for history to be placed in schools. The text does not specifically identify curricular patterns or specific lessons for elementary schools.

Goodlad, J. (1984). *A place called school: Prospects for the future.* New York: McGraw-Hill.

This is the standard work on public schooling. Goodlad provides an excellent overview of what's happening in public schools (circa 1980s).

Jarolimek, J., & Walsh, H. (1970). *Readings for social studies in elementary education.* New York: Macmillan.

Thomas, R. M., & Brubaker, D. L. (1972). *Teaching elementary social studies readings.* Belmont, CA: Wadsworth.

At one time social studies reading texts were fairly common in elementary education programs; today they are rarely seen or used. These two texts are representative of the best available (you will find them in libraries/interlibrary loan). Each contains brief, well written articles about the teaching of social studies that remain timely. If possible, elementary teachers should review these texts very carefully.

Jenness, D. (1990). *Making sense of social studies.* New York: Macmillan.

A comprehensive account of social studies from the 1920s to 1990, this book does not specifically address elementary themes, although readers will be able to reconstruct the movement of social studies from the progressive era through the 1960s.

Parker, W. C. (1991). *Renewing the social studies curriculum.* Alexandria, VA: Association for Supervision and Curriculum Development.

This book must be read by all those involved in curricular development.

Saxe, D. (1991). *Social studies in schools: A history of the early years.* Albany: State University of New York Press.

This book offers an accounting of the beginnings of the social studies. Particular attention is given to the transition from history to social studies in curricular design.

Shannon, P. (1990). *The struggle to continue.* Portsmouth, N.H.: Heinemann.

Written by a teacher and scholar who knows elementary schools well (he is a former kindergarten teacher), this book helps to make sense of the whole language movement by casting present efforts into proper historical perspective. As Shannon's themes and topics are closely allied to the synoptic method, this interesting and easily read book is a must for elementary teachers seeking to understand the politics and promise of working out better solutions for helping children learn and thrive in elementary settings.

Shaver, J. P. (1991). *Handbook of research on social studies teaching and learning.* New York: Macmillan.

This is the most recent and thorough examination of social studies theory and practice available. Every school library should have this excellent source readily available to faculty.

Stratemeyer, F., Forkner, H., McKim, M., & Passow, H. (1957). *Developing a curriculum for modern living.* New York: Bureau of Publications, Teachers College.

A master of putting ideas into application, Stratemeyer and associates developed one of the earliest spiral curriculum patterns for social studies. Stratemeyer's idea was to take a persistent life theme and repeat the theme over a number of years, adding complexity and thoroughness in the process. Though only available through interlibrary loan or at major teaching centers or universities, Stratemeyer's work is closely allied to holistic and synoptic themes; every elementary teacher should become familiar with Stratemeyer's ideas and materials.

Taba, H. (1967). *Teacher's handbook for elementary social studies.* Palo Alto, CA: Addison-Wesley.

One of the best sources available for teaching elementary social studies through concept formation. Although the examples are now dated, Taba's work is well respected within the social studies community. Every elementary teacher should investigate how Taba uses discovery methods to teach social studies.

Tanner, D., & Tanner, L. (1990). *History of the school curriculum.* New York: Macmillan.

This text is the standard work available on the history of public school curricula. Tanner and Tanner provide useful charts that help explain and present the complexity of school curricula in theory and practice.

References on Research in Elementary Schools

Armento, B. J. (1986). Research on teaching social studies. In Wittrock, M.C., Ed. *Handbook of research on teaching,* 3rd ed. New York: Macmillan.

Berkowitz, M. W., & Gibbs, J. C. (1983). Measuring the developmental feature of a moral discussion. *Merrill-Palmer Quarterly* 29:339–440.

Crabtree, C. (1974). *Children's thinking in the social studies.* Los Angeles: University of California.

Edwards, C. P. (1986). *Promoting social and moral development in young children.* New York: Teachers College Press.

Geographic Education National Implementation Project (GENIP), *K–6 geography: Themes, key ideas, and learning opportunities.* Washington, DC: GENIP.

Greenstein, F. I. (1969). *Children and politics.* New Haven, CT: Yale University Press.

Hatcher, B. (1983). Putting young cartographers "On the map." *Childhood Education.* 59:311–15.

Hess, R. D., & Torney, J. V. (1967). *The development of political attitudes in children.* Chicago: Aldine.

Hewes, D. W. (1982). Preschool geography: Developing a sense of self in time and space. *Journal of Geography* 81:94–97.

Katz, P. A. (1976). *Toward the elimination of racism.* New York: Pergamon Press.

Kennedy, K. J. (1983). Assessing the relationship between information processing capacity and historical understanding. *Theory and Research in Social Education.* 11(2): 1–22.

Kohlberg, L. (1976). This special section in perspective. *Social Education* 40:213–15.

Lanegran, D. A., Snowfield, J. G., & Lavent, A. (1970). Retarded children and the concepts of distance and direction. *Journal of Geography* 69:157–60.

Levstik, L. (1986). The relationship between historical response and narrative in a sixth grade classroom. *Theory and Research in Social Education* 41(1):1–15.

Liben, L. S., Moore, M. L., & Golbeck, S. L. (1982). Preschooler's knowledge of their classroom environment. *Childhood Development* 53:1275–84.

Muessig, R. (1987). An analysis of developments in geographic education. *The Elementary School Journal* 87(5):571–89.

Park, D. C., & James, C. Q. (1983). Effects of encoding instruction on children's spatial and color memory. *Child Development* 54:61–68.

Regan, W., & McAulay, J. (1973). *Social studies for today's children.* New York: Appleton-Century-Crofts.

Semaj, L. (1980). The development of racial evaluation and preference: A cognitive approach. *Journal of Black Psychology* 6:59–79.

Stanley, W. B. (1985). *Review of research in social studies education.* Washington, DC: National Council for the Social Studies.

Stone, L. C. (1986). International and multicultural education. In Atwood, V., Ed. *Elementary social studies: Research as a guide to practice.* Washington, DC: National Council for the Social Studies.

Appendix A

ORDERING CATALOGS

For the price of a postage stamp the world (and a lot of useful information and teaching ideas) can be brought directly into your classroom! Think of ordering a catalog as one of our edventures. It's fun to explore, to look at new things, and dream. The following is a listing of companies and organizations that offer catalogs at no cost. Not only does each catalog offer up-to-date products to choose from that can make social studies exciting, children can also make use of catalog pictures and graphics to create collages, posters, and more. Be sure to order your catalogs in time for teaching. A formal letter stating your intentions is always appreciated.

Active Learning Systems
P. O. Box 1984
Midland, MI 48640

Addison-Wesley Publishing Company
Alternative Publishing Group
P. O. Box 10888
Palo Alto, CA 94303

Addison-Wesley Publishing Company
2725 Sand Hill Road
Menlo Park, CA 94025

Agency for Instructional Technology
Box A
Bloomington, IN 47402

Ambrose Video Publishing, Inc.
381 Park Avenue South, Suite 1601
New York, NY 10016

American Forum for Global Education
45 John Street, Suite 908
New York, NY 10038

American Guidance Service, Inc.
Publishers Building
Circle Pines, MI 55014

AMSCO School Publications
315 Hudson Street
New York, NY 10013

Anti-Defamation League of B'nai B'rith
823 United Nations Plaza
New York, NY 10017

Apple Computer, Inc.
20525 Mariani Avenue
Cupertino, CA 95014

Arab World and Islamic Resources and School
    Services
2095 Rose Street, Suite 4
Berkeley, CA 94709

Association for Supervision and Curriculum
    Development
1250 North Pitt Street
Alexandria, VA 22314

Beagle Brothers, Inc.
6215 Ferris Square, Suite 100
San Diego, CA 92121

BFA Educational Media
2211 Michigan Avenue
Santa Monica, CA 90404

Broderbund Software
17 Paul Drive
San Rafael, CA 94903

Center for Applied Research in Education
West Nyack, NY 10995-9901

Center for Civic Education
5146 Douglas Fir Drive
Calabasas, CA 91302-1467

Center for Teaching International Relations
University of Denver
2201 South Gaylord
Denver, CO 80208

Chelsea Curriculum Publications
P. O. Box 5186
Yeadon, PA 19050

The Children's Book Council, Inc.
568 Broadway
New York, NY 10012

Childrens Press/Goldencraft
5440 North Cumberland Avenue
Chicago, IL 60656

Close-Up Foundation
1235 Jefferson Davis Highway
Arlington, VA 22202
Congressional Quarterly Books
1414 22nd Street, NW
Washington, DC 20037

Coronet Film & Video
108 Wilmot Road
Deerfield, IL 60015

The George F. Cram Company
P. O. Box 426
Indianapolis, IN 46206

Crestwood House
Dillon Press
New Discovery Books
866 Third Avenue
New York, NY 10022

Cross-Cultural Software
5385 Elrose Avenue
San Jose, CA 95124

D. C. Heath and Company
School Division
125 Spring Street
Lexington, MA 02173

Denoyer-Geppert Company
5235 Ravenswood Avenue
Chicago, IL 60640

Disney Educational Productions
108 Wilmot Road
Deerfield, IL 60015

Eastern National Park & Monument Association
1100 East Hector Street, Suite 105
Conshohocken, PA 19428

Econo-Clad-Brooks
P. O. Box 1777
Topeka, KS 66601

Educational Program Service (EPS)
P. O. Box 50008
Columbia, SC 29250

Educational Resources
1550 Executive Drive
Elgin, IL 60123

Educator's Guide to Free Curriculum Materials
in Social Studies
Educator's Progress Service
Randolph, WI 53956

Encyclopaedia Britannica Educational
Corporation
425 North Michigan Avenue
Chicago, IL 60611

ERIC
Clearinghouse for Social Studies/Social Science
Education
2805 East Tenth Street
Bloomington, IN 47408

Ethnic American Minorities Guide
R. R. Bowker
P. O. Box 1807
Ann Arbor, MI 48106

Films Incorporated
5547 North Ravenswood Avenue
Chicago, IL 60640-1199

Glencoe
Macmillan/McGraw-Hill
P. O. Box 508
Columbus, OH 43216

Globe Book Company
4350 Equity Drive
P. O. Box 2649
Columbus, OH 43216

Good Apple
1204 Buchanan Street
P. O. Box 299
Carthage, IL 62321-0299

Great Plains National Instructional Television
  Library
1800 North 33rd Street
P. O. Box 80669
Lincoln, NE 68501

Greenhaven Press, Inc.
P. O. Box 289009
San Diego, CA 92198-0009

Grolier Electronic Publishing, Inc.
Department 336 Sherman Turnpike
Danbury, CT 06816

Gryphon House
Early Childhood Books
P. O. Box 275
Mt. Rainier, MD 20712

Hammond
515 Valley Street
Maplewood, NJ 07040

Harcourt Brace Jovanovich, Inc.
6277 Sea Harbor Drive
Orlando, FL 32887

Hartley Courseware, Inc.
133 Bridge Street
Dimondale, MI 48821

Highsmith Co.
W5527 Highway 106
P. O. Box 800
Fort Atkinson, WI 53538-0800

Holt, Rinehart, and Winston
School Division
1627 Woodland Avenue
Austin, TX 78741

Houghton Mifflin
One Beacon Street
Boston, MA 02108

Hubbard Company
1846 Raymond Drive
Northbrook, IL 60062

Interact
P. O. Box 997-S91
Lakeside, CA 92040

International Telecommunication Services, Inc.
2942 Freeton Drive
Reston, VA 22091

Jackdaw Publications
P. O. Box A03
Amawalk, NY 10501

Journal Films, Inc.
930 Pitner Avenue
Evanston, IL 60202

K–12 MicroMedia, Inc.
6 Arrow Road
Ramsey, NJ 07446

Kimbo Educational
Department R
P. O. Box 477
Long Branch, NJ 07740-0477

Knowledge Unlimited
Box 52
Madison, WI 53701-0052

Krell Software
1320 Stony Brook Road
Stony Brook, NY 11790

Laureate Learning Systems, Inc.
110 East Spring Street
Winooski, VT 05404

Learning Corporation of America
108 Wilmot Road
Deerfield, IL 60015

Libraries Unlimited
Teacher Idea Press
P. O. Box 3988, Department 550
Englewood, CO 80155-3988

Longman Inc.
95 Church Street
White Plains, NY 10601-1505

Macmillan/McGraw-Hill
220 East Danieldale Road
DeSoto, TX 75115

Macmillan Publishing Company
866 Third Avenue
New York, NY 10022

Media Materials, Inc.
1821 Portal Street, Department 910301
Baltimore, MD 21224

Millbrook Press, Inc.
2 Old Milford Road
Brookfield, CT 06804

Modern Curriculum Press
13900 Prospect Road
Cleveland, OH 44136

MTI Film & Video
108 Wilmot Road
Deerfield, IL 60015

National Archives Publications
Trust Fund Board
Washington, DC 20408

National Council for the Social Studies
3501 Newark Street, NW
Washington, DC 20016

National Geographic Society
Educational Services
Washington, DC 20036

National History Day
11201 Euclid Avenue
Cleveland, OH 44106

National Wildlife Federation
1412 16th Street, NW
Washington, DC 20036

National Women's History Project
7738 Bell Road
Windsor, CA 95492-8518

Nystrom
3333 Elston Avenue
Chicago, IL 60618-5898

Opportunities for Learning, Inc.
20417 Nordhoff Street
Chatsworth, CA 91311

Oxford University Press
200 Madison Avenue
New York, NY 10016

PBS Video
1320 Braddock Place
Alexandria, VA 22314-1698

PC Globe, Inc.
4700 South McClintock
Tempe, AZ 85282

Prentice-Hall
113 Sylvan Avenue Route 9W
Englewood Cliffs, NJ 07632

Pro*Ed
8700 Shoal Creek Boulevard
Austin, TX 78758-6897

Rand McNally
Educational Publishing Division
P. O. Box 1906
Skokie, IL 60076-8906

Reach Center
239 North McLeod
Arlington, WA 98223

Salisbury-Gordan
Catalog of Free Teaching Materials
P. O. Box 1075
Ventura, CA 93003

Scholastic Inc.
P. O. Box 7501
2931 East McCarty Street
Jefferson City, MO 65102

Scott Foresman
1900 East Lake Avenue
Glenview, IL 60025

Silver Burdett & Ginn
4350 Equity Drive
P. O. Box 2649
Columbus, OH 43216

Silver Burdett Press, Inc.
P. O. Box 1226
Westwood, NJ 07675-1226

Simon & Schuster
15 Columbus Circle
New York, NY 10023

Social Issues Resources
P. O. Box 2507
Boca Raton, FL 33432

Social Science Education Consortium, Inc.
855 Broadway
Boulder, CO 80302

Social Studies School Service
1000 Culver Boulevard
Culver City, CA 90230

South Carolina ETV Marketing
2712 Milwood Avenue
Columbia, SC 29250

SouthWestern Publishing
5101 Madison Road
Cincinnati, OH 45227

Stanford Program on International and Cross-
Cultural Education (SPICE)
Littlefield Center, Room 14
300 Lasuen Street
Stanford, CA 94305-5013

Steck-Vaughn Company
P. O. Box 26015
Austin, TX 78755

Sunburst Communications
39 Washington Avenue
Pleasantville, NY 10570

Superintendent of Documents
United States Government Printing Office
Washington, DC 20402

Teachers College Press
Teachers College, Columbia University
New York, NY 10027

The Teachers Press
3731 Madison Avenue
Brookfield, IL 60513

Technomic Publishing
851 New Holland Avenue, Box 3535
Lancaster, PA 17604

Tom Snyder Productions
90 Sherman Street
Cambridge, MA 02140

TVOntario
United States Sales
143 West Franklin Street, Suite 206
Chapel Hill, NC 27514

Twayne Publishers/G. K. Hall
70 Lincoln Street
Boston, MA 02111

United States Memorial Council
2000 L Street, NW Suite 588
Washington, DC 20036

University Press of America
4720 Boston Way
Lanham, MD 20706

Wadsworth School Group
10 Davis Drive
Belmont, CA 94002-3098

J. Weston Walch, Publisher
321 Valley Street
P. O. Box 658
Portland, ME 04014-0658

Wagner & Christopher
Free Learning Materials for Classroom Use
State College Extension Service
Cedar Falls, IA 50613

WETA/TV Educational Activities
Box 2626
Washington, DC 20013

WGBH Educational Foundation
125 Western Avenue
Boston, MA 02134

Word Associates, Inc.
3096 Summit Avenue
Highland Park, IL 60035

The World Bank Educational Materials
1818 H Street, NW
Washington, DC 20433

World Eagle, Inc.
64 Washburn Avenue
Wellesley, MA 02181

Appendix B

INFORMATION SOURCES

The following represents a selected list of organizations that support special interest positions or certain ideas, and/or promote particular actions that may be of interest to you and your children. While no specific endorsement of any of the following organizations is offered here, I do support the notion that as liberal democratic citizens we should protect a citizen's access to information. Again, for the price of a stamp, these organizations will send information and materials to your door. A word of caution: whereas some sell or promote certain products, each represents ideas or positions on issues (some controversial, others not). In addition, by contacting these groups, unless you specifically request otherwise, your name may be placed on a mailing list that the group will use to solicit initial and continued financial support.

Action for Children's Television
20 University Road
Cambridge, MA 02138

African Studies Program Outreach
Indiana University
Woodburn Hall 221
Bloomington, IN 47405

Afro-American Distributing Company
910 South Michigan Avenue, Suite 556
Chicago, IL 60605

Agricultural History Society
1301 New York Avenue, NW
Room 928
Washington, DC 20250

Air and Waste Management Association
P. O. Box 2861
Pittsburgh, PA 15230

Al-Anon Family Groups
P. O. Box 862
Middletown Station
New York, NY 10018

American Anthropological Association
1703 New Hampshire Avenue, NW
Washington, DC 20009

American Automobile Association (AAA),
    Traffic Safety and Education
8111 Gatehouse Road
Falls Church, VA 22042

American Bar Association
1155 East 6th Street
Chicago, IL 60637

American Civil Liberties Union
633 South Shatto Avenue
Los Angeles, CA 90005

American Agricultural Economics Association
80 Heady Hall
Iowa State University
Ames, IA 50001

American Council on Alcohol Problems
3426 Bridgeland Drive
Bridgeton, MO 63044

American Council on Education
One Dupont Circle, NW #800
Washington, DC 20036

American Federation of Arts
41 East 65th Street
New York, NY 10021

American Forum
45 John Street, Suite 1200
New York, NY 10038

American Historical Association
400 A Street, SE
Washington, DC

American Institute for Character Education
P. O. Box 12617
San Antonio, TX 78212

American Kennel Club
51 Madison Avenue
New York, NY 10010

American Legion
700 North Pennsylvania Street
Indianapolis, IN 46204

American Peace Society
4000 Albemarle Street, NW
Washington, DC 20016

American Red Cross
17th and D Streets, NW
Washington, DC 20006

American Society for Prevention of Cruelty to
  Animals
441 East 92nd Street
New York, NY 10128

Amnesty International
102 Greenwich Avenue
Greenwich, CT 06830

Animal Welfare Institute
1686 34th Street, NW
Washington, DC 20007

Anti-Defamation League of B'nai B'rith
823 United Nations Plaza
New York, NY 10017

Antique Automobile Club of America
501 West Governor Road
Hershey, PA 17033

Archaeological Institute of America
675 Commonwealth Avenue
Boston, MA 02215

Asia Monitor Resource Center
444–46 Nathan Road
8-B
Kowloon, Hong Kong

The Asia Society
725 Park Avenue
New York, NY 10021

Asian-Pacific Heritage Council
Box 11036
Alexandria, VA 22312

Association for the Study of Afro-American Life
  and History
1401 14th Street, NW
Washington, DC 20005

Association for World Education
P. O. Box 589
Huntington, NY 11743

Association of Arab-American University
  Graduates
556 Trapelo Road
Belmont, MA 02178

Association of Junior Leagues
660 First Avenue
New York, NY 10016

Association on American Indian Affairs
245 Fifth Avenue
New York, NY 10016

Association for Childhood Education
  International
11141 Georgia Avenue
Suite 200
Wheaton, MD 20902

Better Business Bureaus
4200 Wilson Boulevard
Arlington, VA 22203

Big Brothers/Big Sisters of America
230 North 13th Street
Philadelphia, PA 19107

B'nai B'rith International
1640 Rhode Island Avenue, NW
Washington, DC 20036

Boy's Clubs of America
771 First Avenue
New York, NY 10017

Boy Scouts of America
1325 Walnut Hill Lane
Irving, TX 75015-2079

Brigham Young University
Center for International and Area Studies
Box 61 FOB
Provo, UT 84602

CARE
660 First Avenue
New York, NY 10016

Catholic Educational Association
1077 30th Street, NW
Suite 100
Washington, DC 20007

Center for Civic Education
5115 Douglas Fir Road, Suite 1
Calabasas, CA 91302

Center for International Relations
University of Denver
Denver, CO 80208

Center for Teaching about China
2025 Eye Street, NW
Suite 715
Washington, DC 20006

Center for United States-Mexican Studies
D-010 University of California-San Diego
La Jolla, CA 92093

Chamber of Commerce of the USA
1615 H Street, NW
Washington, DC 20062

Chemical Manufacturers Association
2501 M Street, NW
Washington, DC 20037

Child Welfare League of America
440 First Street, NW
Washington, DC 20001

Children's Aid Society
105 East 22nd Street
New York, NY 10010

Children's Book Council
568 Broadway, Suite 404
New York, NY 10012

Children's Defense Fund
122 C Street, NW
Washington, DC 20001

Church World Service
Office of Global Education
P. O. Box 968
Elkhart, IN 46515

Close-Up Foundation
1235 Jefferson Davis Highway
Arlington, VA 22202

Colonial Williamsburg Foundation
Williamsburg, VA 23187

Committee on Teaching about Asia
5633 North Kenmore, #24
Chicago, IL 60660

Common Cause
2030 M Street, NW
Washington, DC 20036

Congress of Racial Equality (CORE)
1457 Flatbush Avenue
Brooklyn, NY 11210

Congressional Quarterly
1414 22nd Street, NW
Washington, DC 20037

Consortium of Social Studies Associations
1200 17th Street, NW
Suite 520
Washington, DC 20036

Constitutional Rights Foundation
1510 Cotner Avenue
Los Angeles, CA 90025

Consumer Protection Institute
5901 Plainfield Drive
Charlotte, NC 28215

Council on Basic Education
725 15th Street, NW
Washington, DC 20005

Council on Indian Education
517 Rim Rock Road
P. O. Box 31215
Billings, MT 59107

Council on Interracial Books for Children
1841 Broadway
New York, NY 10023

Democratic National Committee
430 South Capital Street, NE
Washington, DC 20003

Earthpost
163 Amsterdam Avenue
Suite 381
New York, NY 10023

Education Development Center, Inc.
55 Chapel Street
Newton, MA 02160

Educators for Social Responsibility
23 Garden Street
Cambridge, MA 02138

Facts-On-File
460 Park Avenue
New York, NY 10016

Foreign Policy Association
205 Lexington Avenue
New York, NY 10016

Forest Council
1250 Connecticut Avenue, NW
Washington, DC 20036

Foundation for Economic Education
30 South Broadway
Irvington-on-Hudson, NY 10533

4-H Clubs
Extension Service
U.S. Department of Agriculture
Washington, DC 20250

Freedom of Information Center
20 Walter Williams Hall
University of Missouri
Columbia, MO 65211

Friends of the Earth
530 7th Street, SE
Washington, DC 20003

Future Farmers of America Organization
5632 Mt. Vernon Memorial Highway
Alexandria, VA 22309-0160

General Society of Colonial Wars
840 Woodbine Avenue
Glendale, OH 45246

Geographic Education National
    Implementation Project (GENIP)
Association of American Geographers
1710 16th Street, NW
Washington, DC 20009

Girls Clubs of America
30 East 33rd Street
New York, NY 10016

Girl Scouts of the United States of America
830 Third Avenue
New York, NY 10022

Global Perspectives in Education
218 East 18th Street
New York, NY 10003

InterAction
200 Park Avenue South
New York, NY 10003

International Committee of the Red Cross
780 Third Avenue
New York, NY 10017

Japan Institute for Social and Economic Affairs
1333 Gough Street, Suite 6F
San Francisco, CA 94109

Jefferson Foundation
1529 18th Street, NW
Washington, DC 20036

JC Penney Company
1301 Avenue of the Americas
New York, NY 10019

The Joint Council on Economic Education
51 River Street
Wellesley Hills, MA 02181

Kiwanis International
3636 Woodview Trace
Indianapolis, IN 46268-3196

League of Women Voters of the United States
1730 M Street, NW
Washington, DC 20036

National Aeronautics and Space Administration
    (NASA)
Central Operation of Resources for Educators
    (CORE)
Lorain County JVS
15181 Route 58 South
Oberlin, OH 44074

National Archives and Records Administration
Office of Public Programs
Pennsylvania Avenue at 8th Street
Washington, DC 20408

National Association for the Advancement of
    Colored People (NAACP)
4805 Mt. Hope Drive
Baltimore, MD 21215

National Association of Secondary School
    Principals
1904 Association Drive
Reston, VA 22019

National Audubon Society
950 Third Avenue
New York, NY 10022

National Baseball Congress
P. O. Box 1420
Wichita, KS 67201

National Coalition Against Censorship
132 West 43rd Street
New York, NY 10036

National Collegiate Athletic Association
6201 College Boulevard
Overland Park, KS 66211-2422

National Civic League
55 West 44th Street
New York, NY 10036

National Conference of Christians and Jews
71 Fifth Avenue, Suite 1100
New York, NY 10003

National Congress of Parents and Teachers
  (PTA)
700 North Rush Street
Chicago, IL 60611

National Council for Geographic Education
Department of Geography
University of Houston
Houston, TX 77004

National Council for the Social Studies
3501 Newark Street, NW
Washington, DC 20016

National Council on Family Relations
3989 Central Avenue NE
Suite 550
Minneapolis, MN 55421

National Dairy Council
6300 North River Road
Belmont, IL 60018

National Education Association
1201 16th Street, NW
Washington, DC 20036

National Fisheries Institute
2000 M Street
Washington, DC 20036

National Health Council
350 Fifth Avenue, Suite 1118
New York, NY 10118

National Model Railroad Association
4121 Cromwell Road
Chattanooga, TN 37421

National Safety Council
444 North Michigan Avenue
Chicago, IL 60611

National Society for the Prevention of Blindness
500 East Remington Road
Schaumburg, IL 60173

National Wildlife Federation
1412 16th Street, NW
Washington, DC 20036

National Women's Hall of Fame
P. O. Box 335
Seneca Falls, NY 13148

National Women's History Project
P. O. Box 3716
Santa Rosa, CA 95402

National Trust for Historic Preservation
1785 Massachusetts Avenue, NW
Washington, DC 20036

New York Stock Exchange
11 Wall Street
New York, NY 10005

Opportunities for Learning
8950 Lurline Avenue
Chatsworth, CA 91311

Organization of American Historians
112 North Bryan Street
Bloomington, IN 47408

Organization of American States
17th and Constitution Avenue, NW
Washington, DC 20006

Population Institute
110 Maryland Avenue, NE
Washington, DC 20002

Procter and Gamble Education Service
P. O. Box 599
Cincinnati, OH 45201

Public Affairs Committee
381 Park Avenue
New York, NY 10016

Republican National Committee
310 1st Street, SE
Washington, DC 20003

Social Issues Resource Series
P. O. Box 2507
Boca Raton, FL 33432

Social Science Education Consortium
855 Broadway
Boulder, CO 80302

Society for American Archaeology
Committee on Public Education
Bureau of Reclamation
P. O. Box 25007, D-5611
Denver, CO 80225-0007

Southern Africa Media Center
630 Natoma Street
San Francisco, CA 94103

Third World Resources
464 19th Street
Oakland, CA 94612

United Nations
Room DC 1-0522
United Nations, NY 10017

United Nations Association of USA
300 East 42nd Street
New York, NY 10017

U.S. Committee for United Nations Children's
  Fund (UNICEF)
333 East 38th Street
New York, NY 10016

Wilderness Society
900 17th Street, NW
Washington, DC 20006

Women's International League for Peace and
  Freedom
1213 Race Street
Philadelphia, PA 19107

World Bank
1818 H Street, NW
Washington, DC 20433

World Council of Churches
158 Route de Ferney
CH-1211
Geneva 20, Switzerland

World Health Organization
20 Avenue Appia
1211 Geneva, Switzerland

World Policy Institute
777 United Nations Plaza
New York, NY 10017

Young Americans for Freedom
Box 1002 Woodland Road
Sterling, VA 22170

Young Astronaut Council
1211 Connecticut Avenue, NW
Washington, DC 20036

Appendix C

WRITING TO PEOPLE OF OTHER NATIONS

Writing letters to people from other countries of the world is exciting. As you communicate with others you can find out all sorts of interesting things. For a child, the writing of a letter can be made fun, but the receiving of a response can be terribly exciting! The addresses are for you to use in this class as well as with your children. A reminder: these addresses are current as of spring 1993, however, nations often change mailing addresses and some even change the name of the country! Again, a brief letter explaining your requests is always in order and appreciated. I have listed nations of the world first, by embassy, if possible. I have also listed those that have tourist and information centers. Note: All embassy addresses in the United States are operated by citizens of the particular countries (that is, the German Embassy is run by Germans, Afghan Embassy by Afghans, Chinese Embassy by Chinese etc).

Afghanistan
  Embassy of Afghanistan
  2341 Wyoming Avenue, NW
  Washington, DC 20008

Albania
  Embassy of the Republic of Albania
  1150 18th Street, NW
  Washington, DC 20036

Algeria
  Embassy of Algeria
  2118 Kalorama Road
  Washington, DC 20008

Andorra
  Andorra Information and Tourism
  1923 Irving Park Road
  Chicago, IL 60613

Angola
  British Embassy
  Rua Diogo Cao 4 (Caixa Postal 1244)
  Luanda, Angola

Anguilla
  Anguilla Department of Tourism
  40 East 49th Street
  New York, NY 10017

Antigua and Barbuda
  Embassy of Antigua and Barbuda
  3400 International Drive, NW
  Washington, DC 20008

Argentina
  Embassy of Argentina
  1600 New Hampshire Avenue, NW
  Washington, DC 20009

Armenia
    Embassy of the Republic of Armenia
    122 C Street, NW, Suite 360
    Washington, DC 20001

Aruba
    Aruba Tourist Bureau
    399 NE 15 Street
    Miami, FL 33132

Australia
    Embassy of Australia
    1601 Massachusetts Avenue, NW
    Washington, DC 20036

    Australian Tourist Commission
    630 Fifth Avenue, Room 467
    New York, NY 10111

Austria
    Embassy of Austria
    3524 International Court, NW
    Washington, DC 20008

    Austrian National Tourist Office
    3440 Wilshire Boulevard
    Los Angeles, CA 90010

Bahamas
    Embassy of the Commonwealth of the
        Bahamas
    2220 Massachusetts Avenue, NW
    Washington, DC 20008

    Bahamas Ministry of Tourism
    Bay Street
    Box n-3701
    Nassau, Bahamas

Bahrain
    Bahrain Embassy
    3502 International Drive, NW
    Washington, DC 20008

Bangladesh
    Bangladesh Embassy
    2201 Wisconsin Avenue, NW, Suite 300
    Washington, DC 20007

Barbados
    Barbados Embassy
    2144 Wyoming Avenue, NW
    Washington, DC 20008

    Barbados Board of Tourism
    800 2nd Avenue
    New York, NY 10017

Belarus
    Embassy of the Republic of Belarus
    1511 K Street, NW
    Washington, DC 20005

Belgium
    Belgium Embassy
    3330 Garfield Street, NW
    Washington, DC 20008

    Belgian Tourist Office
    Rue Marche Aux Herbes 61
    1000 Brussels, Belgium

Belize
    Belize Embassy
    2535 Massachusetts Avenue, NW
    Washington, DC 20008

Benin
    Benin Embassy
    2737 Cathedral Avenue, NW
    Washington, DC 20008

Bhutan
    Permanent Mission to the United Nations
    2 United Nations Plaza, 27th Floor
    New York, NY 10017

    Bhutan Travel Service
    120 East 56th Street
    New York, NY 10022

Bolivia
    Bolivia Consulate General
    3014 Massachusetts Avenue, NW
    Washington, DC 20008

Botswana
    Botswana Embassy
    3400 International Drive, NW
    Washington, DC 20008

Brazil
    Brazil Embassy
    3006 Massachusetts Avenue, NW
    Washington, DC 20008

    Brazilian Tourist Authority
    60 East 42nd Street, Suite 1336
    New York, NY 10165

Brunei Darussalam
    Embassy of the State of Brunei Darussalam
    Watergate
    2600 Virginia Avenue, Suite 300
    Washington, DC 20037

Information Department, Ministry of
   Culture, Youth, and Sport
Box 2318 Bandar Seri Begawan
Negara Brunei Darussalam

Bulgaria
   Bulgaria Embassy
   1621 22nd Street, NW
   Washington, DC 20008

   Bulgarian Tourist Office
   161 East 86th Street
   New York, NY 10028

Burkina Faso
   Burkina Faso Embassy
   2340 Massachusetts Avenue, NW
   Washington, DC 20008

Burundi
   Republic of Burundi Embassy
   2233 Wisconsin Avenue, NW
   Washington, DC 20007

Cameroon Republic
   Cameroon Embassy
   2349 Massachusetts Avenue, NW
   Washington, DC 20008

Canada
   Embassy of Canada
   501 Pennsylvania Avenue, NW
   Washington, DC 20001

   Canadian Consulate General
   235 Queen Street
   Ottawa, ON KIA OH6
   Canada

Cape Verde Islands
   3415 Massachusetts Avenue, NW
   Washington, DC 20007

Central African Republic
   Central African Republic Embassy
   1618 22nd Street, NW
   Washington, DC 20008

Chad
   Republic of Chad Embassy
   2002 R Street, NW
   Washington, DC 20008

Chile
   Chile Embassy
   1732 Massachusetts Avenue, NW
   Washington, DC 20036

China (People's Republic of China)
   China Embassy
   2300 Connecticut Avenue, NW
   Washington, DC 20008

   China International Travel Service
   6 East Chang'an Avenue
   Beijing, China

Colombia
   Colombia Embassy
   2118 Leroy Place, NW
   Washington, DC 20008

Cook Islands
   Cook Islands Tourist Authority
   Box 14 Rarotonga
   Cook Islands

Comoros
   Embassy of Comoros
   336 East 45th Street
   New York, NY 10017

Congo
   Embassy of the People's Republic of the
      Congo
   4891 Colorado Avenue, NW
   Washington, DC 20011

Costa Rica
   Costa Rica Embassy
   1825 Connecticut Avenue, NW
   Washington, DC 20009

   Costa Rican Tourist Board
   200 SE 1st Street, Suite 402
   Miami, FL 33131

Croatia
   Embassy of the Republic of Croatia
   236 Massachusetts Avenue, NW
   Washington, DC 20002

Cuba
   Permanent Mission to United Nations
   315 Lexington Avenue
   New York, NY 10016

   Cuban Tourist Board
   440 Dorchester Boulevard, Suite 1202
   Montreal PQ H2Z IV7
   Canada

Cyprus
   Cyprus Embassy
   2211 R Street, NW
   Washington, DC 20008

Cyprus Tourist Office
18 Th. Theodotou Street Box 4535
Nicosia, Cyprus

Czech and Slovak Federal Republic
Embassy of the Czech and Slovak
3900 Linnean Avenue, NW
Washington, DC 20008

Czechoslovak Travel Bureau
10 East 40th Street, Suite 1902
New York, NY 10016

Denmark
Embassy of Denmark
3200 Whitehaven Street, NW
Washington, DC 20008

Danish Tourist Board
655 Third Avenue
New York, NY 10017

Djibouti
Djibouti Embassy
1156 15th Street, NW
Washington, DC 20005

Dominica
Dominica Tourist Board
Box 73, Roseau
Dominica, W. I.

Dominican Republic
Dominican Republic Embassy
1712 22nd Street, NW
Washington, DC 20008

Dominican Tourist Information Center
485 Madison Avenue
New York, NY 10022

Ecuador
Embassy of Ecuador
2535 15th Street, NW
Washington, DC 20009

Ecuador Tourist Commission
Reina Victoria 514
Quito, Ecuador

Egypt
Embassy of Egypt
2310 Decatur Place, NW
Washington, DC 20008

Egyptian Tourist Authority
630 Fifth Avenue
New York, NY 10111

El Salvador
Embassy of El Salvador
2308 California Street, NW
Washington, DC 20008

El Salvador Tourist Commission
200 West 58th Street, Suite 10B
New York, NY 10019

Equatorial Guinea
Embassy of Equatorial Guinea
57 Magnolia Avenue
Mount Vernon, NY 10553

Estonia
Office of the Consulate General
9 Rockefeller Plaza
New York, NY 10020

Ethiopia
Embassy of Ethiopia
2134 Kalorama Road, NW
Washington, DC 20008

Ethiopia Tourist Commission
Box 2183
Addis Ababa, Ethiopia

European Community
Delegation of the Commission of the
European Community
7th Floor, 2100 M Street, NW
Washington, DC 20037

Fiji Islands
Fijiian Embassy
2233 Wisconsin Avenue, NW
Washington, DC 20007

Fiji Visitor's Bureau
Thomson Street, Box 92
Suva, Fiji

Finland
Finland Embassy
3216 New Mexico Avenue, NW
Washington, DC 20016

Finnish Tourist Board
Pohjoisesplanadi 19, 00100
Helsinki, Finland

France
Embassy of France
4101 Reservoir Road, NW
Washington, DC 20007

French Government Tourist Office
127 Ave des Champs-Elysees
75382 Paris, France

Gabon
  Gabon Embassy
  2034 20th Street, NW
  Washington, DC 20009

Gambia
  The Embassy of the Republic of The Gambia
  1155 15th Street, NW
  Washington, DC 20005

Germany
  Embassy of Germany
  4645 Reservoir Road, NW
  Washington, DC 20007

  German National Tourist Office
  Gutleut Street 7
  6000 Frankfurt/Main
  Frankfurt, Germany

Ghana
  Embassy of Ghana
  3512 International Drive, NW
  Washington, DC 20008

Gibraltar
  Gibraltar Government Tourist Office
  Cathedral Square, Box 303
  Gibraltar, Gibraltar

Greece
  Greece Embassy
  2221 Massachusetts Avenue, NW
  Washington, DC 20008

  Greek National Tourist Office
  2 Amerikis Street
  Athens, Greece

Grenada
  Grenada Embassy
  1701 New Hampshire Avenue, NW
  Washington, DC 20009

  Grenada Tourist Department
  141 East 44th Street, Suite 803
  New York, NY 10017

Guatemala
  Guatemala Embassy
  2220 R Street, NW
  Washington, DC 20008

  Maya Information Service
  501 Fifth Avenue, Suite 1611
  New York, NY 10017

Guinea
  Republic of Guinea Embassy
  2112 Leroy Place, NW
  Washington, DC 20008

Guinea-Bissau
  Embassy of Guinea-Bissau
  918 16th Street, NW
  Washington, DC 20006

Guyana
  Embassy of Guyana
  2490 Tracy Place, NW
  Washington, DC 20008

Haiti
  Haiti Embassy
  2311 Massachusetts Avenue, NW
  Washington, DC 20008

  Haiti National Office of Tourism
  1270 Avenue of the Americas, Suite 508
  New York, NY 10020

Honduras
  Embassy of Honduras
  3007 Tilden Street, NW
  Washington, DC 20008

  Instituto Hondureno De Turismo
  Apartado Postal 154-C
  Tegucigalpa, Honduras

Hungary
  Hungary Embassy
  3910 Shoemaker Street, NW
  Washington, DC 20008

  Tourist Office of Hungary
  Rakoczi ut 52
  1443 Budapest
  Budapest, Hungary

Iceland
  Iceland Embassy
  2022 Connecticut Avenue, NW
  Washington, DC 20008

  Iceland Tourist Office
  Laekkjartorg Municipal Information Center
  Reykjavik, Iceland

India
  India Embassy
  2107 Massachusetts Avenue, NW
  Washington, DC 20008

  Government of India Tourist Office
  Transport Bhawan 1, Parliament Street
  Delhi, India 110001

Indonesia
  Indonesia Embassy
  2020 Massachusetts Avenue, NW
  Washington, DC 20036

Directorate General of Tourism
Jalan Kramat Raya 81
Jakarta, Indonesia

Iran
Iran Embassy
411 Roosevelt Avenue
Ottawa, ON K2A 3X9
Canada

Iraq
Embassy of the Republic of Iraq
215 McLeod Street
Ottawa, ON K2P 0Z8
Canada

Embassy of Iraq
1801 P Street, NW
Washington, DC 20036

Ireland
Embassy of the Republic of Ireland
2234 Massachusetts Avenue, NW
Washington, DC 20008

Irish Tourist Office
14 Upper O'Connell Street
Dublin 1, Ireland

Israel
Embassy of Israel
3514 International Drive, NW
Washington, DC 20008

Israel Government Tourist Office
Empire State Building
350 Fifth Avenue
New York, NY 10118

Italy
Embassy of Italy
1601 Fuller Street, NW
Washington, DC 20009

Italian Government Travel Office
Via Parigi 11
Rome, Italy

Ivory Coast (Cote d'Ivoire)
Embassy of the Ivory Coast
2424 Massachusetts Avenue, NW
Washington, DC 20008

Ivory Coast Tourist Bureau
c/o Air Afrique
1350 Avenue of the Americas
New York, NY 10019

Jamaica
Embassy of Jamaica
1850 K Street, NW
Washington, DC 20036

Jamaica Tourist Board
36 South Wabash Avenue, Suite 1210
Chicago, IL 60603

Japan
Embassy of Japan
2520 Massachusetts Avenue, NW
Washington, DC 20008

Japan National Tourist Organization
6-6 Yurakucho 1-Chome, Kotani Building
Tokyo, Japan

Jordan
Embassy of Jordan
3504 International Drive, NW
Washington, DC 20008

Jordan Information Bureau
1701 K Street, NW 11th Floor
Washington, DC 20006

Kazakhstan (temporary)
Embassy of Kazakhstan
1125 16th Street, NW
Washington, DC 20036

Kenya
Embassy of Kenya
2249 R Street, NW
Washington, DC 20008

Kenya Tourist Office
Dheny Plaza 9100 Wilshire Boulevard, Suite 111
Beverly Hills, CA 90212

Kiribati
British High Commission
P. O. Box 61 Bairiki
Tarawa, Kiribati

Korea
Embassy of the Republic of Korea (South)
2450 Massachusetts Avenue, NW
Washington, DC 20008

Korea National Tourist Corporation
Kukdong Building 3rd Floor
60-1 3-ga Chungmu-ro Box 903
Seoul, Korea

Kuwait
Embassy of the State of Kuwait
2940 Tilden Street, NW
Washington, DC 20008

Kyrgyzstan
    Embassy of Kyrgyzstan
    705 1511 K Street, NW
    Washington, DC 20005

Laos
    Embassy of Laos
    2222 S Street, NW
    Washington, DC 20008

Latvia
    Embassy of Latvia
    4325 17th Street, NW
    Washington, DC 20011

Lebanon
    Embassy of Lebanon
    2560 28th Street, NW
    Washington, DC 20008

Lesotho
    Embassy of the Kingdom of Lesotho
    2511 Massachusetts Avenue, NW
    Washington, DC 20008

Liberia
    Embassy of Liberia
    5201 16th Street, NW
    Washington, DC 20011

Libya
    Libyan Diplomatic Mission
    5 St. James's Square
    London, SW1
    England

Liechtenstein
    British Consul General
    Dulfourstrasse 56
    8008 Zurich, Switzerland

    Liechtenstein National Tourist Office
    Box 139 FL-9490 Vaduz
    Liechtenstein

Lithuania
    Embassy of Lithuania
    2622 16th Street, NW
    Washington, DC 20009

Luxembourg
    Luxembourg Embassy
    2200 Massachusetts Avenue, NW
    Washington, DC 20008

    Luxembourg National Tourist Office
    77 Rue d'Anvers
    Luxembourg

Madagascar
    Embassy of Madagascar
    2374 Massachusetts Avenue, NW
    Washington, DC 20008

Malawi
    Embassy of Malawi
    2408 Massachusetts Avenue, NW
    Washington, DC 20008

    Southern Africa Regional Tourism Council
    Box 564
    Blantyre, Malawi

Malaysia
    Embassy of Malaysia
    2401 Massachusetts Avenue, NW
    Washington, DC 20008

    Tourist Development Corporation of
        Malaysia
    17 & 18 Floor Wisma MPI
    JIRaja Chulan Box 10328
    Kuala Lumpur, Malaysia

Maldives Islands
    Republic of Maldives Islands
    Permanent Mission to the United Nations
    820 Second Avenue, Suite 800C
    New York, NY 10017

    Maldives Department of Tourism
    Orchid Building
    Orchid Magu, Male
    Republic of Maldives

Mali
    Embassy of the Republic of Mali
    2130 R Street, NW
    Washington, DC 20008

    Societe Malienne d'Exploitation des
        Resources Touristiques
    Place de la Republique
    B. P. 222
    Bamako, Mali

Malta
    Embassy of Malta
    2017 Connecticut Avenue, NW
    Washington, DC 20008

    Malta National Tourist Organization
    Harper Lane
    Floriana, Malta

Marshall Islands
    Embassy of the Marshall Islands
    2433 Massachusetts Avenue, NW
    Washington, DC 20008

Mauritania
  Embassy of the Islamic Republic of
    Mauritania
  2129 Leroy Place, NW
  Washington, DC 20008

Mauritius
  Embassy of Mauritius
  4301 Connecticut Avenue, NW
  Washington, DC 20008

  Mauritius Tourist Information Service
  401 Seventh Avenue
  New York, NY 10001

Mexico
  Embassy of the United Mexican States
  1911 Pennsylvania Avenue, NW
  Washington, DC 20006

  Mexican Government Tourism Office
  2 Illinois Center
  233 North Michigan Avenue
  Chicago, IL 60601

Micronesia
  Embassy of Micronesia
  1725 N Street, NW
  Washington, DC 20036

Monaco
  Monaco Consulate General
  845 Third Avenue
  New York, NY 10022

  Monaco Tourist Office
  2/A Boulevard Des Moulins
  Monte Carlo

Mongolia
  Embassy of Mongolia
  2833 M Street, NW
  Washington, DC 20007

Morocco
  Embassy of Morocco
  1601 21st Street, NW
  Washington, DC 20009

  Moroccan National Tourist Office
  20 East 46th Street, No. 503
  New York, NY 10017

Mozambique
  United States Embassy
  35 Rua da Mesquita, 3rd Floor
  Box 783
  Maputo, Mozambique

Embassy of Mozambique
1990 M Street, NW
Washington, DC 20036

Myanmar
  Embassy of the Union of Myanmar
  2300 S Street, NW
  Washington, DC 20008

  Tourist Myanmar
  Hotel & Tourist Corporation
  77-91 Sule Pagoda Road
  Box 559
  Rangoon, Myanmar

Namibia
  Embassy of Namibia
  1605 New Hampshire Avenue, NW
  Washington, DC 20009

Nauru
  Consulate of the Republic of Nauru
  841 Bishop Street
  Honolulu, HI 96813

Nepal
  Embassy of Nepal
  2131 Leroy Place, NW
  Washington, DC 20008

  Ministry of Tourism
  Tripureswor
  Katmandu, Nepal

Netherlands
  Embassy of Netherlands
  4200 Linnean Avenue, NW
  Washington, DC 20008

  Netherlands National Tourist Office
  Box 85973, The Hague 2508 CR
  Netherlands

New Zealand
  New Zealand Embassy
  37 Observatory Circle, NW
  Washington, DC 20008

  New Zealand Tourist & Publicity Department
  Private Bag
  Wellington, New Zealand

Nicaragua
  Embassy of Nicaragua
  1627 New Hampshire Avenue, NW
  Washington, DC 20009

Niger
  Embassy of the Republic of Niger
  2204 R Street, NW
  Washington, DC 20008

Nigeria
  Embassy of Nigeria
  2201 M Street, NW
  Washington, DC 20037

  Nigerian Tourist Association
  Tatawa Balewa Square Complex
  Box 2944
  Lagos, Nigeria

Norway
  Embassy of Norway
  2720 34th Street, NW
  Washington, DC 20008

  Norwegian Tourist Office
  Slottsgaten 1
  5000 Bergen, Norway

Oman
  Oman Embassy
  2342 Massachusetts Avenue, NW
  Washington, DC 20008

Pakistan
  Embassy of Pakistan
  2315 Massachusetts Avenue, NW
  Washington, DC 20008

  Pakistan Tourism Development Corporation,
    Ltd.
  House No. 2 Street 61 F-7/4
  Islamabad, Pakistan

Panama
  Embassy of Panama
  2862 McGill Terrace, NW
  Washington, DC 20008

  Panama Government Tourist Bureau
  2616-A Hyperion Avenue
  Los Angeles, CA 90027

Papua New Guinea
  Embassy of Papua New Guinea
  1615 New Hampshire Avenue, NW
  Washington, DC 20009

Paraguay
  Embassy of Paraguay
  2400 Massachusetts Avenue, NW
  Washington, DC 20008

Peru
  Embassy of Peru
  1700 Massachusetts Avenue, NW
  Washington, DC 20036

Peruvian National Tourist Office
489 Fifth Ave, Suite 3001
New York, NY 10017

Philippines
  Embassy of the Philippines
  1617 Massachusetts Avenue, NW
  Washington, DC 20036

  Philippine Ministry of Tourism
  Agrifina Circle
  Rizal Park Box 3451
  Manila, Philippines

Poland
  Embassy of Poland
  2640 16th Street, NW
  Washington, DC 20009

  Orbis Polish Travel Bureau
  500 Fifth Avenue
  New York, NY 10110

Portugal
  Embassy of Portugal
  2125 Kalorama Road, NW
  Washington, DC 20036

  Portuguese National Tourist Office
  Avenue Antonio Augusto de Aguiar 86
  Lisbon 1000, Portugal

Qatar
  Embassy of Qatar
  600 New Hampshire Avenue, NW
  Washington, DC 20037

Romania
  Embassy of Romania
  1607 23rd Street, NW
  Washington, DC 20008

  Romanian National Tourist Office
  Carpati 7 Magheru Boulevard
  Bucharest, Romania

Russia
  Embassy of Russia
  1125 16th Street, NW
  Washington, DC 20036

  Russia Intourist Information Office
  16 Marx Prospect
  Moscow 103009
  Russia

Rwanda
  Embassy of Rwanda
  1714 New Hampshire Avenue, NW
  Washington, DC 20009

Saint Lucia
Embassy of St. Lucia
2100 M Street, NW
Washington, DC 20037

Saint Vincent & The Grenadines
High Commission of St. Vincent & The
Grenadines
10 Kensington Court
London W8
England

Embassy of Saint Vincent and the Grenadines
1717 Massachusetts Avenue, NW
Washington, DC 20036

Saint Kitts and Nevis
Embassy of Saint Kitts and Nevis
2100 M Street, NW
Washington, DC 20037

San Marino
Consulate General of San Marino
150 East 58th Street
New York, NY 10155

Sao Tome' and Principe
Sao Tome' and Principe Permanent Mission
to the United Nations
801 Second Avenue
New York, NY 10017

Saudi Arabia
Royal Saudi Arabian Embassy
601 New Hampshire Avenue, NW
Washington, DC 20037

Arab Tourism Union
Box 2354
Aman, Jordan

Senegal
Embassy of Senegal
2112 Wyoming Avenue, NW
Washington, DC 20008

Seychelles
Embassy of the Seychelles
820 Second Avenue
New York, NY 10017

Sierra Leone
Embassy of the Republic of Sierra Leone
1701 19th Street, NW
Washington, DC 20009

Singapore
Embassy of Singapore
1824 R Street, NW
Washington, DC 20009

Singapore Tourist Promotion Board
131 Tudor Court
Tanglin Road
Singapore 1024

Slovenia
Embassy of the Republic of Slovenia
1300 19th Street, NW
Washington, DC 20036

Solomon Islands
Solomon Islands Mission to the United
Nations
820 Second Avenue
New York, NY 10017

Solomon Islands Tourist Authority
Box 321
Honiara, Solomon Islands

Somalia
Embassy of Somalia
600 New Hampshire Avenue, NW
Washington, DC 20037

Somalia National Agency for Tourism
Box 553
Mogagishu, Somalia

South Africa
Embassy of the Republic of South Africa
3051 Massachusetts Avenue, NW
Washington, DC 20008

South Africa Tourism Board
747 Third Avenue
New York, NY 10017

Spain
Embassy of Spain
2700 15th Street, NW
Washington, DC 20009

Spanish National Tourist Office
845 North Michigan Avenue
Chicago, IL 60611

Sri Lanka
Sri Lanka Embassy
2148 Wyoming Avenue, NW
Washington, DC 20008

Sri Lanka Tourist Board
228 Havelock Road
Columbo 5, Sri Lanka

Sudan
Sudan Embassy
2210 Massachusetts Avenue, NW
Washington, DC 20008

Sudanese Tourist Corporation
Box 2424
Khartoum, Sudan

Suriname
Embassy of Suriname
4301 Connecticut Avenue, NW
Washington, DC 20008

Swaziland
Embassy of the Kingdom of Swaziland
3400 International Drive, NW
Washington, DC 20008

Sweden
Embassy of Sweden
600 New Hampshire Avenue, NW
Washington, DC 20037

Swedish Tourist Office
Sverigehuset
Hamngatan 27
10392 Stockholm, Sweden

Switzerland
Embassy of Switzerland
2900 Cathedral Avenue, NW
Washington, DC 20008

Swiss National Tourist Office
104 South Michigan Avenue
Chicago, IL 60603

Syria
Embassy of Syria
2215 Wyoming Avenue, NW
Washington, DC 20008

Ministry of Tourism
Abi Fara El-Hamadani Street
Damascus, Syria

Taiwan
Taiwan Coordination Council for Northern
    American Affairs
801 Second Avenue
New York, NY 10017

Ministry of Communications
280 Chunghsiao East Road, Section 4
Box 1490
Taipei, Taiwan

Tanzania
Embassy of Tanzania
2139 R Street, NW
Washington, DC 20008

Tanzania Tourist Corporation
201 East 42nd Street
New York, NY 10017

Thailand
Embassy of Thailand
2300 Kalorama Road, NW
Washington, DC 20008

Tourism Authority of Thailand
4 Ratchademnoen Nok Avenue
Bangkok 10100, Thailand

Togo
Embassy of the Republic of Togo
2208 Massachusetts Avenue, NW
Washington, DC 20008

Togo Tourist Board
1625 K Street
Washington, DC 20006

Tonga
Kingdom of Tonga High Commission
New Zealand House
Haymarket
London, SW1
England

Tonga Visitor's Bureau
Box 37
Nuku'alofa, Tonga

Transkei
Transkei Consulate
1511 K Street, NW
Washington, DC 20005

Trinidad & Tabago
Embassy of Trinidad & Tabago
1708 Massachusetts Avenue, NW
Washington, DC 20036

Trinidad & Tabago Tourist Board
400 Madison Avenue, Suite 712
New York, NY 10017

Tunisia
Embassy of the Republic of Tunisia
1515 Massachusetts Avenue, NW
Washington, DC 20005

Turkey
Embassy of the Republic of Turkey
1714 Massachusetts Avenue, NW
Washington, DC 20036

Uganda
Uganda Embassy
5909 16th Street, NW
Washington, DC 20011

Uganda Tourist Information
5909 16th Street, NW
Washington, DC 20011

Ukraine
Embassy of the Republic of Ukraine
1828 L Street, NW
Washington, DC 20036

United Arab Emirates
Embassy of the United Arab Emirates
600 New Hampshire Avenue, NW
Washington, DC 20037

United Kingdom (England, Scotland, Wales,
    and Northern Ireland)
Embassy of Great Britain/United Kingdom
3100 Massachusetts Avenue, NW
Washington, DC 20008

England Tourist Office
Victoria Station Forecourt
London, SW1
England

Northern Ireland Tourist Office
River House
48 High Street
Belfast, Northern Ireland

Scottish Tourist Office
23 Ravelston TR
Edinburgh, Scotland EH4 3EU

Welsh Tourist Office
3 Castle Street
Cardiff, Wales

Uruguay
Embassy of Uruguay
1918 F Street, NW
Washington, DC 20006

Vanuatu
Vanuatu Embassy
c/o United Kingdom Embassy
3100 Massachusetts Avenue, NW
Washington, DC 20008

Vatican City State (Holy See)
Apostolic Nunciature
3339 Massachusetts Avenue, NW
Washington, DC 20008

Venezuela
Embassy of Venezuela
1099 30th Street, NW
Washington, DC 20007

Western Samoa
1155 15th Street, NW #510
Washington, DC 20005

Yemen
Embassy of the Republic of Yemen
2600 Virginia Avenue, NW
Washington, DC 20037

Yugoslav
Embassy of the Yugoslav Federal Republic
2410 California Street, NW
Washington, DC 20008

Zaire
Embassy of Zaire
1800 New Hampshire Avenue, NW
Washington, DC 20009

Zaire National Tourist Office
1259 Boulevard du 30 Juin
Box 9502
Kinshasa, Zaire

Zambia
Embassy of Zambia
2419 Massachusetts Avenue, NW
Washington, DC 20008

Zambia National Tourist Office
237 East 52nd Street
New York, NY 10022

Zimbabwe
Embassy of Zimbabwe
1608 New Hampshire Avenue, NW
Washington, DC 20009

Zimbabwe Tourist Board
35 East Wacker Drive, Suite 1778
Chicago, IL 60601

Appendix **D**

STATES OF THE UNITED STATES

The United States is a very large country; explore it with your children. If you request information from the following addresses, your mailbox will be stuffed with valuable information and colorful pictures. Encourage your children to write letters to the different states, compare and contrast the various places, plan trips. Again, always include a formal letter requesting information.

Alabama
   State Chambers of Commerce
   468 South Perry Street
   P. O. Box 76
   Montgomery, AL 36195

Alaska
   Alaska Division of Tourism
   P. O. Box E
   Juneau, AK 99811-0800

Arizona
   Arizona Convention Bureau
   One Arizona Center
   400 East Van Buren, Suite 600
   Phoenix, AZ 85004

Arkansas
   Chamber of Commerce
   One Spring Street
   Little Rock, AR 72201

California
   Chamber of Commerce
   1027 10th Street
   Sacramento, CA 95814

Colorado
   Colorado Travel
   1625 Broadway, Suite 1700
   Denver, CO 80202

Connecticut
   State Department of Economic Development
   865 Brook Street
   Rocky Hill, CT 06067

Delaware
   Chamber of Commerce
   One Commerce Center
   Wilmington, DE 19801

Florida
   Florida Division of Tourism
   126 Van Buren Street
   Tallahassee, FL 32399-2000

Georgia
   Chamber of Commerce
   235 International Boulevard
   Atlanta, GA 30303

Hawaii
   Chamber of Commerce
   Dillingham Building
   735 Bishop Street
   Honolulu, HI 96813

Idaho
   Department of Commerce
   700 West State Street
   Boise, ID 83720

Illinois
Illinois Department of Commerce and
Community Affairs
620 East Adams Street
Chicago, IL 62701

Indiana
Chamber of Commerce
One North Capital, Suite 200
Indianapolis, IN 46204

Iowa
Division of Tourism
200 East Grand Avenue
Des Moines, IA 50309

Kansas
Kansas Department of Commerce
Travel and Tourism
200 SW 8th Street, 5th Floor
Topeka, KS 66603

Kentucky
Chamber of Commerce
452 Versailles Road
P. O. Box 817
Frankfort, KY 40602

Louisiana
State Department of Culture, Recreation, and
Tourism
P. O. Box 94291
Baton Rouge, LA 70804-9291

Maine
Chamber of Commerce
126 Sewall Street
Augusta, ME 04330

Maryland
Chamber of Commerce
60 West Street, Suite 405
Annapolis, MD 21401

Massachusetts
Massachusetts Office of Travel & Tourism
100 Cambridge Street, 13th Floor
Boston, MA 02202

Michigan
Chamber of Commerce
200 North Washington Square
Lansing, MI 48933

Minnesota
Minnesota Office of Tourism
375 Jackson Street
250 Skyway Level
St. Paul, MN 55101

Mississippi
Chamber of Commerce
P. O. Box 1849
Jackson, MS 39205

Missouri
Chamber of Commerce
400 High Street, P. O. Box 149
Jefferson City, MO 65101

Montana
Chamber of Commerce
2030 11th Avenue
P. O. Box 1730
Helena, MT 59624

Nebraska
Chamber of Commerce
1320 Lincoln Mall
Box 95128
Lincoln, NE 68501

Nevada
Commission on Tourism
Capitol Complex
Carson City, NV 89710

New Hampshire
Department of Resources and Economic
Development
Division of Tourism
P. O. Box 856
Concord, NH 03302-0856

New Jersey
Chamber of Commerce
51 Commerce Street
Newark, NJ 07102

New Mexico
New Mexico Department of Tourism
P. O. Box 20003
Santa Fe, NM 87503

New York
New York State Department of Economic
Development
1 Commerce Plaza
Albany, NY 12245

North Carolina
Division of Travel and Tourism
430 North Salisbury Street
Raleigh, NC 27603

North Dakota
Chamber of Commerce
P. O. Box 2467
Fargo, ND 58108

Ohio
  Chamber of Commerce
  35 East Gay Street
  Columbus, OH 43215

Oklahoma
  Tourism Department
  P. O. Box 60000
  Oklahoma City, OK 73146-6000

Oregon
  Economic Development Department
  775 Summer Street, NE
  Salem, OR 97310

Pennsylvania
  Chamber of Commerce
  222 North 3rd Street
  Harrisburg, PA 17101

Rhode Island
  Chamber of Commerce
  30 Exchange Terrace
  Providence, RI 02908

South Carolina
  Chamber of Commerce
  930 Richard Street
  P. O. Box 1360
  Columbia, SC 29201

South Dakota
  South Dakota Tourism
  711 Wells Avenue
  Pierre, SD 57501-3335

Tennessee
  Department of Tourist Development
  Rachel Jackson Building, 5th Floor
  Nashville, TN 37219

Texas
  Chamber of Commerce
  900 Congress, Suite 501
  Austin, TX 78701

Utah
  Utah Travel Council
  Council Hall
  Salt Lake City, UT 84114

Vermont
  Vermont Travel Division
  134 State Street
  Montpelier, VT 05602

Virginia
  Chamber of Commerce
  9th South Fifth Street
  Richmond, VA 23219

Washington
  Chamber of Commerce
  P. O. Box 658
  Olympia, WA 98507

West Virginia
  Department of Commerce
  State Capitol
  Charleston, WV 25305

Wisconsin
  Wisconsin Department of Development and
    Tourism
  123 West Washington Avenue
  Madison, WI 53702

Wyoming
  Travel Commission
  Etchepare Circle
  Cheyenne, WY 82002

Other United States Areas:

Puerto Rico
  Chamber of Commerce
  100 Tetuan
  P. O. Box S-3789
  San Juan, PR 00904

Virgin Islands
  Department of Economic Development, St.
    Thomas
  P. O. Box 6400
  St. Thomas, VI 00801

Appendix E

PROFESSIONAL ORGANIZATIONS FOR TEACHERS

While none of these organizations has an all-elementary focus, each of these important educational groups offers materials and ideas on teaching in elementary schools. You should seriously consider joining one or two professional organizations. They not only provide valuable information on new research and keep you up to date on the latest developments, but they also offer opportunities for you to interact with other educators through professional publications and/or national and regional conventions. Write each for details about membership. Because these groups often have special membership benefits for elementary teachers, be sure to identify what grade level you teach. Once again, remember to use a formal letter to request information. (Major publications for social studies are in parentheses.)

American Education Research Association
1230 17th Street, NW
Washington, DC 20036-3078
(Review of Educational Research, Annual
  Yearbook)

American Federation of Teachers (AFT)
11 Dupont Circle
Washington, DC 20036
(American Teacher)

Association for Childhood Education
  International
11141 Georgia Avenue, Suite 200
Wheaton, MD 20902
(Childhood Education)

Association for Supervision and Curriculum
  Development
1250 North Pitt Street
Alexandria, VA 22314
(Educational Leadership)

Geographic Education National
  Implementation Project
Association of American Geographers
1710 16th Street, NW
Washington, DC 20009

International Reading Association
800 Barksdale Road
P. O. Box 8139
Newark, DE 19711
(The Reading Teacher)

National Council for Teachers of
   English
1111 Keyon Road
Urbana, IL 61801
(Language Arts)

National Council for History
   Education
26915 Westwood Road, Suite B-2
Westlake, OH 44145-4656
(History Matters)

National Council for the Social Studies
3501 Newark Street, NW
Washington, DC 20036
(Social Education, Theory and Research in
   Social Education, Social Studies and the
   Young Learner)

National Council of Mathematics Teachers
1906 Association Drive
Reston, VA 22091

National Education Association
1201 16th Street, NW
Washington, DC 20036
(Today's Education)

National Science Teachers Association
1742 Connecticut Avenue, NW
Washington, DC 20009

Phi Delta Kappa
8th & Union Street
P. O. Box 789
Bloomington, IN 47402
(Phi Delta Kappan)

HOUGHTON MIFFLIN
SOCIAL STUDIES SERIES:
SCOPE AND SEQUENCE

This Scope and Sequence has been designed to provide students with the comprehensive knowledge, civic values, and intellectual skills they will need to meet the challenge of citizenship in the 21st century. The three strands of the program have been tightly integrated at all levels, so that skills are always taught in the context of the lesson content, and knowledge is enhanced by the application of sound values. The goals of each strand are listed on the following two pages. References in the Teachers' Edition key all learning objectives to these goals. Typically the student is introduced to a subject or skill at an early level, taught to actively use it at an intermediate level, and encouraged to analyze and critique it at an advanced level.

KNOWLEDGE AND UNDERSTANDING
- History
- Geography
- Economics
- Culture
- Ethics and Belief Systems
- Social and Political Systems

CIVIC UNDERSTANDING AND VALUES
- National Identity
- Constitutional Heritage
- Citizenship

SKILLS
- Study Skills
- Visual Learning
- Map and Globe Skills
- Critical Thinking
- Social Participation

KNOWLEDGE AND UNDERSTANDING

HISTORY	GEOGRAPHY	ECONOMICS

HISTORY

1. Develop an understanding of the reasons for studying history and of the relationships between the past and the present
2. Develop an awareness of the ways in which we learn about the past and the methods and tools of the historian
3. Create a sense of empathy for the past
4. Understand the meaning of time and chronology
5. Analyze the sometimes complex cause-and-effect relationships of ideas and events, recognizing also the effects of the accidental and irrational on history
6. Understand the reasons for both continuity and change
7. Recognize the interrelatedness of geography, economics, culture, belief systems, and political systems within history
8. Comprehend the history of women, minorities, and the full range of social classes, not just the history of the elite or the notable individual

GEOGRAPHY

1. Develop locational skills and understanding
2. Develop an awareness of place
3. Understand human and environmental interaction
4. Understand movement of people, goods, and ideas
5. Understand world regions and their historical, cultural, economic, and political characteristics

ECONOMICS

1. Identify and apply basic concepts of economics (basic wants and needs, scarcity, choices, decision making, opportunity costs, resources, production, distribution, consumption, markets, labor, capital)
2. Develop an awareness of past and present exchange systems
3. Recognize and analyze the economic systems of various societies, including the United States, and their responses to the three basic economic questions: what to produce (value), how and how much to produce (allocation), and how to distribute (distribution)
4. Recognize the economic global interdependence of societies
5. Recognize the impact of technology on economics

CULTURE

1. Understand the concept of culture and how it is transmitted
2. Develop an appreciation for the rich complexity of a society's culture and an understanding of how the parts of a culture interrelate
3. Recognize and appreciate the multicultural and multiethnic dimensions of our society and the contributions made by various groups
4. Appreciate the cultural similarities and differences that exist among societies of different times and places
5. Recognize the special role literature and the arts play in reflecting the inner life of a people and in projecting a people's image of themselves to the world
6. Learn about the mythology, legends, myths of origin, and heroes and heroines of societies of different times and places

ETHICS & BELIEF SYSTEMS

1. Recognize that all societies have ideals and standards of behavior
2. Understand that the ideas people profess affect their actions
3. Recognize the importance of religion in human society and its influence on history
4. Become familiar with the basic ideas of major religions and ethical traditions of other times and places
5. Develop an understanding of how different societies have tried to resolve ethical issues when conflicts occur between individuals, groups, and societies

SOCIAL & POLITICAL SYSTEMS

1. Develop an awareness of the reciprocal relationship between the individual and various social and political groups: family, community, and nation
2. Understand the role of law and its relationship to social and political systems
3. Develop an appreciation for the tension between opposing ideals in human affairs
4. Develop an awareness of the structure of social classes and the changes in status of women and racial and ethnic minorities in U.S. society and other societies
5. Understand comparative political systems, past and present
6. Understand the complex relationship and interdependence that exists among the world's nations

CIVIC UNDERSTANDING AND VALUES

NATIONAL IDENTITY

1. Develop an appreciation for the multicultural, pluralistic nature of U.S. society
2. Understand the basic principles of democracy
3. Understand and appreciate American ideals, as expressed in historical documents, speeches, songs, art, and symbolic representations and activities
4. Recognize that the American patriotic ideals are not yet fully realized and that to be protected they must constantly be reaffirmed

CONSTITUTIONAL HERITAGE

1. Develop an appreciation for the balance of power established by the Constitution between majority and minority, the individual and the state, and government by and for the people
2. Understand the historical origins of the Constitution and how it has been amended and changed over time
3. Recognize the Constitution as an expression of democratic ideals that is reinterpreted from time to time

CITIZENSHIP

1. Recognize the reciprocal relationship between the individual and the state in a democracy
2. Understand and appreciate the kind of behavior necessary for the functioning and maintenance of our democratic society
3. Learn the duties and method of selection of our leaders
4. Develop a respect for human rights, including those of individuals and of minorities
5. Develop an understanding and appreciation for the rational settlement of disputes and for compromise
6. Recognize the special strategies required to allow the different elements within our pluralistic society to live together amicably
7. Develop an understanding of the processes that have led to the fall of democracies

SKILLS

STUDY SKILLS

1. Locate, select, and collect information by interviewing or by using appropriate reference materials
2. Organize information from reference sources to address issues or problems
3. Present information convincingly in spoken or written forms

VISUAL LEARNING

1. Develop careful and directed observation of images, objects, and the environment
2. Understand, use, and create graphic information (timelines, charts, tables, other graphic organizers, graphs, diagrams)
3. Interpret and respond to photographs, paintings, cartoons, and other illustrative materials
4. Understand and use symbols
5. Express meaning through sensory forms of representation

MAP & GLOBE SKILLS

1. Identify and use map and globe symbols; identify and use different map projections
2. Understand and use locational terms; locate places and positions on a map or globe
3. Interpret and use directional terms and symbols on a map or globe
4. Understand and use terms to describe relative size and distance; identify and use map scales
5. Construct and use maps and geographic models

CRITICAL THINKING	SOCIAL PARTICIPATION
1. Define and clarify problems, issues, and ideas	1. Develop interpersonal skills
2. Evaluate and judge information related to a problem, an issue, or an idea	2. Work successfully in groups
3. Solve problems and draw conclusions related to an issue or idea*	

*Critical thinking is taught both in a problem-solving and in a decision-making context.

KNOWLEDGE AND UNDERSTANDING

				Grade
	K	1	2	3
HISTORY				
1. Links to the past	Compare travel now and long ago	Parents and grandparents	Discuss traditions and their origins	
2. How we know		Family histories		Physical evidence Journals of pioneers
3. Empathy	Identification through literature		Biographies	Real people of the past
4. Time and chronology	Understand and use time sequence terms Identify seasons of the year			Read and use timelines
5. Cause and effect	Introduce through group dynamics	Changes in community	Effects of war Inventions	Migration and settlement Conservation issues
6. Continuity and change	In individuals, families	In community	Histories of families How basic needs were met	Bust of a boom town long ago and today
7. Interrelated-ness	Of economics with history	Of geography with history	Origins of Thanksgiving	Of geography, economics with history
8. Women, minorities	Through stories, illustrations	Diversity of people presented		
GEOGRAPHY				
1. Location	The self in space	Home, school, community	Beyond the neighborhood	Relative location
2. Place	Elementary land and water forms	Map locations	Global climates	Place characteristics
		Identify and analyze microenvironments		
3. Human-environment interaction	Adjustment of dress to climate	Environmental changes in area		Environmental changes Community interactions
4. Movement	Movement of goods and people			Historical movements of people
5. Regions			Identify regions other than one's own	Regional characteristics

4	5	6	7	8
State, region placenames Family histories	Origins of today's institutions Cultural heritage of self, others		Global interaction today Origins of law, government	Personal, national identity Redefinition of the past
Archaeological evidence Primary sources, artifacts	Historian's techniques; archaeologist's discoveries Limitations of information about the past			Historical record, newspapers, photos; points of view
Past settlers of the state, region	With pioneers, slaves, American Indians	With people of ancient times	Literature, art primary sources, artifacts	With pioneers, American Indians, slaves, immigrants
Read and use timelines	Use of B.C./A.D.	Developments in concurrent civilizations		
Settlement, expansion Cultural diversity	Analysis of settlement, expansion, wars	Of territorial expansion, cultural diffusion	Exploration, Reformation, technology	Of settlement, expansion, Industrial Revolution
Of region over time	Analyze reasons for	Steps to civilizations Analysis of a civilization over time		Regional development, urbanization
Of geography, economics, religion, culture	Of belief systems	Of trade and religion in the spread of ideas Of class structure		Of belief systems Of class structure
Role of American Indians, Hispanics, blacks, Asians, women in early U.S. society		Women, social classes, in ancient cultures, in past societies		Diverse groups in U.S. history
Factors that influence locations	Why different activities are in different locations	Evaluate reasons for a city's location	Historical significance of	Competition for locations
Rural/urban areas	Comparative historical analysis of places	Influences of physical, cultural geography on history		Effect of place on population distribution
Environmental changes at different times	Use of natural resources Effect on technology	Origin of the city Changes in cities Environmental changes over time		Use of natural resources Effect on technology
Reasons for migrations	Migrations of people; movement of goods	Ancient migrations Ancient trade routes	Global movements Effect of technology	Migrations to America
Nature and characteristics of regions	Compare/contrast of regions over time	Identify and analyze criteria used to define regions		

(Continued)

KNOWLEDGE AND UNDERSTANDING *(Continued)*

			Grade	
	K	1	2	3
ECONOMICS				
1. Basic concepts	Differences between wants and needs	Discuss how needs are met Identify and discuss community jobs		Compare how needs met over time, space
2. Exchange systems	Role-playing (stores)	Trade of surpluses	How systems are learned (immigrants)	American Indian exchange systems
3. Basic economic questions	Distribution of goods from production to market		Production and distribution	
4. Interdepend-ence		Interdependence of producers and consumers	Inventions	To and from community
5. Technology				Production and transportation
CULTURE				
1. Cultural understanding	Appreciation through participation		Role of family	How transmitted
2. Cultural complexity	Identify through literature		Compare traditions	American Indians
3. Multicultural society			Biographies	American Indians
4. Similarities and differences	Compare through literature			American Indians
5. Literature and the arts	Recognize and respond through examples			Of other times and places
6. Myths and legends	Listen and respond to folk tales			Of American Indians, cowboys, settlers
ETHICS & BELIEF SYSTEMS				
1. Present in all societies				In American Indian societies
2. Ideas affect behavior				In American Indian societies

4	5	6	7	8
How wants met over time History of businesses	Distribution of resources	How met long ago Scarcity; specialization	In different societies Rise of merchant class	Colonial markets/materials Divisions of labor
Use of barter Trace money flow	Early exchange systems Role of trade routes		Banking systems	Trade partnerships
Economic cycles	In early U.S. history Role of government	In ancient times	At different times and places	Analyze economic decisions Roles of governments
Within, between regions Effect of natural disasters	Between people, states, nations	Ancient global trade Transportation changes	International trade routes	Debtor/lender nations Imports/exports
Post-World War II developments; pollution	Industrial Revolution	Effects of new technologies	Key inventions in world history	Industrial revolution; mass production
How transmitted	Role of education	Define culture Analyze how culture is transmitted	Define and identify	
Recognize through state's, region's history	Identify in U.S. at different time periods	Analyze prehistoric, ancient cultures	Analyze other cultures	Analyze in U.S. historically
Contributions to local history	Contributions of Indians, blacks, immigrants	Identify origins of contemporary cultures		Contributions of Indians, slaves, immigrants
American Indians Other groups in region	Interactions and conflicts of cultures in U.S.	Analyze interaction and conflict in other cultures		Among U.S. population Interaction and conflict
Throughout area's history	Understand and appreciate cultural images presented			Analyze cultural images presented
American Indian, cowboy, settlers	Analyze heroes, heroines	Importance in ancient cultures	Analyze legends and tales of others	Analyze American legends, tall tales
In historical past in state, region, country		Comparison of past societies		Analyze ethical standards in past U.S. history
Role of missionaries Beliefs of immigrants	Pilgrims, puritans, attitudes about slavery	Buddhist, Jewish, Christian examples	Crusades, from two points of view	The Great Awakening Church and Abolitionists *(Continued)*

KNOWLEDGE AND UNDERSTANDING *(Continued)*

	K	1	2	Grade 3
ETHICS & BELIEF SYSTEMS *(Continued)*				
3. Influence of religion				Among American Indians, Pilgrims
4. Basic belief systems				Of American Indians
5. Resolution of ethical issues	Introduce through literature			Discuss examples in literature
SOCIAL & POLITICAL SYSTEMS				
1. Belonging to groups	Recognize membership in groups Identify public/private sectors			Responsibilities of individual to group
2. Law	Recognize and observe the need for rules			Rules among other societies
3. Opposing ideals				American Indians and settlers
4. Social structure				Social structure in other societies, times
5. Comparative political systems				Recognize not all political systems are alike
6. Global inter-dependence	Recognize world neighbors	Recognize interdependence	Recognize other nations	International trade

4	5	6	7	8
Conflict between belief systems	Pilgrims, puritans, attitudes toward slavery	Spread through missionaries, diffusion	Split among Christians; Islam; missionaries	Slavery; Manifest Destiny; 2nd Great Awakening
American Indians	Of American Indians, slaves, immigrants	Origins, early history of major world religions	Origins, history of Islam; Japanese Buddhism	Of Indians, slaves, early immigrants
Discuss examples in literature	Freedom to dissent; slavery; tolerance	Examples from ancient civilizations	Through religious wars	Attempts to resolve slavery issue
Political subunits	Early U.S. political units / Origins of public/private	Identify social, political units in ancient times	Identify world social and political units	Conflicting group memberships in U.S. history
Who enforces laws	Reinterpretations of law over time	Identify origins of law	Recognize non-Roman systems of law	How law is enacted, changed; dissent
Conflicting goals in state, regional history	In early U.S. history	In and among prehistoric, ancient societies	In and among world societies, over time	At various times in U.S. history
Recognize differences in treatment over time	Analyze reasons for changes	Analyze social status in ancient times	Analyze changes over time	Analyze reasons for change
Recognize variety of political systems	Of American Indian, British, French, Spanish	Among ancient civilizations	Note changes over time	Among nations that have affected U.S. history
Trade, foreign affairs	Identify relationships of U.S. with others	Analyze interdependence in ancient times	Identify and analyze interdependencies	History of U.S. relationship with other nations

CIVIC UNDERSTANDING AND VALUES

	K	1	2	Grade 3
NATIONAL IDENTITY				
1. Pluralism	Recognize national identity Recognize diversity of U.S. citizens			Through examples
2. Democracy	Practice through classroom examples			Through historic, contemporary examples
3. American ideals and symbols	Recognize flag, songs Role-play	Learn national symbols, Pledge of Allegiance, patriotic songs		
4. Reaffirmation of American ideals				Conservation of resources
CONSTITUTIONAL HERITAGE				
1. Balance of power	Fair treatment of all in the classroom			In other societies
2. Origin of Constitution				
3. Reinterpretation of ideals				
CITIZENSHIP				
1. Individual and state	Through family, classroom examples			In conservation of natural resources
2. Democratic behavior	Recognize problems that arise in groups			Develop awareness of need for rules
3. Selection of leaders			Identify office of U.S. president	Awareness of Presidents' Day
4. Human rights	Develop respect for others			Through examples in the past
5. Settlement of disputes	Through classroom examples			Through group activities
6. Strategies for pluralism		Through classroom examples		

4	5	6	7	8
Through examples	Origins of pluralism	Discuss identities of ancient civilizations	Discuss identities of other nations	Tensions of assimilation
Through historic, contemporary examples	History of, in U.S.	Origins of, in ancient times	Historical origins of democracy	History and development of U.S. democracy
Learn state symbols	As expressed in U.S. history	Ancient national symbols	Symbols of other nations and empires	As expressed in U.S. history
Focus on state's or region's future	Identify past crises in U.S. history	Compare and contrast examples from ancient, historical times, with U.S.		Identify and discuss past crises in U.S.
Examples in state, regional history	Checks and balances Historical examples	Balance of power in ancient civilizations	How balance of power achieved elsewhere	Checks and balances Historical examples
State constitutions	Writing of Constitution Passage of amendments		Influence of Enlightenment ideas	Writing of Constitution Passage of amendments
Changes in state laws over time	Meaning then and now			Discuss reasons for reinterpretations
Through examples in state history	Identify examples in U.S. history	Identify examples in ancient times	Identify examples in other societies	Analyze examples in U.S. history
Need for rules Violations in past	Discuss examples in U.S. history	Analyze behavior in ancient times	Analyze behavior in other societies	Discuss examples in U.S. history
Selection of state leaders	Analyze, using past U.S. examples	Compare selection process of long ago	Compare selection process of others	Analyze, using past U.S. examples
Through examples in state history	Evaluate cases from U.S. history	Discuss minority rights long ago	Discuss minority rights of others	Evaluate cases from U.S. history
Through examples in state history	Identify examples from U.S. history	Analyze disputes in ancient times	Analyze disputes in other societies	Analyze examples from U.S. history
Through examples in state history	Identify examples from U.S. history	Analyze pluralism in ancient times	Analyze pluralism in other societies	Analyze examples from U.S. history

SKILLS

			Grade	
	K	1	2	3

STUDY SKILLS

	K	1	2	3
1. Collecting information	Interview others Visit a library	Learn book parts Picture dictionary	Use a library; reference materials Interview for information	
2. Organizing information	Listen to story and relate what happened	Identify and make categories	Identify main ideas and details	Summarize a paragraph
3. Presenting information	Tell events in sequence		Tell events and ideas in sequence Write simple paragraphs	

VISUAL LEARNING

	K	1	2	3
1. Observation	Classroom materials	School, neighborhood	Neighborhood, community features	
2. Timelines	Know the seasons	Read and make simple timelines		
Graphic organizers	Use a chart	Read charts, tables		
Graphs	Use simple picture, bar graphs	Read and make picture, bar graphs		Read line, circle graphs
Diagrams		Read process and cut-away diagrams; also, cross-section diagrams		
3. Interpretation	State main idea of illustrations	Gather information from and respond to photos, illustrations; also, fine art		
4. Symbols	Traffic signs; U.S. flag	National symbols; flag		
5. Visual self-expression	Drawings, constructions	Class activities		

MAP AND GLOBE SKILLS

	K	1	2	3
1. Symbols	Compare maps, photos, and real environments		Color as symbol Continents and oceans	Read a physical map Use a map key, rose
2. Location	Use simple locational terms		Use grids to find locations Relative location	Latitude, longitude
3. Direction	Orient self in space; use directional terms		Cardinal directions Describe routes	Intermediate directions Follow routes on map
4. Scale and distance	Use relative terms	Judge relative sizes, distances		Use map scale Time/distance
5. Construction and use	Construct table or floor 3-dimensional maps of community, neighborhood			

4	5	6	7	8
Use a library catalog Interview for information		Use atlas; primary sources	Use Reader's Guide Conduct interviews	Use special reference resources
Combine information Give directions	Take notes, make outlines	Identify text patterns	Code notes Interpret primary sources	Make bibliography cards
Develop oral discussion skills Plan and write reports			Use a variety of oral and written genres, debates, skits, to present reports	
Regional features	Apply to historical artifacts, photographs, fine art			
Read U.S. time zone maps; timelines	Understand B.C./A.D.	Read and make telescopic and parallel timelines		
Read charts, tables		Read and make cluster, cause-and-effect graphic organizers		
Read bar, line, circle graphs	Make line graphs	Compare graphs	Choose, assess graphs	
Read and use variety of diagrams		Analyze cross-section, process diagrams		
Interpret illustrative materials; cartoons; Compare media		Identify limitations of illustrative materials		
State symbols	Learn history of national symbols	Religious, historical symbols		History of U.S. symbols
As class activities		Making a mural, a Moment in Time	As class activities	
Area characteristics Making symbols	Parallels/meridians tied to earth/sun	Read cartograms Draw inferences	Use topographical map	Make inferences Relate routes/topography
Hemispheres Global reference points	Use latitude/longitude to locate, specify places		Earth/sun relationship and time of day	Analyze locations
Use directional terms to describe routes	Trace explorers' routes	Formulate hypotheses Movement of people over time		Cultural diffusion
Large- and small-scale representations	Evaluate large- and small-scale maps	Compute distances and travel time	Vertical profiles Trace and analyze routes	
Make a map	Use landmarks to draw map	Make a map	Make a map, vertical profile	Design map based on information given

(Continued)

SKILLS *(Continued)*

	K	1	2	Grade 3
CRITICAL THINKING				
1. Define and clarify	Similarities and differences Organize categories	Formulate questions		Identify problems or central issues
2. Evaluate and judge	Identify evidence	Sequence of events		Evidence supporting main idea
3. Solve and conclude	Identify cause and effect Draw conclusions based on evidence			Cause and effect Make "if . . . then" statements
SOCIAL PARTICIPATION				
1. Interpersonal	Develop self-respect and confidence Develop good listening skills			Others' points of view Express one's own ideas
2. Group work	Show willingness to participate in group activities	Accept group decisions	Practice collaborative learning roles	Identify goal

4	5	6	7	8
Identify problems or central issues	Ask good questions	Interpret values and ideologies of individuals, groups	Identify central issues	Analyze points of view
Facts and opinions Evaluate information	Identify facts, opinions	Distinguish among facts, opinions, and reasoned judgements	Recognize bias	Judge bias, propaganda Analyze arguments
Cause and effect Draw conclusions	Interpret cause and effect Draw conclusions from evidence		Make hypotheses Predict consequences	Compare causes/effects Identify alternatives
Listen to others Express one's own ideas	Recognize the social needs of others Provide positive feedback		Overcome stereotypes Recognize and respect others' points of view	
Participate in discussions	Participate in setting and planning goals Develop collaborative learning roles		Analyze and support group decisions	Appreciate and practice compromises

INDEX